THE
HORSESHOE
TABLE

THE HORSESHOE TABLE

An Inside View of the UN Security Council

Chinmaya R Gharekhan

Foreword by
Dr Boutros Boutros Ghali

PEARSON
Longman

An imprint of **Pearson Education**

ISBN 81-7758-453-7

Second Impression, 2006

Published by Dorling Kindersley (India) Pvt. Ltd., licensees of Pearson Education in South Asia.

Head Office: 482, F.I.E., Patparganj, Delhi 110 092, India.
Registered Office: 14 Local Shopping Centre, Panchsheel Park, New Delhi 110 017, India.

Laser typeset by InoSoft Systems, NOIDA

Printed in India by Sanat Printers.

Photographs courtesy: The United Nations

By God's grace, I dedicate this book to

my parents
Surbhilaxmi and Rajaninath

my wife
Rita

my children
Darshini, Nikhil-Mandira

and

my grandchildren
Rohan and Rishabh

The author with Kofi Annan.

CONTENTS

FOREWORD

Peace is the supreme goal, the very raison d'être of the whole United Nations system. There can be no development in time of war, and there can be no democracy when war is going on. Development as a goal is mentioned in the Charter, but it is a kind of a secondary goal, one that, so to speak, helps in peace keeping. Democracy, on the other hand, has not been one of the UN's goals, even though the preamble of the Charter begins with the celebrated phrase 'We the peoples of the United Nations'. Democracy was not a goal, because there was never any question of asking states that wanted to belong to the Organisation to adopt a democratic system. The only requirement for membership was that states should be peace loving and willing and able to carry out the decisions of the United Nations. The UN has routinely admitted states that were far from democratic. It was only after the end of the Cold War that democracy became one of the goals of the UN, and it was only after 1992 that a section in charge of electoral assistance was set up in the secretariat.

While domestic or national democracy is or can be a reality, can there be such a thing as genuine international democracy? A further question is: How is it that the increase in the number of democratic states has not gone hand-in-hand with more democratic relations among states? How can one explain the reluctance of democracies to extend their model of governance to inter-state relations?

There is no gainsaying the fact that the structure of the UN is outdated. There is no international democracy, in the sense that democracy obtains in many states around the world. Perhaps it is not possible to have democracy at the international level since states, unlike individuals within a country, in a legal sense as well as increasingly, in a social sense, are not equal entities. There are differences in geographical size, population, military and economic power, physical attributes, and so on. An important point of difference among states is the ability and willingness to use the power of the state to impose its values on others or to promote its interests at the expense of the interests of others. A question which suggests itself automatically is: What is, or what will be the impact on democracy at a national level, of the absence of democracy at the international level, or the hegemony of a super power? Will not democracy, already weakened by transnational movements, be further weakened by the presence of an undemocratic international system?

Perhaps the only way to make the international system less undemocratic, or more responsive to world public opinion is for a group of states, obviously less powerful individually than the most powerful state in the international arena, to assert themselves, to speak up and take positions together to defend the system based on respect for international legality and legitimacy. During the era of the Cold War, countries such as Cuba and Yugoslavia exercised influence far beyond their intrinsic strength. I believe that the aspirants for permanent membership of the Security Council will not contribute much to the democratisation of international relations unless they are willing to take a risk, which I believe will be minimal, of a temporary set back to their national interests for the sake of promoting and defending international morality. Individually, and even more so collectively, they can exercise an extremely healthy influence in the functioning of the international political, juridical and security order.

Apart from anything else, the high level panel appointed by the current Secretary General of the United Nations to examine the new challenges facing the international community in the 21st century has helped focus the attention of the world on the need for reform of the United Nations. It is entirely reasonable that most of the discussion has concerned itself with reform of the Security Council. Members of the public at large, and not just professional diplomats, have begun to ask questions about the role of the Security Council, the body entrusted with maintaining peace and security in the world, as well as about its functioning.

Ambassador Gharekhàn has rendered a most useful service to all those concerned about the functioning of the international security system by giving an intimate, honest and highly professional account of the manner in which this extremely important organ of the United Nations conducts its business. *The Horseshoe Table* brings out, as no other book has, the compulsions which members of the Council feel, in the face of the pressure which public opinion exerts through the media, to 'do something' in difficult situations. The book helps understand the chasm between the often unrealistic expectations and demands of the Council and the human and material resources which it is willing and able to make available to the Secretary General to achieve those objectives. There is also the tension, of which the Secretary General becomes the intended victim, which arises when members pursue their own national agenda, without worrying about wider considerations of morality or even legality. Ambassador Gharekhan's book is an excellent, instructive contribution to the understanding of what is undoubtedly the most crucial organ in the international security structure today.

Dr Boutros Boutros Ghali

ABBREVIATIONS

CAS	Close Air Support
CIS	Commonwealth of Independent States
CSCE	Conference on Security and Cooperation
DPKO	Department of Peacekeeping Operations
EC	European Community
ECOSOC	Economic and Social Council
FRY	Federal Republic of Yugoslavia
GCC	Gulf Cooperation Council
IAEA	International Atomic Energy Agency
ICFY	International Conference on Former Yugoslavia
ICJ	International Court of Justice
JNA	Yugoslav National Army
MICIVIH	International Civilian Mission in Haiti
MNF	Multinational Force
OAS	Organisation of American States
OAU	Organisation of African Unity
OIC	Organisation of Islamic Countries
PKF	Peace Keeping Force
PKO	Peace Keeping Operations
PLO	Palestine Liberation Organisation
PROP	Provisional Rules of Procedure
RPF	Rwanda Patriotic Forces

RSK	Republika Srpska Krajina
SFRY	Socialist Federal Republic of Yugoslavia
UNAMIR	United Nations Assistance Mission in Rwanda
UNCRO	United Nations Confidence Restoration Operation
UNHCR	United Nations High Commission for Refugees
UNIKOM	United Nations Iraq Kuwait Observation Mission
UNMIH	United Nations Mission in Haiti
UNMO	United Nations Military Observers
UNMOVIC	United Nations Monitoring, Verification and Inspection Commission
UNPAs	United Nations Protected Areas
UNPREDEP	United Nations Preventive Deployment Force
UNPROFOR	United Nations Protection Force
UNSCOM	United Nations Special Commission
UTA	Union des Transports Arienne
WMD	Weapons of Mass Destruction

INTRODUCTION

THE 38-STOREY GLASS Tower on East River in New York City, global head-quarters of the United Nations Organisation, is a symbol of humankind's aspiration for peace. The principal purpose behind the creation of the world body, as a successor to the discredited League of Nations, was to ensure that future generations never again suffered from the scourge of war. The international community thus has a right and duty to inform itself about how the UN goes about discharging this mandate.

The 1990s saw an unprecedented expansion in the peacekeeping operations (PKO) of the United Nations. This growth in the PKOs coincided with the end of the Cold War and the demise of the Soviet Union. It was as if the Security Council had felt stymied and frustrated during all the years of the Cold War and wanted to make up for the lost time by getting involved in all kinds of situations without worrying about whether it would be able to handle them competently or about the impact in case its assumption of unmanageable mandates led to undesirable and unexpected consequences. The fact that the new threats to peace and stability occurred for the most part within the territorial confines of states, and did not arise as a result of disputes between states, coupled with the lack of experience in the UN bureaucracy, did not augur well for the success of the operations. For their part, member states of the United Nations, feeling compelled to 'do something' in response to the carnage going on in some 'failed states', entrusted the Secretary General of the UN with difficult mandates, without providing him the resources, financial and human, which were indispensable for the proper discharge of those mandates.

Article 24 of the Charter of the United Nations has entrusted the 'primary' responsibility for maintaining international peace and security to the Security Council. The use of the word 'primary' would suggest that the General Assembly has at least a 'secondary' or 'residual' responsibility in this field. The General Assembly sought to legislate this 'residual' authority in the form of a resolution commonly known as 'Uniting for Peace' in which it proclaimed for itself the right to set up even a peacekeeping operation in the event that the Security Council was stalemated into inaction because of the use of veto by one or more permanent members. The Uniting for Peace resolution did come in useful on one occasion, in a conflict between Israel and Arab states. For the past four decades, it has been invoked at times by the Palestinians to give vent to their frustration with the Americans who routinely veto resolutions critical of Israel. Thus, it has its uses. However, for the citizens of the world, it is only the Security Council which comes to their mind when issues of war and peace are discussed.

In recent years, the Council has acquired the propensity to deal with all kinds of issues by the simple stratagem of defining peace in holistic terms. Since there is consensus in the international community that peace cannot, and should not, be defined solely in military or security terms but must include other dimensions such as poverty, environment, health, aid, education, and so on, it has become legitimate for some powerful members of the Council to raise all these issues

2

as well in the Council chamber. The developing countries are, in a manner of speaking, the victims of their own cleverness since it was they who took the initiative in defining peace in such broad terms to squeeze funds from the affluent countries for their development plans. Now, with the global war on terror being the highest priority for all nations, there is practically no restriction on the authority of the Security Council to legislate on any subject. There is, thus, a need to critically examine the functioning of the Security Council.

Closely linked to the propensity of the Security Council to expand its jurisdiction in new areas is the question of its representative character. The international community has reached broad consensus on the need to enlarge the membership of the Council in both categories— permanent and non-permanent. For the Council to acquire legitimacy for its decisions, it must more realistically reflect the power equations in the contemporary world which have changed significantly during the past 60 years. Kofi Annan, the Secretary General, has repeatedly called for such expansion. He set up a High Level Panel of 16 eminent men and women in November 2003 to make recommendations on how the UN could be reformed or restructured to deal with the challenges of the modern era. The report of the panel was released in December 2004. The most important, certainly the most eagerly awaited recommendation of the panel deals with the question of how to make the Security Council more representative of contemporary realities. The Secretary General presented his own report titled 'In Larger Freedom' in March 2005. Both these reports were discussed at the General Assembly in the autumn of 2005.

The Security Council is unique in the sense that it combines in itself both legislative and executive functions. It decides whether or not a particular situation warrants its attention; whether it amounts to a threat to peace; what, if anything, it should do about it and then proceeds to do it. Since there are no definitions of terms such as threats or breaches of peace, it is left to the members of the Council to decide how they ought to react in a given situation. What this means in practice is that the permanent members decide everything.

The Security Council also considers itself to be above the law. In theory, the Council is bound by the provisions of the Charter. But the Charter does not contain any constraints on the functioning of the Council except laying down the majority required for adopting decisions. Nowhere does the Charter say that the Council cannot deal with a particular subject or issue. The only restraint on the authority of the Council is the practical one of a country intending to raise an issue mustering the necessary political support within the Council. Thus, USA, UK, and France were able to browbeat other members into going along with their plan to bring to the Council their complaint against Libya on the issue of the Pan Am crash over Lockerbie in Scotland and the crash of the UTA airliner over Chad, even though most members were not at all happy about it. When Libya approached the International Court of Justice for its opinion on the legality of raising the issue in the Council, the three countries concerned made it clear that they would not accept any limitation, even from the International Court of Justice (ICJ), on the authority of the Council in the matter. India toyed with the idea of bringing to the Council the question of the hijackers of an Indian civilian plane who were given asylum in Pakistan, but gave up since it had no chance whatsoever of finding the necessary backing for it. If Pakistan wishes to raise Kashmir, which is already on the official agenda of the Council, it must first ascertain how much support it would be able to mobilise.

This book is the first ever of its kind—an intimate, first hand account of the functioning of the most important organ of the United Nations. It describes, in detail, with dates and names of participants, how the Security Council handled the crises in different regions of the world since the end of the Cold War era, starting with the first Gulf War in 1991. It offers an insight into the secret confabulations that go on in the consultations room, the small and somewhat oppressive room next to the Council chamber, where all important decisions are arrived at. It exemplifies the characteristics of the Council mentioned above.

Fortunately for the United Nations, the very first crisis it was called upon to deal with after the end of the Cold War was of the classic type. Iraq's invasion of Kuwait in August 1990, in an attempt to swallow it, was precisely the type of situation for which the UN was created. It was a clear-cut case of aggression by one state against another. There was no room for any doubt or debate as to who was the aggressor and who the victim. Despite the existence of different and conflicting national interests of great powers, unanimity was achieved among the permanent members on facing up to Iraq's aggression. Even if Iraq had undertaken the operation during the Cold War, the Soviet Union would have found it extremely difficult not to join in the condemnation of the aggression and the demand for withdrawal from Kuwait. It would, however, be safe to assume that the United States would not have been able to impose the kind of sanctions and inspection mechanism that it was able to, if the Cold War had continued. The system of collective security enshrined in the Charter delivered, as it was meant to.

Soon, however, the Security Council was confronted with unforeseen challenges for which the UN and the member states were ill prepared, politically as well as logistically. Some of the crises, such as the one in former Yugoslavia, presented features of civil war as well as of external involvement. Furthermore, by the time the Yugoslav crisis broke, the Russian Federation, which had replaced Soviet Union in the Council, had acquired enough confidence, and felt sufficient domestic pressure, not to give in to every proposal put forward to punish one party to the conflict, namely, the Serbs with whom the Russians had ethnic affinity. The United Nations Secretariat, which was anxious to preserve its impartiality vis-à-vis the parties, often had to give in to pressures from the Americans, who, in turn, had begun to pay attention to the numerically, and hence politically, influential Islamic group. The crisis in former Yugoslavia and Bosnia also exposed the inability and unwillingness of the Europeans to deal on their own with problems in their 'backyard'. (This experience of the early 1990s directly led to the proposal ten years later for the creation of a European Defence Force, independent of NATO and the US.) The United States, most reluctantly, agreed to assume leadership and eventually hammered out the package solution in Dayton.

Most of the other situations of active UN involvement during the 1990s were primarily cases of internal strife or civil war, such as Somalia, Rwanda, Mozambique, Angola, and so on. But even in these crises, external aspects were present. Angola, and to an extent Mozambique, were holdovers from the Cold War era when the rival ideological alliances backed one or the other side in the civil war. Even Rwanda, which was overwhelmingly an ethnic conflict, had an external dimension in the form of active assistance to the Rwanda Patriotic Force, a Tutsi army, by the Uganda government of President Musevini, without which General Kagame could not have succeeded in defeating the largely Hutu Rwandan government armed forces. The common feature in all those situations was that the big powers did not have conflicting interests there. Rather, the problem was precisely the fact that big powers had no interest at all in Somalia, or the other situations, once the Cold War had ended. The Security Council and the Secretariat blundered their way into those crises, often with irreversible damage to their credibility.

The first chapter sets the stage, as it were, for subsequent chapters. It explains, in less than reverent terms, the rules of procedure, the formal framework within which the Council is supposed to operate, as well as the practices that have evolved over time which have come to acquire more importance for the permanent members than the official rules of conduct. A reading of Chapter 1 would help in a better understanding of some of the procedural terms used in the other chapters and in following the day-to-day discussions in the Council of each of the crises dealt with by it.

The subsequent chapters are case studies of the various threats or breaches of peace which came before the Council during my asssociation with it. The intention is not to provide a definitive and exhaustive history of the different crises or of the peacekeeping operations launched by the Council following its consideration of the particular crisis. The aim is to describe how the Council responded to the crises, how the national perspectives of its members, rather than the merits of each case, dominated the thinking, positions, and actions of the members of the Council.

Chapter 2 gives an insight into how Iraq's invasion of Kuwait in August 1990 spontaneously produced a near-unanimous reaction among members condemning the aggression and demanding withdrawal of Iraqi troops from Kuwait. However, when the 'coalition' forces launched disproportionate and indiscriminate strikes against Iraq, causing immense suffering to the ordinary Iraqis, differences emerged. The chapter brings out the not-so-hidden agenda of some members behind sanctions and 'use of all necessary means', with the US and UK making it clear that they wanted a 'regime change' in Baghdad. It reveals how members quibbled about whether Iraq should implement 'all resolutions' or 'all relevant resolutions' and about when the ceasefire between the coalition and Iraqi forces should come into effect. The negotiating story behind Resolution 687, 'the mother of all resolutions', would be of particular interest.

Chapter 3 on Iraq, WMD, and Oil-for-Food, traces the early history of the frequent confrontations between the UN weapons inspectors and Iraq, and of Iraq's deep suspicion, shared by some members of the Council, of the inspectors and their espionage activities. It describes the effort made by the Secretary General to persuade Iraq to agree to the oil-for-food programme, the negotiations between the Secretariat and Iraqi officials on the details of the plan, and the continuous pressure exerted by the Americans and British to influence these negotiations.

Chapters 4 and 5 on former Yugoslavia and Bosnia trace the history of UN involvement in that region and how the UN was gradually dragged into adopting positions which severely damaged its credibility as an impartial body. They bring out the conflicting interests between US and Russia which, for domestic compulsions and ethnic affinity, became increasingly reluctant to endorse harsh measures against the Serbs. Readers would also get a glimpse into the horse-trading which the Russians attempted to indulge in to get recognition for their special position in what they regard as their front yard or 'near abroad'. The rise in the influence of the 'Islam' factor became noticeable for the first time during the Balkan crisis.

Chapter 6 on Middle East gives an account of Secretary of State Baker's travels in the region following the conclusion of the Gulf War and his efforts, ultimately successful, in persuading the Arabs and Israelis to attend the Madrid Conference in October–November 1991. The Palestinian issue is easily the most intractable item which the Council has to handle from time to time. Given Israel's influence with the US, the American representatives on the Council have absolutely no leeway in negotiating the text of any resolution censuring Israel. At the same time, when circumstances demanded it, as was the case during the Gulf War, the Americans readily fell in line with the rest of the members in condemning the deportation of Palestinians from the West Bank and Gaza.

Chapter 7 on Libya—The Lockerbie Disaster highlights the extreme reluctance among most members of the Council to support the Anglo–American–French initiative in bringing to the Security Council an issue which most felt did not belong there. The non-aligned were keen to defuse the problem by bringing the Secretary General into the search for a peaceful, non-sanctions solution, and the latter was only too willing to help. But the three sponsoring countries did not brook any interference, either from the Secretary General or from the International Court of Justice and managed to have their way into imposing sanctions against Libya.

Chapter 8 on Haiti bears much resemblance to the recent events in that unfortunate country. It brings out how the US went to the extent of sending its own military forces to restore Jean-Bertrand Aristide to his presidency, the same Aristide whom the Americans unceremoniously expelled from his country ten years later.

Rwanda Genocide, Chapter 9, was a stark example of the conflict between professions of respect for human rights and lives on the one hand, and cold calculations of national interests on the other, and the prevalence of the latter over the former. UN's image suffered almost irreparably because of the perception, which the Western members of the Council assiduously and successfully propagated, that it was the UN which failed to stop the genocide. This chapter would hopefully help in correcting this impression and in exposing the responsibility of the United States and its friends in denying the required resources to the UN which just might have enabled it to act with some measure of firmness to avert or minimise the massacre. It also exposes the weakness in the United Nations Secretariat which, for reasons of expediency, failed to take a more principled and firm stand in the crisis.

There are two chapters on the election of the Secretary General, Chapters 10 and 11. The one on the election of Dr. Boutros Ghali in 1991 contains a detailed account of how the UN goes about selecting the occupant of what is perhaps the most demanding diplomatic job in the world. The Charter does not contain any guidance on how the search for the Secretary General has to be conducted or what the qualifications for the job ought to be. The permanent members perhaps did this on purpose since the absence of any criteria gives them absolute control over the process. The chapter on the election of Kofi Annan in 1996 recounts how the United States, single-handedly, blocked Dr. Boutros Ghali's bid for a second term. Hopefully, both these chapters would offer some guidance to the United Nations when it embarks on the election of its next Secretary General in the autumn of 2006.

In the final chapter, I have offered some observations on the current debate on reform of the Security Council.

The Security Council and the Secretary General are the two main organs of the United Nations intimately concerned with the principal function of the UN, namely, maintenance of international peace and security. The Secretary General is basically the Chief Administrative Officer of the UN, but public opinion the world over regards him as the keeper of the world's conscience and expects him to uphold the highest standards of integrity and independence in the discharge of his responsibilities. This book would hopefully bring out the tension between the Secretary General and the Security Council, which at times vitiated the relationship between the two most important organs of the United Nations responsible for maintaining peace and security in the world. The relationship between him and the Security Council is crucial to the smooth functioning of the United Nations in the vital sphere of peace and security.

I was associated with the Security Council for six years, as India's representative in 1991–92, and the Secretary General's personal representative to the Council from 1993–96. I have written this book almost entirely on the basis of the notes that I had kept at the time. I did not smuggle out a copy of a single official memo or document or cable. I have one main objective. I want the readers to get a 'feel' of the Security Council. It is not my intention to provide a definitive history of each of the conflicts covered in the book, nor of the policies pursued by the members of the Council nationally, nor indeed of the peace-keeping operations concerned. It is however a definitive history of the handling of those conflicts by the Security Council. My hope is that the readers would obtain a lively and accurate picture of the atmosphere in the Security Council as it battled with the first Gulf War or the problem of air strikes in Bosnia or the horrible genocide in Rwanda. I would wish the readers to be able to visualise the small room in which the Council meets to conduct informal consultations as the ambassadors of the

Informal consultations room. Madeleine Albright is in the middle, with Secretary General Boutros Boutros Ghali to her right. The author is to the right of the Secretary General.

various countries argue back and forth, spending endless hours over what must appear to outsiders as trivial matters such as whether the Council should issue a presidential statement or a resolution or whether the Council should meet at all.

I remain a firm believer in the relevance of the United Nations to the contemporary world despite the blow to its image and credibility by the tragedies in Rwanda and Somalia and especially, by the Iraq-related events of the spring of 2003. In my opinion, the failure or refusal of the Council to pass the 'second resolution' sought by the British and the Americans, whereby they would have the automatic right to strike Iraq, was a rebuff, not so much to the UN as to the two governments concerned which had convinced themselves that they could use the Council on any issue and at any time to serve their national purposes. If the Council had indeed passed the 'second resolution', it would have conferred legitimacy on the military intervention against Iraq whose legality was challenged by no less an authority than Secretary General Kofi Annan. Is that what the international community, so critical and dismissive of the UN in the wake of that war, would have preferred?

1

PROCEDURES AND PRACTICES OF THE SECURITY COUNCIL

THE SECURITY COUNCIL held its first meeting on January 17, 1946, at Church House, Dean's Yard, Westminster, London. After having met for as many as 23 times within a month, it adjourned for transfer to New York-Hunter College from February until August 1946 and to Lake Success from August 28, 1946.

Any organisation needs rules of business to ensure discipline and orderly conduct. The Security Council adopted its provisional rules of procedure at its first meeting. They had been prepared earlier by the Preparatory Commission in San Francisco which was also given the task of proposing the draft agenda for the first meeting. At that first meeting, the Council appointed a Committee of Experts consisting of representatives of all its 11 members to examine and report on the rules of procedure. The Committee made a few recommendations relating to the credentials of representatives and provision for the President to stand down under certain circumstances. After nearly 60 years, the Council has yet to adopt its final or definitive rules of procedure! The rules were amended six times—in May and June 1946, June and December 1947, February 1950, January 1969, January 1974, and December 1982. Nearly all the amendments had to do with the question of official and working languages. The Council has not found it necessary or possible to undertake another exercise of amending its rules for the past 23 years. The Committee of Experts could not reach agreement on a few issues. One such issue was the requirement of quorum, which it decided to come back to later. Then there was the difficult point of the privilege or right of a state, which was not a member not only of the Council but even of the United Nations. Should such a state be allowed to take part in the work of the Council? This issue too was left for later consideration. These probably are some of the reasons why the rules have remained provisional.

The absence of a definitive set of rules, however, has not affected the Council's working negatively. The manner of its functioning cannot be attributed to its rules of procedure but is the result of the fact, often not appreciated by outsiders, that the Council is a political organ and not a juridical body or a court of law. The highest judicial body in the UN system is the International Court of Justice (ICJ), which is based in The Hague. The Council, however, does not consider itself obliged to respect the verdicts of the ICJ. The Security Council takes its decisions on the issues brought before it by member states on the basis of the political equations prevailing on each occasion. Naturally, parties argue about a particular dispute or question and they are listened to, most of the time, by members of the Council. Decisions in the form of resolutions are then worked out in ways which are only slightly less opaque than the ones in which the head of the Roman Catholic Church is elected. More about this, later.

The mandate of the Security Council is, of course, to maintain international peace and security. The first thing that has to happen for the Council to maintain or restore peace in the world is that it has to hold a meeting. One would think that *that* should not be a big deal. Not so. The issue for decision would be whether the Council should meet and if yes, whether they should meet in an official mode or whether they should meet in a mode which is dear to the hearts of all of them, namely, informal consultations. The differences in the two formats are enormous. In the case of an official or formal meeting, should it be an open meeting or a closed meeting? If an open meeting, should non-members of the Council be allowed to speak—or make statements as it is formally and somewhat pompously called? If it is to be a closed meeting, should non-members be allowed to be present in the Council chamber and make statements? Should the records of the meeting be made available to the other members of the UN and/or the media? At the risk of only a slight exaggeration, it can be said that the members, especially some western permanent members, seem to be allergic to official meetings and prefer to avoid them as much as possible.

The most elementary thing about informal meetings is that they have no legal standing. It does not mean that they are illegal, just that the rules do not make any mention of them. The implication of this silence on informal consultations in any official document is that they are not governed by any rules. This is not to suggest that informal meetings are unruly. Over time, practices have developed which, as a body, like the unwritten British constitution, have served the meetings quite well. 'The Security Council is the master of its procedures' is a maxim, which is often heard in the consultations room, almost always from delegates of the same permanent members referred to earlier, when they want to go against established practices and, often, written rules.

And there is the question of languages. The UN has six official languages—English, French, Spanish, Russian, Chinese, and Arabic. The first five have been official languages since the beginning of the Organisation. Arabic was added in December 1982 when the Arab countries collectively lobbied for it and offered to meet the costs involved. The rules regarding languages had to be modified a few times. Initially, of the five official languages—English, Spanish, French,

Russian, and Chinese—only two—English and French—were designated working languages. In 1969, four of them, excluding Chinese,
were made working languages. In 1974, Chinese was also made a working language; by that date, the People's Republic had taken its rightful
place in the UN displacing the Taiwan regime. When Arabic became an
official language of the UN in late 1982, it automatically became an
official as well as working language of the Security Council.

In the early years, there was an additional requirement. Since the
Council dealt with matters of such vital import, it was deemed indispensable for its members to understand and follow precisely what the
parties to a dispute, or indeed other members said and meant in their
interventions, which is yet another term for statements or speeches.
Those sitting in judgment over issues of war and peace had to make sure
that they did not miss any nuance in the presentations of the parties.
Consequently, it was the practice in the Council for each speech to be
translated consecutively in all the working languages. When a statement was made in Russian or Chinese, it was interpreted in other languages one by one! This was in addition to the simultaneous
interpretation, which was available to members as the statements were
delivered. The real reason for this absurd, time-consuming, and highly
expensive practice was that it gave time to diplomats to seek instructions from their governments, since consecutive interpretation could at
times take several hours. Very often, delegates left their seats and either
went home for meals with their families or, more likely, patronised the
bar and 'held consultations' with fellow delegates. It is a fact that many
a knotty issue is thrashed out over a glass of appropriate beverage,
depending on the time of night or evening or, rarely, day.

Official meetings are held in the Security Council chamber, situated in the south-east corner of the UN building. The chamber has the
famous horseshoe table around which members sit in an alphabetical
order. In an act of great generosity, which they might have regretted at
times, the French acquiesced in the seating order to follow the English

alphabet. At its very first meeting in January 1946, the representative of the first country in the English alphabetical order of names, which happened to be Australia, became the first President of the Council. The President sits in the middle, surrounded on his right by the Secretary General and, on his left, by the Secretary of the Council, a Secretariat official who is expected to be the repository of all the rules of procedure as well as the practices followed by the Council over the years. It is the Secretary of the Council who is the more useful to the President since he is the one who must instantly advise the President in case he is confronted with a difficult issue relating to a point of order from a member quoting some rule of procedure of which the President almost certainly has never heard. Mercifully, members of the Council themselves hardly have a nodding acquaintance with the rules of procedure and are understandably reluctant to expose their ignorance. As a result, the Secretary is seldom put to test about his knowledge of the rules.

To come back to the seating order. The other members sit in English alphabetical order starting from the President's left. This means that the member on his right, right to the Secretary General that is, is always the President of the previous month and the member to his left, left of the Secretary that is, is always the president designate for the following month. Thus, there are seven countries seated to the right and seven to the left of the President. Infrequently, this order can change in the middle of the month, when a country changes its official name. When Ivory Coast insisted, to show its solidarity with its erstwhile metropolitan power, on being known as Cote d'Ivoire, its place had to be changed. Yemen changed its name a couple of times during its membership of the Council. USSR became Russian Federation in December 1991. One of the unintended, or perhaps not so unintended, consequences of the change in name is that the country concerned might get to preside over the Council more times than might have otherwise been the case. Most non-permanent members get the privilege to act as the President on an average twice during their 2-year lifetime on the

Council. Incidentally, the right to become President is treated in conformity with impeccable democratic practices; permanent members have to take their turn in the alphabet. Since, however, they *are* permanent, their ambassadors invariably have more shots at the job than others.

The same seating order is observed in the informal consultations room. It is a small room where the Security Council meets to conduct informal consultations, not to be confused with or referred to as the chamber. It has a more intimate character and does lend itself to informality, sometimes even in matters such as dress code over weekends when delegates would risk attending in non-pinstripes or non-dark suits. Being small, the room has less accommodation for delegations— three economy class seats for each member as opposed to five, one first class and four economy class, seats in the chamber. There is no restriction on the number of persons each member can have in the room; it is not unusual for delegates to keep standing when a particularly exciting subject is being discussed. The smaller countries usually have small delegations; their seats are gratefully accepted by larger delegations.

Because of the nature of the issues which the Security Council is called upon to handle, 'consultations' have always been an inseparable part of the process of reaching decisions. In the early days of the UN, these consultations were conducted either in the offices of member states, usually permanent members, or in the delegates' lounge over endless cups of tea and coffee or whiskey. Over time, the need was felt for a room in which the members could collectively consult one another and, so, the 'room next door' was constructed. What has not changed with the passage of years is that real decisions are still arrived at outside of the UN building, certainly outside the 'room' or the 'chamber'. Before they come to the consultations room, all good professional delegates have a pretty good idea of the positions that the other delegates would adopt during the formal informals. Since 'informal consultations' have no official standing, the Council is not supposed to take 'decisions' in the small room. The Council can take decisions, in the form of resolutions, only at its official sessions in the chamber. It follows, therefore, that the President ought not to announce during the course of informal meetings, words to the effect: 'it is so decided' nor should they bang the gavel; ideally, the President should not even be provided with a gavel in the consultations room.

When I represented India in the Council during 1991–92, I often perceived myself in the role of a purist and objected every time the President used his gavel or announced a 'decision'. For example, it is standard practice to finalise the agenda for a formal meeting at the informal meeting that precedes the formal meeting. The President invariably declares at the informal meeting that 'the agenda is adopted'; this is technically wrong. But I was in a minority of one and soon gave up my futile attempts to enforce respect for proper form.

Before assuming presidency, the chief delegate of the country concerned, usually its ambassador or, to give the post its proper designation, permanent representative, calls on the Secretary General, a day or two before its month starts. The Secretary General briefs the president-designate about all the issues which the Council would have to deal with in the coming month; this would be decided in terms of previous decisions of the Council, reports of the Secretary General on various items on its agenda, and so on. Sometimes, of course, new, unexpected issues come up though before they are actually raised in the meeting, quite a lot of consultations take place particularly among the permanent members. The President spends the first couple of days of his presidency in individual or bilateral consultations with the other 14 members about the 'programme of work'. He receives them in his room, next to the 'room' as well as the chamber; his room is conveniently situated exactly opposite the Secretary General's room in the same area. He announces the programme of work for the whole month at the first collective consultations meeting. This is helpful since it enables delegates to prepare themselves in advance for the work ahead in terms of studying reports, getting instructions from their capitals, and the like.

There is no mention of a 'quorum' in the Provisional Rules of Procedure (PROP). The Committee of Experts, appointed on January 17, 1946, examined this question. Some experts would have preferred to include a provision on quorum but others pointed out that it would create serious difficulties. Therefore, there is no requirement of quorum. Theoretically, the Council can hold a meeting without all the 15 members in attendance. In practice, this is unthinkable. How can a country, entrusted with the task of maintaining peace and security—a responsibility which it has had to lobby hard to be given to it—not be present at all the meetings of the Council? The one time the Soviet Union decided to absent itself from an official meeting of the Council in the early 1950s—when the Americans got through the resolution on Korea—it lived to regret that decision for most of the remaining years of its existence. Even at the informal consultation meetings, members are always present. If the ambassador happens to be preoccupied with even more weighty affairs of state, such as accompanying his or her foreign minister who happens to be in town for a shopping expedition with his spouse, a junior member of the delegation would definitely deputise for him.

A party to a dispute, which is before the Council, is barred from voting on it according to PROP but is not disqualified from attending its meetings. In 1994, Rwanda, a member of the Security Council at the time, was represented by the regime that was involved in the genocide and did not feel inhibited from using its presence to influence the decisions of the Council. But in July 1994, the Council decided to suspend Rwanda's presidency for the month of September. On August 28, the Secretary General received the credentials of the new permanent representative of Rwanda, signed by the foreign minister of the new regime that had assumed power in Kigali. The Secretary General certified the credentials as being in order. The Council, thereupon, decided on September 16 that Rwanda would become President in December 1994. It is of interest to note that the representative of the previous regime did not avail himself of Rule 20 under which he could have voluntarily stepped down or declined the presidency.

Some ambassadors, when they become President of the Council, make a feeble but well-meaning effort to enforce discipline; they announce that they would not wait for more than 10 minutes before starting meetings, whether or not all members were present. During my six years in the Council, only once did a meeting start with 14 members present.

Rule 1 of PROP says that the Security Council shall meet whenever convened by the President, but not more than two weeks shall lapse between two meetings. This is one rule which needs to be amended. If it refers to official meetings, which it does, there are times when the Council does not meet for much more than two weeks. But it is Rule 2 whose violation has at times caused much resentment and frustration. The rule says that the Council shall meet when asked by a member of the Council. The verb 'shall' has a mandatory meaning to it; the President must convene an official meeting when even one member of the Council demands it. When the Gulf War was unleashed on January 16, 1991, five countries of the Maghreb asked for a meeting of the Council on January 23. A day later, all the six members of the Gulf Cooperation Council (GCC) wrote to the President opposing the proposal for a meeting. To remove ambiguity about the rules of procedure, Yemen, which was a member of the Council, formally asked for an official meeting on 24th. Cuba, also a member, joined in the demand two days later. India too supported the request for an official meeting. The President, representative of Zaire, was not inclined to convene the meeting since the Americans, British, Soviets, and some others did not favour a public meeting for fear that it would provide a forum for Iraq's friends to make anti-coalition speeches. Days passed without agreement on the matter. On one particular day, January 31, 1991, members discussed for three hours the importance of the rules of procedure and the authority of the President to interpret them. At one stage, the President suggested two options: (a) either Cuba or Yemen could propose inclusion of the item relating to the Gulf War when the Council met to discuss another item, or (b) the item would be included in the provisional agenda and approved at the official meeting, but some member would immediately propose postponing consideration of the item until a later, unspecified date. No one bought his ideas. The argument of the Americans and others was that while they recognised the validity of the rules, the Council had the right and duty to decide on the timing and nature of the meeting. They also made the point that the outcome of the meeting—whether a resolution or a presidential statement or anything else—should be known before going into official meetings. An impartial President would have called a meeting after a week or so. It was left to the President for the following month, Zimbabwe, to declare that he had no alternative but to call a meeting. Thereupon, the idea of a closed meeting was thrown up by someone. When that was agreed, the next question was whether or not to allow non-members to participate and make statements at the official meeting. All this procedural wrangling served the purpose of the principal coalition leaders; the meeting, a closed one, was not held until five weeks later.

There was one more point to be settled. The coalition demanded that they should have the right to put questions to the representatives of non-members at the meeting. No one had any objection to that, but what would be the procedure for that? A non-member (of the Council) has to leave his seat at the table after reading out his statement. Also, others would have inscribed their names in the speakers' list; would they have to wait till the so-called question-answer session was over? The President was clear and firm. His ruling was that a member of the Council could ask questions when his turn to speak came. The answers would be provided when it was the turn of the concerned non-member state to speak. At the official meeting, Saudi Arabia offered to cede its place to Kuwait to whom a question had been asked. But when the President clarified that in that case, Saudi Arabia would have to go to the bottom of the list, it promptly withdrew its generous offer to Kuwait.

One would think that at the informal meetings, the members would dispense with protocolaire and other formalities. Not at all. At his first informal meeting, the President pays tribute to his predecessor for the 'outstanding manner in which he presided over the work of the Council' during his presidency and appeals for the 'same spirit of co-operation' from members. The members reciprocate his sentiments and pledge 'the full co-operation of my delegation' to the President in the discharge of his 'heavy and important' responsibilities. Peter Hohenfellner, the much admired ambassador of Austria, pleaded with his colleagues not to spend time on congratulating him when he assumed the 'high office' of President in April 1991. Everyone agreed with him and promptly proceeded to compliment him on his presidency! Even in smaller groups such as the non-aligned caucus, which had seven members in 1991, the 'distinguished' delegates could not take the risk of not conforming to the practice of offering congratulations and promises of co-operation every time a country became convener of the group. The author never had the opportunity of attending meetings of the P-5, who also had the system of monthly co-ordinators, to find out if they too suffered from the same disease. Incidentally, the P-5 have their own consultations room, located between the Economic and Social Council and Security Council chambers.

Unlike in the official meetings where delegates almost invariably read out prepared statements, it is seldom that they have written texts in informal meetings. The reason is simple. Every word spoken in the official meetings is recorded and distributed to anyone interested enough in learning who said what in the Council. This makes delegates cautious since they do not want to be quoted from their own statements against their government's positions. In the informals, no records, either summary or verbatim, are kept. Delegates have the great advantage of deniability. They all keep their own respective records, as does the

Secretariat, but nothing can be quoted against anybody. This can at times give rise to serious differences among delegations and between them and the Secretariat. The most controversial example of such a situation arose in 1996. (For details, see Chapter 9 on Rwanda.)

It had been the practice for the Secretary General to attend consultations meetings until 1991. He was always present, available to brief members on any matter the Council might be discussing. Often he would be accompanied by the senior officials concerned with the particular subject, but he alone would speak. Xavier Perez de Cuellar was the last Secretary General to follow this tradition. The very first time he did not attend, even though he was present in his office, was in March of 1991. He explained his absence to me as due to pressures of work and to the much-increased frequency of Council meetings. But on the whole he continued to attend the meetings and missed them on very few occasions.

His successor, Boutros Ghali, started his tenure in January 1992 by being respectful to the Council and religiously attended its meetings, formal and informal. He too soon started to attend fewer and fewer meetings, for two reasons. He found the meetings a bit of a bore. He did not form a high opinion of most of the ambassador members of the Council and he just could not cope, in terms of the management of his time, to do justice to all his other responsibilities. When he invited me to join his team of senior advisers in January 1993, he entrusted me with the work relating to the multilateral track of the Middle East peace process started by the Madrid conference.

To mine, and everyone else's surprise, the Secretary General asked me, within two months of my appointment, to act as his personal representative to the Security Council, to speak in his name and answer questions on his behalf. When I joined his office, I had told the Secretary General that the Council was not happy with him since he seldom attended the consultations meetings. He said, with a good deal of justification, that unlike his predecessor, the Council now met every day and twice a day on most days. If he spent all his time in the Council how would he attend to his other work? He was also against his Under Secretaries General wasting their time sitting in the Council. I suggested that the Secretary General ought to explain his difficulties to the Council. It was not a healthy situation when there was an air of hostility between two principal organs of the UN. He promised to think it over. A few days later, at an internal meeting, he consulted, for the sake of form only since his mind had been made up, about his idea of appointing me as his personal representative to the Council. A few of the Under Secretary Generals were distinctly unhappy at the proposal since it would deprive them of the opportunity of interacting with Council members and of the high profile that such interaction provided to them. The Secretary General invited the P-5 and informed them of his decision. His strong point was that I had recently served on the Council and knew the diplomatic corps as well as all the issues on the Council's agenda. The P-5 of course had no choice but to acquiesce. The Secretary General promised to attend personally any time I recommended his personal presence.

The ambassadors on the Security Council were not happy with Boutros Ghali's decision. They took it as an affront to their importance, which it was, at least to an extent. But gradually, they seemed to be not only reconciled with it but to actually welcome it. They now had someone who was continuously in attendance on them, who answered all their questions, who collected information for them, and, most important, who could be used to take their ire out against the Secretary General. Most of them became quite vocal in expressing their unhappiness with the Secretary General in his absence; in his presence they would not say anything except in his praise. For the Secretary General, it was a big relief not to have to put up with the mediocrity, as he saw it, of the ambassadors. The other senior advisors in the Secretariat, at first minded missing out on all the action in the Council. Perhaps what they missed most was the monthly lunches hosted by the President of the Council! After the appointment of the personal representative, only the Secretary General and the personal representative were invited to these lunches. But, over time, even the senior officials came to appreciate the positive side of things. For one, it left them more time to devote to their substantive work. For another, they did not have to face the music in the Council. On some issues such as Bosnia, the atmosphere became extremely uncomfortable when the question of air strikes came up. Many members, especially USA, wanted the UN to launch air strikes against the Serbs, but the force commander, who was French, was not in favour, nor was the civilian head of the United Nations Protection Force in former Yugoslavia. The head of Department of Peace Keeping Operations (DPKO) at the time was grateful that he did not have to deal with questions, framed in not-so-polite terms, from the Americans. I had to take the flak on behalf of my colleagues and at times that was not at all pleasant. But I had the full support of the Secretary General who told me not to take nonsense from anyone. After a while, things settled down and a correct, mutually respectful relationship developed between Secretary General's personal representative and the members of the Security Council. I came to be known as the sixth permanent member of the Council!

When Kofi Annan became Secretary General in January 1997, he was under pressure from the major contributors to effect economy in the expenses of the organisation. In addition to me, there were two other senior advisors in the Secretary General's cabinet on the 38th floor. It was the easiest thing for the new Secretary General to abolish these three senior level posts and to show instant savings. The new Secretary General himself was most decent about the whole thing. He consulted me and other senior staff. He said it was his intention to personally attend meetings of the Council as much as possible, and so on. Importantly, he offered me a politically attractive assignment, albeit not at the headquarters but out in the field.

The Security Council takes decisions usually in the form of reso-lutions. The initiative for drafting resolutions, particularly since the end of the Cold War and the dawn of the new era, is almost always taken by the western permanent members. During my association with the Council, China never tabled a draft resolution in its name alone. It is also reluctant to affix its name to drafts prepared by others. The British delegation in most cases initiates a draft, even when it is the Americans who may be more interested in a particular subject. Thus, most Anglo-American drafts are prepared by the British in the first instance. The usual practice, at least during my association with the Council, was for the US and UK to prepare the first draft which was then shared with either France or/and Russia; China was often the last among the per-manent members to be taken into confidence. Depending on the issue, fellow western members would also be informed, rather than con-sulted, ahead of others. Once the P-5 had taken care of one another's concerns, the draft would be made available to the second-class mem-bers. Over the years, American diplomacy has become sophisticated enough to leave some room for others to propose amendments, a few of which the US would graciously accept. If the subject were of great importance to the Americans, they would go straight to the capitals of the state members of the Council, before sharing their thoughts with them in New York.

It is of course not essential that the draft should command general acceptance before it is put to vote. But the sponsors would like to make sure that their draft would muster the requisite majority without at-tracting a veto. Once the sponsors have decided to table their draft, it is circulated in blue ink among members of the Council. For a draft to become an official document, it is circulated in black ink with a proper document number.

As for actual voting, veto has been the subject of innumerable studies and proposals in recent years. There is widespread sentiment against veto and demand for its abolition or modification. According to one proposal to dilute veto, at least two permanent members should cast a negative vote for the veto to be effective. There is not the slightest chance that any of the permanent members would ever agree to even dilute the right of veto. It is interesting to recall that the provisions relating to veto had generated the maximum controversy at the San Francisco conference in 1945 where the Charter of the UN was hammered out. One of the proposals was that veto should not apply to peaceful settlement of disputes dealt with by the Council under Chapter VI of the Charter, but only to threats or breaches of peace brought to the Council under Chapter VII. The Americans at one stage were willing to consider this idea but the Soviets would not agree to any dilution of the veto. A British delegate—even at that time the British had to take on the job of handling uncomfortable briefs—admitted that the veto provision might not be too democratic but it was not unreasonable, given the immense responsibility the permanent members were going to shoulder. The Indian delegate, perhaps reflecting the view of others, said that it was better to have an imperfect organisation than none at all.

Interestingly, the Charter makes no mention anywhere of the word 'veto'. All it says in Article 27, Para 3, is that decisions of the Council on all matters other than procedural shall be taken with the concurring votes of the permanent members. In the initial years of the UN's existence, there was some discussion on what 'concurring' meant. Did it mean that all five permanent members must actually vote 'yes' for a resolution to pass? Consensus, backed by convenient legal opinion, soon emerged that that was not the case. All that was required was that a permanent member should not cast a negative vote. Thus, abstention by a permanent member was good enough to let a resolution be adopted. The practical effect of this legal interpretation is that an abstention by a permanent member is virtually the same as a positive vote. In case of non-permanent members, however, abstention almost always amounts to a negative vote; the country concerned would actually like to vote against the resolution in question but prefers, for political reasons, to abstain. Abstention, thus, has very different implication depending upon whether it is cast by a permanent or a non-permanent member.

The demand for the abolition of veto has lost much of its force in recent years, because veto has hardly been exercised by permanent members. China has used its veto power on a few occasions involving extensions of peacekeeping operations, all of them having to do with some country having established diplomatic relations with the Taiwan regime. The US invokes veto when a resolution seeking to condemn Israel comes up. There have been instances, very rare, when a certain threat of a veto has deterred intending sponsors from approaching the Council with a draft resolution, as was the case with Kosovo in 1999 when the certainty of Russian veto dissuaded the Americans and others from bringing their plan to bomb Kosovo to the Council, and Iraq in 2003 when the threat of multiple veto from France, Russia, and possibly China frustrated the British, and to a lesser extent, the Americans in their initiative to obtain the so-called second resolution. These two instances are the exceptions to the general rule that the major powers have had their way in the Security Council all these decades without having to suffer setbacks.

Chapter VII of the Charter lays down a graduated response that the Council ought to follow while dealing with threats to or breaches of peace and acts of aggression. Ideally, the first step should be economic and other sanctions. At some stage down the line, the Council ought to decide that sanctions had not and would not bring about the desired result and only thereafter proceed to take enforcement measures prescribed in Article 42 onwards. The Council also ought to state the specific article under which it proposes to act. In practice, however, the Council has found it convenient to simply state that it is acting under Chapter VII, without specifying any article. In August 1990, the Security Council imposed comprehensive sanctions against Iraq. Before proceeding to adopt Resolution 678 in November 1990 which authorised member states to use all necessary means to throw Iraq out of Kuwait, the Council should have determined that the sanctions had not and would not reverse Iraq's aggression against Kuwait. Both procedurally and politically that should have been the correct way to proceed. The Americans would have experienced no difficulty in obtaining such a decision from the Council, but they did not want to take the slightest risk of a veto from the Soviets.

There is a practice in the Council according to which resolutions are not put to vote unless members have received it at least 24 hours earlier. Often, this practice is waived on grounds of urgency, almost always at the insistence of the permanent members. The same is true of presidential statements. There are advantages and disadvantages in resorting to presidential statements. Since a statement is supposed to reflect general consensus, every member technically has a veto over it. In practice, however, non-permanent members are not able to hold up or deny consensus over a statement except by getting at least one permanent member, preferably a western one, to align on its side. The other advantage is that as it is meant to convey the general sense of the Council on a given situation, members can always explain away their consent to it by saying that they would have taken a different position had it been a resolution. This, in fact, is the great advantage of a presidential statement, namely, members do not have to vote on it. The disadvantage is that in the spirit of compromise, members do end up agreeing to more than they would have liked to. In that sense, a resolution is better because it enables members to accurately demonstrate and record their views on the matter under consideration. For a presidential statement too, 24 hours notice is supposed to be available, but this requirement is more often than not waived at the request of interested parties. The thing about serving on the Council is that since members are dealing with questions of war and peace, they have always to be ready to show flexibility and co-operation; in other words, to accommodate the demands of the major powers. The second-class members always have to think and worry about the implications of their actions in the Council on their bilateral relations with the big powers.

An interesting point often came up in connection with presidential statements. Should the statement refer to 'the Council' or to 'members of the Council'? To outsiders this may sound like splitting hair, but to those engaged in preparing the statements, it was a very serious matter. If the statement referred to 'the Council', it meant that the statement reflected the common position of the whole Council. But if it spoke of 'members of the Council', it could be speaking on behalf of only a majority of members. Whatever the merits of the respective phrases, the agreed practice, at least in the 1990s was that if the statement was read out in an official meeting, it could be either on behalf of the Council or members of the Council. But if the statement was issued as an official document without being read out by the President in an open, official meeting, it could only be on behalf of members of the Council.

One unwritten rule, never violated so far, forbids non-members of the Council from participating in the meetings of informal consultations. Attempts have been made by non-members to attend the consultations, but never very seriously because everyone knows that it is a 'no go' matter. Non-members can try to influence discussions and the nature of the decisions by either conveying their views to the President of the Council and/or, more likely, through their contacts with members of the Council. If India-Pakistan questions came up, delegates from both countries would be spending enormous amount of their energy in keeping in touch with permanent members as well as with most of the non-permanent members to ensure an outcome which would not be too unpalatable for them. The first priority of India would be to block altogether any discussion of the problem in the small room. At one time, the permanent mission of India had to cover a lot of ground to keep references to the Kashmir question out of the Secretary General's annual reports on the work of the organisation. If the Secretary General felt that he had to say something about the situation in Kashmir in his report, it opened up possibilities to Pakistan and its friends to raise the issue in their statements to the General Assembly and in all other forums of the UN system including the Security Council.

A unique practice, which has since acquired the status of an institution, is called the 'Arria' formula. It is named after the then permanent representative of Venezuela, Diego Arria. He was dynamic, extremely active on the Bosnian crisis, almost always on the side of Bosnian Muslims. He got so involved with the Bosnian Muslims that he came to be known as 'Don Diego of Sarajevo'! He came up with the idea that if members of the Council thought it would be useful to listen to someone who was not a delegate of a country or an official of the UN, they could invite him or her to another room. It would not be a consultations meeting and would not be shown as such in the UN journal. It would not be obligatory for members to attend it; only those interested in what the visitor might have to share with them would attend. Arria's idea found resonance among many members and was accepted by all. Soon, meetings under the Arria formula became a fact of life in the UN. To the author's recollection, no member of the Council missed any of such meetings. At times, the Arria formula presented headaches for some members. For example, in 2003, Pakistan wanted to arrange a meeting with Kashmiri militants under the Arria formula. Pakistan was at the time a member of the Security Council. Nearly all other members had agreed to attend. The Indians had a hard time, in New York and in Washington, to sabotage it. They succeeded in preventing it, thanks to timely and crucial support of the Americans.

The Cyprus problem is a good example of how a country that is not member of the Security Council influences the contents of a resolution. The two parties directly involved—Greek Cypriots and Turkish Cypriots—have to work through Greece and Turkey respectively. The delegates of these two member states, among the most active in the UN, use all available channels to bring pressure on those drafting the resolution, US and UK. Sometimes, the Under Secretary General dealing with Cyprus would take the initiative in preparing the first draft; he always consulted with the powers concerned. The Greeks had more channels available to them than the Turks, such as the non-aligned group, the Commonwealth, and so on but the Turks made up by having the most influential member of the UN on their side.

During my presidency, the permanent representatives of UK and US came to my room to work out a compromise. Both were very able— Tom Pickering of the US and David Hannay of the UK. The latter was forceful enough to have prevailed over any adversary, but he often had to defer to Pickering. It seems Pickering also managed to convince the Turks of the merits of any deal that he struck with Hannay as being in their best interests. The Greeks were more at ease with Hannay. During my six years with the Security Council, all the resolutions on Cyprus were adopted without a vote and without any statements by anyone on most occasions. This was a great success for the diplomats concerned as well as for the unwritten but respected practices developed by the Americans and the British in dealing with one of the most vexing problems on the UN's agenda.

Sometimes, it becomes essential to give access in some form to non-members to an item being considered by the Council. This is particularly the case for countries contributing troops to peacekeeping operations. It stands to reason that when countries are willing to put the lives of their soldiers and policemen on the firing line, they ought to have an opportunity to interact with the Council and the Secretariat to know how their troops were going to be utilised. Regular meetings were and are being held for the purpose, not in the consultations room but in some other conference room. This practice was put on a more regular and institutional basis in the 1990s when the peacekeeping operations proliferated like never before.

In an effort to improve the image of the Council vis-à-vis the rest of the membership of the UN, some members of the Council, New

Zealand in particular, suggested, and the others agreed, that the meetings with troop-contributing countries, which earlier were chaired by the head of the DPKO, should be jointly chaired by the President of the Council and the Secretariat. We in the Secretariat were not happy about it but we could do nothing to stop it. It was taken for granted, that the Secretariat co-chair would be the chief of DPKO. However, the Secretary General decided that I, as his special representative to the Council, would co-chair the meetings along with the Council President. I tried to persuade the Secretary General to nominate the DPKO, but his answer was that anything to do with the Council would be handled by Gharekhan. DPKO probably thought that I had used my proximity with the Secretary General to have myself nominated, but this was not the case. The head of DPKO was justifiably resentful of the Secretary General's decision and sent a note to him, protesting the decision, adding, 'I was a little surprised that there was no prior consultation with me before the instruction was issued'. The Secretary General's chief of staff showed me the note. I advised him to suppress it and not to show it to the Secretary General. He agreed with me and the note was never shown to the Secretary General.

A pernicious practice developed in the 1990s when the peacekeeping operations expanded exponentially. The affluent countries took over the Organisation. Because of financial constraints, resulting almost exclusively from America's non-payment of its dues to the UN, many of the programmes were funded by the so-called voluntary grants by the rich countries through 'trust funds'. These funds became the legitimate instruments for the developed countries to run the UN. Since they supplied the money, they also supplied the required human resources and sold the necessary equipment and other supplies. This practice had particularly undesirable consequences in the DPKO. It had more than 110 military officers placed at its disposal 'pro buono' to man its situation centre, to help the office of the military adviser to the Secretary General. Nearly all of them were from western countries.

Since the UN did not pay them, they owed no allegiance to it. They brought with them their own concepts and they saw to it that the UN procured its supplies from their countries. They provided intelligence to their governments. There was tremendous dissatisfaction among delegations with this practice of 'freebies'.

This was also true of field stations. In Afghanistan, for instance, the head of the operation was a German. His staff officers, political and military, five or six in number, were provided by countries on a pro buono basis. Naturally, they all came from Japan, UK, Russia, France, and the like. Then, a few countries formed themselves into a group called 'friends of the rapid deployment headquarters'! They came up with a proposal for Rapidly Deployable Headquarters. The idea was that every peacekeeping operation needed a headquarters in the field. These 'friends' undertook to provide the officers and to transport them to the field. Sometimes, they would recruit a few people from the developing countries for the sake of appearance. The ambassador of Pakistan made a scathing attack on DPKO in October 1996 for letting itself become part of this exercise.

Since the Security Council is the place where all the action takes place, there is enormous interest among members to find out what goes on behind the closed doors of the consultations room. Delegates from many non-members hover around in the south or the Security Council lounge, using their contacts, which they would have cultivated over a period of months, both among member states and Secretariat, to acquaint themselves with the activities of the Council. As an exercise in public relations, a practice developed in the 1990s for the President of the Council to hold monthly meetings where he briefed all non-members on the activities of the Council. This concern for image was a new phenomenon in the history of the Council. Other initiatives were also started at about the same time such as publishing in the journal of the UN the date, time and even the subjects for informal consultation meetings. In addition, there was the 'stake out' at the entrance to the council where delegates as well as the Secretariat officials, especially the Secretary General, stop over, usually on their way out after the meeting, and spend a few minutes talking to the media. That is also the place where representatives of the media corner delegates of their choice to ferret out more information.

One of the questions which the Council has to deal with is the admission of new members. Over the years, the number of fresh admissions has declined for the obvious reason that there are fewer and fewer new states being born. A significant item which was never brought on the agenda of the Security Council in the month of December 1991 related to the permanent seat occupied by the Soviet Union. It became clear by the middle of the month that the Soviet Union as such would cease to exist before the end of the year. While it was obvious that the Russian Federation would occupy the Soviet seat, the question was how this would or should be done. One possibility was for the Russian Federation to apply for membership of the UN and claim the Soviet seat in the Security Council after its admission to the UN. The second alternative was for the Russian Federation to straightaway claim the Soviet seat as a successor state to the Soviet Union. The preferred option of the permanent members as well as of many others was for the former constituent republics of the Soviet Union, which were all independent states by now, to collectively declare that the Russian Federation was the successor state and, as such, would occupy the Soviet Union's permanent seat in the Security Council. This is how it eventually happened.

The Commonwealth of Independent States (CIS) meeting in Alma Ata, adopted a unanimous resolution to the effect that the Russian Federation should occupy the permanent seat in the Security Council. President Boris Yeltsin wrote a letter to the Secretary General, merely informing him of the Alma Ata decision and asking him to inform UN members that henceforth the Russian Federation would take the seat formerly occupied by the Soviet Union. There was no debate, no discussion, no resolution, nothing. The transition from Soviet Union to

Russian Federation almost went unnoticed and unreported. Yulie Vorontsov, who started his presidency of the Security Council as the permanent representative of the Soviet Union, ended it as the permanent representative of the Russian Federation.

The Soviet Union was assertive, even ruthless, in protecting and promoting its interests in the world. By comparison, Russia was somewhat timid in the beginning, almost defensive, even when it came to its interests in its backyard and beyond. Russian diplomacy under foreign minister Kozyrev attached overriding priority to maintaining friendly relations with the West, Americans in particular. This approach manifested itself fully at the United Nations. Ambassador Vorontsov, a veteran diplomat with over 45 years experience, hugely admired for his professionalism, faithfully implemented his minister's policy. A time came when most members of the UN stopped bothering to find out the Russian position on a given issue and how Russia would vote on it. India was one of the few countries which were still interested in ascertaining Russian views before deciding its positions. The demise of the Soviet Union was lamented by diplomats from the non-aligned and other developing countries. 'The balancing factor has disappeared' was the refrain most often heard. The Palestinians in particular were shattered; they lost the one friend which could exert some influence in the Security Council on their behalf.

Towards the end of his assignment in New York, Vorontsov became more assertive in defending Russian positions. For the first time, in June–July of 1994, we saw him dig in, in defiance of the Americans. He was concerned with the Americans not treating his country with respect, particularly at their lack of sensitivity to issues of interests to Russia. When he got his chance he fully exploited it. He said unless the Council 'welcomed' Russian and CIS help in the Georgia–Abkhazia conflict, he would not agree to the US draft on Haiti. He repeatedly spoke of double standards. He won his point.

When Sergei Lavrov replaced Vorontsov, things began to change; they became interesting once again. Lavrov was younger, close to Kozyrev, and felt more confident in projecting Russia's independence. He was more willing to use the forum of the Security Council to push for Russian interests, to make deals with the Americans, rather than to acquiesce in what he perceived to be a one-sided traffic. Vorontsov went to Washington as ambassador; he had served there earlier in his career and no doubt regarded it as his dream posting.

The Russians canvassed vigorously for recognition of their special position and responsibility in the near abroad and steadily won support for their role there. The realities of life, realpolitik, began to assert themselves. At the traditional lunch hosted by the Secretary General in honour of the ministers of P-5 on September 29, 1994, Kozyrev personally was very critical of the US, so much so that the French ambassador described the meeting as 'abysmal' and 'incredible'. Under Secretary General Marrack Goulding's remark was: the honeymoon is over. Kozyrev accused the US of adopting double standards.

Another indication of Russian assertiveness came from the Indians. The foreign minister of Pakistan wrote to the President of the Security Council asking for a five-fold increase in the strength of the UN Military Observer Group for India and Pakistan as well as for an enhanced mandate for it. The Russians told India that they had informed Pakistan that they were opposed to its plan to internationalise the issue and would veto it.

In September 1996, UK proposed a draft resolution condemning Saddam Hussein's foray into Irbil in the north to help the Kurdish leader Barzani gain control of the town. The Americans sent down 44 missiles against Iraq's anti-missile batteries in the no-fly zone. The British draft, of course, made no mention of the American activity and sought to justify it implicitly by describing Iraq's action as a violation of Resolution 688. But they ran into a wall of opposition from Russia, China, and France. Russia threatened to veto the draft. There was widespread sympathy for the view that Iraq had acted within its own territory and had merely helped Barzani at his request in his fight with a rival Kurd leader. The British had to withdraw the draft.

SECURITY COUNCIL SUMMIT

At the initiative of the British delegation, it was decided that there should be a special, one-day meeting of the Security Council at the summit level on January 31, 1992. The Heads of State and Government of all the 15 members of the Council approved of the idea. The ostensible purpose was to pledge and demonstrate support for Boutros Ghali, the new Secretary General, who assumed office on January 1, 1992. But the British and other permanent members had their own agenda. The main interest of the British was that the meeting would give high profile publicity to Prime Minister John Major who would preside over the meeting, since it was UK's turn for presidency in January. As for other permanent members, the summit would be an excellent opportunity to enlarge and expand the agenda of the Security Council to new areas. Heads of State and Government are invariably polite to one another and if one of them asks for some favour or special consideration for his proposal, the odds are that the others would not be too difficult about it.

A momentous event such as the Summit of the Security Council could not but issue an equally momentous declaration. The British proposed a draft statement which would be read out by Major at the Summit. It was only on January 22 that the draft was shared with the non-permanent members. The caucus exchanged views about it and found many shortcomings in the text. India in particular had many problems with the draft. India proposed some amendments but was not at all confident that the other non-aligned would want to go against the British draft. US, UK, and France, time and again, came up with suggestions which were not palatable to the non-aligned, but the non-aligned did not wish to appear to be non-co-operative. They did not wish to 'irritate' the permanent members, not only on the occasion of the summit meeting, but as a general rule, and were keen to be perceived by them as 'co-operative'. This was precisely how the permanent members would like the non-permanent members to behave. The Indians took their work more seriously and, consequently, often had to fight a lonely battle.

India's basic point and concern was that since this was a meeting of 15 leaders as members of the Security Council, the statement should deal with matters which were within the Security Council's jurisdiction. The permanent members, especially the western three, wanted to use the opportunity to broaden the Council's mandate without having to amend the Charter. India did manage to some extent in modifying the text to clarify this point. For example, the original draft would have the Secretary General prepare a report on the ways and means of strengthening peacekeeping role and submit it to the Security Council by May 1. India pointed out that while the Council was the appropriate organ to authorize peacekeeping operations, the broad question of peacekeeping principles was the legitimate concern of the entire membership of the UN. Hence, the report should be submitted to the General Assembly. This was accepted.

However, India was not so successful in amending the language relating to weapons of mass destruction and International Atomic Energy Agency (IAEA) safeguards. Regarding the former, India asked that the statement should demand not only the prevention of the spread of such weapons but also the elimination of the existing stocks of such weapons. India also could not agree to a blanket ban on the spread of all technology related to the research for such weapons since much of the technology had civilian application also. Regarding IAEA safeguards, India could not agree with the language which conferred competence on the Security Council to deal with cases of violation of safeguards. On both these points, there was absolutely no support for

India from any of the other members. India was totally isolated. The British threatened to go to the press and publicly blame India for holding up consensus. I called the Indian foreign secretary at Heathrow airport in London. He consulted the prime minister and called me back to say that India should not allow itself to be isolated. India would not hold up consensus but would express its reservations in the statement of the prime minister in the summit meeting.

There was one more tricky problem of protocol, namely, the order of speakers at the summit meeting. India had proposed that the speakers' list should be prepared according to some criteria and not arbitrarily. George Bush wanted to be the first speaker. In that case, India suggested, the President should start the list from his left in a clockwise order. At informal consultations on the 30th, just a day before the summit, Hannay said he had received his instructions from his prime minister. After a few words of welcome by Major, the Secretary General would make his statement. Thereafter Francois Mitterrand would speak since he was the first to have proposed the idea of a summit over a year ago. After that, the speakers would be taken alphabetically, one from the left and one from the right. This was an ingenious arrangement since all the permanent members, except China, would speak first.

This British proposal would have carried if Ayala Lasso of Ecuador had not intervened. He proposed that the usual Council procedure ought to be followed. In other words, the floor should be given in the order in which speakers were inscribed or in an alphabetical order. Others piped in to propose their own ideas. Hannay said he had his instructions but would consult later. He invited some Permanent Representatives to his residence at 9:30 in the evening. A neat compromise was reached as follows: the Heads of State would speak first in alphabetical order, followed by Heads of Government in their own alphabetical order. The foreign ministers of Hungary and Zimbabwe would be the last to speak. Thus, Bush would not be the first speaker; in fact, he would be the last, just before Venezuela.

Boutros Ghali proposed another summit on January 31, 1995, exactly three years after the first one. The idea originated with him but he suggested it to Menem, President of Argentina, who then adopted it as his own. If the meeting happened, Menem would chair it since it would be Argentina's turn for the presidency. Menem was enthusiastic at the prospect of presiding over a high-level meeting. Leaders, however much they might desire fame externally, like nothing better than domestic benefit from forays in international arena. There was not much enthusiasm for the idea among other members. But the Secretary General lobbied hard for it. He spoke personally about it to several leaders, especially to the doubtful ones such as China and Russia. At his instance, I spoke to Emilio Cardenas, the ambassador of Argentina, and conveyed to him the Secretary General's assessment about these two countries and his advice that Argentina better do something about it. Argentina did send special missions to Moscow and Beijing.

The non-permanent members were generally supportive but the P-5 were not. I suspected that the P-5 did not really want their leaders to attend a meeting which would not be chaired by one of them. John Major said he would attend, but he could hardly say otherwise since he had chaired the 1992 summit. Mitterrand promised to attend, health permitting, but it would have been his last show on the international scene. The other three were more honest, they never committed themselves. It was the American position which scuttled the idea. US said it was against the proposal since it would not risk the repeat of what had just transpired at the Conference on Security and Cooperation in (CSCE) summit in Budapest. And nobody wanted to attend a summit meeting if the American president was not going to be there. It was as simple as that. Hannay had been saying that the meeting should be held irrespective of who attended it. But when Bill Clinton decided against, even Major lost all enthusiasm. In any case, Menem certainly lost his.

After every meeting of the Council, formal or informal, some one in the secretariat prepares a summary of the proceedings for internal use. Some times, the person has a delightful sense of humour. An excellent example of secretariat humour is provided by the following extract of the summary prepared after the informal meeting on June 9, 1994:

> The US held up further action during the first round of discussions on the draft resolution (regarding Rwanda) pending instructions from his capital, and came back to the afternoon round, with a number of amendments, to one of which the UK (Hannay) gave remarkably short shrift, even interrupting the US while he did so. All present were highly amused, even the President (Oman). The good humour held up remarkably well thereafter as the Council engaged in its favourite pastime of drafting, drafting and redrafting a text that had been drafted, drafted and redrafted countless times already during the many hours the working group had met yesterday. However, as opposed to others who like short shrift to be given—and the shorter the shrift the better—members seem to be agreed that a fine draft is like a fine painting in that one can never be sure when it is finished. They finally ran out of steam a mere two hours after the afternoon round had begun, with a mere two 'bouts de phrase', neither of them particularly substantive, to show for all their effort.

2

GULF WAR 1991

WHEN SADDAM HUSSEIN invaded Kuwait in the early hours of August 2, 1990, it was late evening on August 1 in New York. The American mission to the UN learnt of the invasion before the Kuwaiti mission. Tom Pickering, the American ambassador, tracked Abulhassan, the Kuwaiti ambassador, to the elegant and posh Russian Tea Room where he was enjoying a leisurely meal with some Arab friends. The US mission had already drafted the first resolution on Iraq by the time the Kuwaiti ambassador was escorted to Pickering's office on First Avenue, opposite the UN Headquarters building. The Security Council met a few hours later and adopted the first of many resolutions on the Iraq–Kuwait question.

Tension between Iraq and Kuwait had been building up during that summer. Iraq had suffered heavily, both in terms of financial set-back and human lives, in the eight-year-long war with Iran, at the end of which Saddam Hussein had nothing to show by way of gain from the war. Iraq had piled up a huge foreign debt and was banking on higher oil price to recover its losses. Saddam Hussein expected Kuwait and other Arabs to waive his debts to them since, he argued, he had waged the war against Iran to save them from Iran. He should have known better. Meanwhile, the oil price declined, further aggravating Iraq's financial woes. Saddam Hussein also accused Kuwait of funnelling away Iraqi oil into Kuwaiti wells. Hectic efforts were made by the Arab League as well by Jordan, Egypt, and Saudi Arabia to ward off the impending conflict, but Saddam Hussein was not inclined to any compromise short of Kuwait agreeing to all his demands. He seemed to have finally made up his mind to invade Kuwait when he interpreted, or misinterpreted, a remark made to him by April Glaspie, the American ambassador to Baghdad, as an indication of American green signal to him to proceed as he wished against Kuwait. He attacked Kuwait, annexed it, and declared it to be Iraq's 19th province.

The one characteristic of Saddam Hussein which stands out throughout the dozen years of his confrontation with the 'coalition' is his awful sense of timing. Even at the height of the Cold War, it would have been difficult for the Soviet Union to support his invasion of Kuwait. But when he attacked Kuwait on August 2, 1990, after the fall of the Berlin Wall the previous November and the consequent end of the Cold War, there was absolutely no possibility for the Soviet Union, which continued to exist as such until December 1991, not to join in the condemnation of Iraqi action and the subsequent resolutions imposing sanctions against Iraq. Saddam Hussein's other serious error was in underestimating American resolve and stakes in the region.

During the months leading up to the Second Gulf War in the spring of 2003, the Americans had deployed their forces in the region before they and the British approached the Security Council for a resolution seeking a mandate to attack Iraq. Perhaps the most compelling reason for not agreeing to give more time to the UN weapons inspectors in 2003 was the extremely high temperatures that would have made life most uncomfortable for their troops which had already been deployed in the region for a few months.

In 1990–91, however, the situation was different. While the US had made up its mind to use force against Iraq to attain its objectives—control over the second richest oil reserves in the world, establishment of base facilities in the region (Osama bin Laden, the implacable enemy of American presence in Saudi Arabia, had not yet emerged on the scene), removal of Saddam Hussein—it needed time to mobilise and deploy its forces, to secure basing facilities in Iraq's neighbouring countries and to build a political and military coalition.

Secretary of State James Baker and his able ambassador to the UN, Tom Pickering, did a marvellous job in putting the coalition together. The toughest challenge for them was to secure a decent majority in favour of a resolution which would authorise the use of 'all necessary means', in other words, the use of military force, to secure Iraq's withdrawal from Kuwait. Baker spoke on telephone to the Malaysian foreign minister while he was having dinner in a restaurant in Tokyo. Other foreign ministers were similarly got hold of without consideration for the time of day or night. Resolution 678, authorising the use of force, was adopted on November 29, without going through the step-by-step approach prescribed in the Charter. Article 42 lays down that the Council may proceed to the measures involving the use of armed forces should it decide that the measures imposed under Article 41, namely economic sanctions, would not be or have proved to be inadequate. The Americans never offered any explanation for not obtaining the determination under Article 42.

Resolution 678 authorised use of force not only to undo Iraq's occupation of Kuwait, but also to 'restore international peace and security in the area'. The sting of the resolution, thus, was in its tail. It is this phrase which made it possible for the Anglo–American combine to maintain the draconian sanctions regime years after Kuwait regained its sovereignty—and a part of the Umm Qasr port in the bargain—and

46

to set up and enforce the elaborate mechanisms to eliminate Iraq's capability for all time to come to acquire mass destruction and other offensive weapons.

Resolution 678 provided Iraq a grace period of 45 days to comply with the demands of the Security Council, which expired on January 15, 1991.

On the 14th, at about 10 a.m., the French ambassador met with the non-aligned caucus and presented an initiative of his government on the Gulf crisis. It was a six-point text, starting with Iraqi withdrawal according to a time table, with speedy and massive withdrawals to take place immediately, and ending with a proposal for an international conference. Much to the delight of the French, all seven non-aligned members spontaneously expressed support for the French peace initiative.

At an informal meeting of the Council on January 10, 1991, the President of the Council informed members of Secretary General Perez de Cuellar's decision to go to Baghdad as a last-ditch effort to avoid war. There was no discussion; no questions were asked. At about 11:30 a.m. on January 14, Perez de Cuellar came to the consultations and presented his report on his mission to Baghdad. It was not an optimistic report. He had been rebuffed by Saddam Hussein who had snubbed him by keeping him waiting for an unconscionably long time before receiving him. Many members asked for the written text of his report. He said he would comply with the request on this occasion, but extremely reluctantly. He reminded the Council that he himself had served on the Council not so long ago and he knew that the well-established practice in the Council was not to circulate such statements in writing. His concern was that in case the text leaked out, it might affect his credibility. The Iraqis, for example, might accuse him of not having reflected their views accurately. His apprehension proved justified. The Iraqis released their version of the Secretary General's discussions which differed in significant details from the latter's.

The following day, January 15, the Soviets and British came to the Council with their own paper, in competition to the French initiative. It was basically a British draft, but they had accepted one sentence proposed by the Soviets which entitled them to claim co-authorship. The Anglo–Soviet paper was in the nature of an ultimatum to Saddam Hussein. There was no support for it in the caucus. The P-5 met in the afternoon to iron out their differences but to no avail. They came to the conclusion that the only practical option was to ask the Secretary General to issue an appeal. In essence, the Council would ask the Secretary General to help it out since it was unable to reach agreement. The Secretary General would thus be bailing the Council out. The Secretary General issued his statement in the evening.

The Security Council was discussing the situation in the Occupied Palestinian Territories on January 16, 1991 in informal consultations. It had adjourned the meeting to give time to members for private consultations among themselves. The Council had been engaged in debating the subject for several weeks, since December of the previous year, without succeeding in arriving at a consensus on how to deal with the issue—through a resolution, or through a presidential statement, or no action at all. It was just before 7 p.m. local time that we learnt about the start of the military operations by the 'coalition' in Iraq in terms of Resolution 678. The deadline or 'grace period' given to Iraq under 678 had expired without Iraq having withdrawn from Kuwait. Everybody was expecting the war to start at any time and was glued to the TV monitor placed thoughtfully by the Secretariat. The source of our information was CNN which remained the speediest, and in most cases, the only avenue for members of the Council on the course of the Gulf War. It took the Council nearly a month to hold an official meeting to take stock of the situation in the Iraq–Kuwait theatre although the war was fought in the name of the Council and in terms of a resolution of the Council.

The President of the Council for the month, Ambassador Bagbeni of Zaire, had scheduled an informal meeting of the Council for 10:30 in the evening of January 16 to discuss Occupied Territories. As soon as the meeting commenced, it was quickly recognised that it would be absurd for the Council to discuss anything except the Gulf War. The President surprised everyone, and shocked many, by proposing a statement to be issued by him to the effect that all peaceful efforts to resolve the Gulf crisis had failed and that, as a consequence, armed action as authorised by the Council was now under way. This would have had the effect of giving the Council's blessings to the war. The President quickly abandoned his idea and consulted permanent members individually and non-aligned caucus collectively. Informal consultations resumed at about midnight. Ambassador Pickering gave an oral report and Ambassador Hannay of UK made a two-line intervention. Ambassador Blanc of France read out extracts from his president's speech delivered earlier and added that French air force planes would take part in the operations when the time came. Ambassador Al Ashtal of Yemen, the longest serving ambassador at the UN, said Yemen regretted the use of force and that sanctions would have achieved the desired objective. Ambassador Alarcon of Cuba, one of the most able diplomats in the UN, said that the Council had no right to authorise any state to use force, except under the provisions of the Charter. He added that Cuba's participation in the meeting did not in any way alter its position that Resolution 678 was illegal and that what we were witnessing was a shameful chapter in history.

The next few weeks were spent by the Council in debating the theological question whether it was incumbent on the President of the Council to convene an official meeting when one or more members of the Council asked for it. Rule 2 of the Provisional Rules of Procedure of the Council is unambiguous. It states that the President shall convene a meeting when requested by a member of the Council, as opposed to a non-member of the Council. Soon after the Gulf War broke out, the five Maghreb countries asked for an official meeting of the Council to discuss the situation in the Gulf. Since none of them was a member of the Council, Rule 2 did not come into play. Besides, the six countries comprising the Gulf Cooperation Council (GCC) conveyed to the President their strong opposition to the proposal for a formal meeting. The Americans and their allies were strongly against the idea of an official meeting since they feared, rightly, criticism of their action, especially its severity and disproportionality.

The first informal consultations were convened on January 24, a week after the start of the war. The President invited members of the 'coalition' to present reports on the course of the war. Pickering, the first to speak, distributed transcripts of Defence Secretary Cheney and Chairman of the Joint Chiefs Colin Powell's press briefings the previous day. He said the campaign was proceeding apace and had been largely successful. He added that there had been no sign as yet of Iraq pulling out or of any change of attitude on the part of Saddam Hussein. Cuba made the point that the meeting could not be accepted as fulfillment of Para 5 of 678 which required the Council 'to remain seized of the matter' which could only be done in an official meeting. Ashtal said the military operations were obviously going far beyond 678 and informed the meeting of his request for a formal meeting. I agreed with Ashtal that the objectives of the coalition seemed to go beyond those authorised under 678, whereupon Hannay chipped in to say that the objectives remained liberation of Kuwait and not destruction or dismemberment of Iraq. I objected to the use of the term 'coalition' since Resolution 678 only spoke of 'countries co-operating with Kuwait' but no one seemed impressed with my profound observation!

At an informal meeting on January 31, Ashtal made a long intervention, saying that the Council was passing through its darkest crisis. 'Large organisations such as the UN would be destroyed when small rules were not respected. The West always lectured countries of the Third World about respect for law, but in fact the respect was only for might. Respect for the rules of procedure was the only guarantee for democracy for big and small states alike.' Both he and Alarcon deplored the practice of taking all decisions in this 'small room which had become more powerful than the Security Council chamber or even the Charter itself'. Alarcon added for good measure that some members seemed to have developed a fear for the larger chamber and to have acquired the habit of meeting only at night, as if they dreaded daylight. When Hannay became irritated at Yemen and Cuba frequently flinging the rules of procedure in support of the demand for an official meeting, the latter replied that the Charter and Rules of Procedure were all that the small states had. Pickering's reaction was quite constructive. He said there were two issues: how to proceed in conformity with the rules of procedure and how to avoid anything which would prejudice the special nature of the conflict the Council was discussing. 'We must guard against the blind application of the rules. The lemmings in Scandinavia throw themselves from the cliff once a year. This seems to be their rule. But we have to use our own judgment.'

Ambassador Vorontsov of Soviet Union who had most effortlessly and professionally taken to the new policy of his government to align itself firmly with the United States recounted the story of the cat and the cook. 'The cat stole a piece of meat, stayed in a corner, and started munching on it. The cook was upset and made an eloquent speech telling the cat that what it had done was wrong. Of course, the cat could not care less about the cook's speech and went on eating. Moral of the story: Saddam would keep swallowing Kuwait while the Council would be listening to eloquent speeches.'

The President, however, had made up his mind; he was not going to agree to anything that would upset his American friends. He kept avoiding giving any ruling and dragged on the process of informal and bilateral consultations until the end of his presidency. Even big powers, however, prefer to give an appearance of being reasonable from time to time. Since the rules were unambiguous, it became increasingly

51

untenable for the Americans to object to the demand for an official meeting forever. An alternative proposal to convene a closed, though official, meeting emerged. The President for February, Mumbengegwi of Zimbabwe, who proved to be an excellent President, eventually managed to find a consensus among members. A formal, open meeting was convened on February 13 at which, after the adoption of the agenda, Hannay proposed that the meeting should be held in private as provided in Rule 48. The motion was carried by a vote of nine in favour, two against (Cuba and Yemen), and four abstentions (India, China, Ecuador, and Zimbabwe). It was a close call and a setback for the Americans since they had got 12 votes in favour of 678.

The Security Council, which is tasked to deal with questions of war and peace, does not lack its own sense of drama. Before convening in an official, closed meeting on the February 14, we were summoned to informals in the 'small room'. Pickering and Hannay suggested that they should be given an opportunity to 'ask questions' to non-members participating in the debate in the Council 'to explore new ideas', as they put it. I asked Hannay who would ask questions to whom and said it would be more appropriate to allow non-members of the Council to interrogate members about what they intended to do to resolve the question peacefully. Ambassador Li Daoyu of China agreed with me. The President said there was obviously a difference of opinion. Hannay asked him: 'Will you give me the floor to ask questions?' The President told him if he put up his hand on a point of order, he was duty bound to give him the floor. But if it was to ask a question, he would follow the usual procedure and Hannay would have to inscribe his name again in the speakers' list. Hannay got a bit impatient, but the President held his ground.

There followed another procedural discussion on whether members of the Council had the right to intervene any time they wished to, superceding non-members inscribed on the list. Pickering said denying that right to members would set another precedent. I pointed out that the matter was not so simple; once a non-member concluded his statement, he had to leave his seat at the Council table. The President added that the order of speakers even among members had to be followed. At the formal meeting, after Ambassador Abulhassan of Kuwait spoke, Pickering, who was already inscribed on the list, asked a few questions to the Kuwaiti. The President gave the floor to Shihabi of Saudi Arabia who was next on the list. Shihabi offered to yield to Abulhassan. The President ruled that he was willing to give the floor to Kuwait on the understanding that Shihabi would then take his turn at the end of the speakers' list! Shihabi was not prepared to take his support for Kuwait and the US that far. He spoke next and Kuwait had to take its turn in the line. The way things turned out, the Americans and the British did ask questions to Kuwait, Saudi Arabia, and Iraq. Since the list of speakers was exhausted, the ambassadors of these countries did not have to wait long to give answers and did not even have to leave their seats at the Council table. Everybody was happy!

The next battle in the Council was waged on the conditions for a ceasefire in the Gulf War. On February 19, Vorontsov informed members about a visit by Iraq's foreign minister Tariq Aziz to Moscow. Mikhail Gorbachev had proposed a peace plan, the key feature of which was the immediate commencement of withdrawal from Kuwait. Vorontsov carefully emphasised that the Soviet plan was not a proposal for ceasefire but a serious diplomatic process, which also stressed the important role of the Security Council in international peace and security. Tariq Aziz would fly to Baghdad for consultations and return to Moscow with Saddam Hussein's response.

The informal meeting of the Council on February 23 was the first occasion when the Secretary General was not present in the room. Perez de Cuellar was most conscientious in attending all the meetings of the Council thus far, even though most of the time he had nothing to say or learn. At the informals on February 8 he had voiced his serious concern at the public perception of the United Nations in all regions of the world. He said he had received expressions of frustration from people everywhere whose trust it was imperative for the UN to retain. In private conversations, de Cuellar made no effort to hide his despair that the war was being fought in the name of the UN. From February 23, he became selective in attending the informal meetings of the Council, a practice his successor, Boutros Ghali, almost completely gave up in the second year of his term. Boutros Ghali's appearances in the Council became so rare that every time he decided to attend, it became a special occasion that attracted considerable attention from the media as well as members of the Council.

On February 25, Vorontsov informed Council members that, in spite of the commencement of ground operations, his government believed that it would be possible to attain the goals of UN resolutions without further loss of life. Saddam Hussein had issued a statement on that very day ordering his troops to withdraw from Kuwait in an organised manner. Vorontsov suggested that the Council could set a very short time limit for Iraq to complete its withdrawal. Soviet Union had reason to believe that Iraq's response would be positive. Pickering, who was not comfortable with the Soviet initiative, said that the key question was whether Iraq was prepared to implement all the resolutions. This reference to 'all resolutions' became very important later.

On February 27, the members saw a letter from Aziz, in which Iraq accepted Resolution 660 as well as 662 and 674 if the Council annulled the three resolutions on sanctions. This was unacceptable to the US, which insisted that Iraq must accept all resolutions unconditionally. At one point, the atmosphere in the room became a bit tense, so Anet of Cote d'Ivoire decided to tell a story. "A lady of certain age was at an immigration checkpoint waiting to cross the border. She filled up the required forms but without mentioning her age. The immigration officer asked her to fill the age column. The lady hesitated for a long time, whereupon the officer told her: 'Madam, the longer you wait, the older you will get'".

On the 28th, the President informed members that he had received a letter from Aziz in which Iraq accepted 660 and all the resolutions. Iraq requested a formal meeting of the Council to consider its response and to arrange a ceasefire. Pickering referred to his president's speech the previous evening and said that a de facto ceasefire was in place since the midnight of February 27. He added that there was still an element of ambiguity in Iraq's response which spoke of 660 and all the resolutions. Hannay echoed Pickering and suggested that the addition of 'relevant' would clarify the situation. Ashtal protested strongly, arguing that it was surely preferable for Iraq to accept all resolutions rather than only all 'relevant' resolutions. The President clarified that Iraq was ready to accept 'all' or 'all relevant' resolutions, but it was he who had advised Iraq to accept 'all' resolutions since it was his impression that the Council demanded compliance with all resolutions, including those that might be irrelevant!

On the evening of February 28, the Americans sprang a draft resolution on their unsuspecting partners in P-5. The Chinese in particular were most upset. The draft sought to extend the scope of Resolution 678 to such an extent that, theoretically, the coalition would have UN-sanctioned authority to resume 'offensive combat operations' even if one Kuwaiti was alleged to be missing or even if one painting was alleged by Kuwait as not returned by Iraq. It asked Iraq to do certain things immediately. The word 'immediately' was mentioned at least a dozen times. Words never before seen in UN resolutions were used such as 'bearing in mind world's need to be assured of Iraq's peaceful intentions'. Li told me that under the draft, Iraq would remain under sanctions until doomsday. 'In fact, Iraq is already under doomsday,' he said. According to Li, he had spoken strongly against the draft in the meeting of the P-5, especially against Para 4 which would authorise the coalition to resume 'offensive combat operations' if Iraq failed to comply with all the demands immediately. Pickering was willing to drop this para but was overruled by John Bolton who had come down from Washington to take personal charge of negotiations.

When the Americans want something, they do not waste time. They approached all the capitals before even sharing the draft with Council members in New York and asked that the draft be adopted on March 1. They almost made it. The resolution was adopted on the evening of March 2 as Resolution 686, with 11 in favour, one less than 678, 1 against (Cuba), and 3 abstentions (China, India, and Yemen). The language was diluted, with all the stuff about offensive combat operations being deleted, but the implication remained the same. Efforts to include language to the effect that if Iraq did all that was demanded of it there would be a ceasefire led nowhere. The word 'ceasefire' was not even mentioned in the resolution. Pickering's argument was that 'ceasefire' came into operation in case of a war between two states or groups of states, whereas this was a war between Iraq and a group of states that were fighting on behalf of the UN. The only purpose Resolution 686 served was to enable the coalition to keep up the myth that it was carrying out Security Council's instructions.

Ecuador and Zimbabwe were expected to abstain on 686 almost until the last moment, but they succumbed to US pressure. Zimbabwe had been the loudest in criticising the draft, but its ambassador told me that Harare had been spoken to, and that was that. India was also under considerable pressure not just from the Americans but also from the Gulf countries and even the Soviet Union, but stood firm. Li later regretted having moderated the offensive language, since the original draft would not have got more than nine votes.

India had prepared a draft resolution proposing lifting of the embargo on food for Iraq. Even such an innocuous resolution was not acceptable to the Americans, not even to all the non-aligned. Pickering asked me to convert it into a presidential statement. I agreed, since the resolution would not have got more than five votes!

An interesting discussion took place in the informals on March 3, The Palestinian observer had met the President to convey to him his concern about the safety of the Palestinian community in Kuwait. Yemen suggested that the President should convey the gist of the Palestinian demarche to Kuwait. Pickering promptly protested, pointing out that this would be a serious precedent and would amount to a violation of Article 2(7) of the Charter regarding non-interference in internal affairs. I immediately agreed with him, with Kashmir in mind. France said that the President could either act on his own or on a specific mandate from the Council. At one stage, Yemen reminded others that the members had stopped talking about Palestinian safety and were discussing how the President should conduct himself. The President summed up, saying that there was agreement that (a) he was the President and (b) that he had common sense!

There was a lull in the Security Council for about three weeks when there were no meetings, formal or informal. The 'coalition' forces were busy in Iraq encouraging, by their mere presence in the country, the Kurds in the north and Shias in the south to rebel against the regime. The Bush administration was hoping that the rebels would accomplish what the coalition had dearly wanted but felt squeamish to bring about, namely, get rid of Saddam Hussein politically and, preferably, physically. The Americans had signed a ceasefire agreement with Iraqi generals on February 27, banning the use of fixed wing aircraft by Iraq but not banning the use of helicopter gunships. Saddam Hussein used the latter with devastating effect in quelling the rebellion, especially in the south. The Americans also got worried about Iran acquiring enormous influence in the region if it was allowed unhindered to help the Shia rebels in the south. Saudi Arabia would prefer to deal with Saddam Hussein than with an Iraq controlled by Iran through the Shia majority in Iraq. Turkey was equally worried about the Iraqi Kurds wresting too much autonomy for themselves for fear of encouraging the Turkish Kurds to make similar demands. At one point, George Bush had claimed that, with Operation Desert Storm, the Americans had managed to rid themselves of the Vietnam Syndrome, but he backtracked on that claim a few days later and admitted that he did not want the US to get bogged down in Iraq. In fact, the more brutal Saddam Hussein became in quelling the rebellion, the more embarrassing it became for the Americans to witness the slaughter of those they had encouraged to rebel in the first place. So, they became desperate to pull out of Iraq, but for that they needed a permanent ceasefire in place which Iraq had to agree to!

On March 20, the Americans presented to their partners in the P-5 what instantly came to be known as the 'mother of all resolutions'. It was a 19-page, 25-preambular and 32-operative paragraph text. It was prepared in Washington and even Pickering was apparently not associated with its drafting. The non-permanent members were given the draft, as became the practice, in the capitals. The Five had intensive consultations over the draft for a week, including even the weekend and, on one occasion, working until three in the morning. Vorontsov got very tired and commented that 'this step-mother of all resolutions' had given him a lot of headache!

It was then for the non-permanent members to work on the draft, not that they could do much to it once the Five had agreed on the text. India and others prepared a series of amendments, some of which, insignificant ones, the Americans accepted. The US deliberately used extreme language in the initial draft to leave scope for them to agree to a few amendments from others who then felt obliged to support the final draft. They use this tactic quite effectively with China, which, having its ideas incorporated, gets on board at least to the extent of not voting against the resolution. On this particular draft, the Chinese did not insist much on any particular point since they had decided to abstain on it. The non-aligned caucus attempted to prepare a set of amendments on which all seven could agree, but Cote d'Ivoire and Zaire made it clear that they would agree only to those amendments that the P-5 could accept!

58

The draft came out in a printed form on the evening of April 1 once it had been agreed to among the Five after they had accommodated one another's concerns. The last remaining point was about the range of the missiles beyond which they would be banned; the Soviets wanted and managed to protect their commercial interests. The Security Council adopted the resolution as Resolution 687 on April 2 by a vote of 12 in favour, 1 against (Cuba) and 2 abstentions (Ecuador and Yemen). Ecuador's vote surprised everyone. Ayala Lasso, Ecuador's ambassador explained privately that he had to abstain because the Congress in Quito had very strong reservations on the paragraphs relating to the border in view of Ecuador's experience with Peru. China's positive vote, though known in advance, was nonetheless a surprise. The Chinese ambassador said privately that he had to vote in favour since he had taken active part in the P-5 meetings where he had got the others to accept many of his suggestions. The real reason, as everybody knew, was Secretary Baker's call to his Chinese counterpart Qian Qichen.

India's affirmative vote also surprised some, especially since its statement in explanation of vote was quite critical and had indicated abstention. India's vote was dictated by pragmatic considerations. The Americans had made it clear to India, in Washington as well as in New Delhi, that failure to support the resolution would make it very difficult for them to help India in the World Bank and the IMF. India was going through a grave balance of payments crisis and badly needed the Bank and the Fund to tide over the crisis. India had also approached Germany and Japan bilaterally but they had said that they could not help unless they had the green light from Washington. India also had to worry about the reaction in the Gulf and Saudi Arabia where it had huge interests. Politically, India would need positive understanding from the Americans and others if and when the Kashmir question came before the Council.

At the official public meeting of the Council when Resolution 687 was adopted, the Iraqi ambassador Anbari described the Kuwaiti ambassador Abulhassan as 'this individual sitting on my right who has no individual or national identity'. He was reprimanded by the President for using such unparliamentary language about a colleague.

Thus, the Americans succeeded, once again, in manipulating the Council. They wanted this resolution since they were anxious to get out of Iraq, but would only do so under an umbrella of a UN-decreed ceasefire. The question was: How long would Iraq take to accept this humiliating resolution? The longer Iraq took to accept 687, the more difficult things would become for the Americans. On the other hand, once the US pulled out, Saddam Hussein would have a clear field to throw everything at the insurgents. Of course, from Iraq's point of view, a delay in agreeing to the resolution also implied a delay in lifting of the sanctions.

At the beginning of April, the Kurdish question came to occupy centre stage. The situation of the Kurds became truly horrendous. TV screens were full of images of Kurdish women and children, thousands of them, on the mountains of northern Iraq bordering Iran and Turkey, shivering and starving in snow. Iran opened and closed its border every alternate day, saying it could not cope with the flood of refugees. It checked every refugee and vehicle for weapons since it did not want a Kurdish problem of its own on its hands. Turkey was equally determined not to let these people establish permanent camp in Turkey; it did not want them to incite its own Kurds even more than they already were. President Bush whom the Kurds at one time affectionately called 'Al Hajj Bush' was now labelled 'the great betrayer'. But more than the Americans, it was the French who were most exercised about the fate of the Kurds. The French mission in New York was under direct and strict instructions from the president, rather from Mme Danielle Mitterand, to take up the issue in the Council. They presented a draft resolution on April 4, condemning Iraq's repression of the Kurds, demanding and insisting that Iraq open a dialogue with the Kurds regarding their safety and return to their homes. Both Turkey and Iran wrote letters to the

Security Council, saying that the influx of the Kurds was a threat to their security thus establishing a rationale for the Security Council to act.

The draft posed problems for some delegations, since it amounted to interference in Iraq's internal affairs. These principles had not lost their validity despite everything, especially for non-permanent members, since the P-5 could always protect themselves through the veto power. India and others proposed amendments which would have made it clear that the Council was only dealing with the aspect of peace and security. India had in mind the 1971 East Pakistan parallel when it had described the presence of 10 million refugees in West Bengal as indirect aggression against it. Even Turkey liked the Indian amendments. But the French had no flexibility whatsoever. It was suggested to China that it should threaten a veto unless the Indian amendments were accepted; its ambassador declined the honour. The Romanian ambassador said he could not sleep for 24 hours as he was extremely troubled by the draft resolution. To calm his nerves, the French inserted a preambular para recalling Article 2 (7) of the Charter which forbids interference in internal affairs of states. The resolution was adopted on April 5 as Resolution 688, with a vote of 10 in favour, 3 against (Cuba, Yemen, and Zimbabwe), and 2 abstentions (China and India).

Stung by the vehement criticism by columnists and Congressmen and pressed by Britain and European allies, the Bush administration was forced to be less squeamish about supporting more forceful measures to provide humanitarian assistance to the Kurds as well as to 'protect' them. John Major, the British Prime Minister who had always to try hard not to appear a wimp, which was what his predecessor. Margaret Thatcher called him, came up with a proposal to create a 'safety zone' in northern Iraq which would be administered by the UN, with the help of military advisers if necessary. He got the idea endorsed by the European Community. Hannay at the New York end had the unenviable task of pushing his boss's proposal which nobody, not even Hannay I suspected, was enthusiastic about.

The Americans were not happy with it at all firstly because Major had not consulted Bush about it in advance and secondly because the proposal raised sensitive issues of sovereignty and interference in internal affairs. During informal consultations, Vorontsov, for the first time, raised reservations regarding an initiative from a fellow P-5 member. The Chinese said privately, 'Enough is enough; at some stage we must stop raising our hand.' Sensing the strength of the opposition, Hannay tried to salvage the situation by explaining that the idea was to create a 'safe haven' and not a 'safety zone'; it would not be a military operation but a civilian exercise of a temporary nature. The Americans were concerned that the tendency of such zones was to perpetuate themselves and, in this particular case, might presage the emergence of Kurdistan and the fragmentation of Iraq. The other countries in the region—Syria, Turkey, and Iran—with significant Kurdish populations, were dead set against the break-up of Iraq.

But Bush was under relentless pressure. His administration resorted to taking ad hoc measures. They first announced a substantial relief programme. Then they declared that US military aircraft would airdrop supplies and warned Iraq against attempting to block them. On April 10, US asked Iraq not to fly any aircraft—fixed wing or helicopters—north of the 36th parallel, thus in effect creating a de facto safety zone, including Mosul. This was a unilateral move; there was no sanction in any resolution for enforcing the no-fly zone. The Americans, however, were still reluctant to embrace Major's proposal in its original form. Hannay said he would try to work through the Secretary General in a pragmatic way.

On April 16, Bush announced a major initiative. US, UK, and France would jointly set up massive refugee camps in northern Iraq and would send troops to provide protection to the Kurds. The US troop strength would be around 10,000. Britain and France would also send thousands. Bush said it would be a purely humanitarian operation and expected that Iraq would not interfere with it in any way. He left no doubt that if Iraq did interfere, the allies would respond with force. Bush admitted that he was not seeking a Security Council resolution for the proposed initiative because some of the friends in the coalition had difficulty supporting it. It was evident that Bush was groping to find a coherent policy and had not thought through the implications of his initiative. How long would the American troops stay in northern Iraq? Would the refugees ever feel safe enough to go back to their homes while Saddam Hussein was in power? They might not wish to go back even if he was dethroned. They would endeavour to prolong American military presence so that a de facto Kurdish area of autonomy would emerge which, who knew, could become a forerunner of an independent Kurdistan. The Kurds had been fighting for Kurdistan for 70 years. There are more Kurds than Jews in the world. They were shrewd enough to scale their demand to one for autonomy, if only for tactical reasons.

By April 25, Operation 'Provide Comfort', as the Bush initiative was called, had led to the deployment of 2000 US army personnel in Zakho. Some British marines and soldiers from France, Canada, and Netherlands had joined the Americans. But the Kurds had not yet come down from the mountains in any significant numbers. On the 25th, the Americans issued an ultimatum to Iraq to clear out of northern Iraq or else... It was not clear whether the US intention was to push Iraq into a corner, since Iraq had already written to the Secretary General that while it rejected the US action as an infringement of Iraq's sovereignty, it would not raise any difficulty since it was a humanitarian operation. Iraq also wanted the UN to take over the entire operation from the Americans as it had signed an MOU with Sadruddin Aga Khan. The Shias in the south, in the meanwhile, were getting worried that Saddam Hussein would turn his full fury against them if and when the Kurds would reach a *modus vivendi* with the government in Baghdad, as appeared to be the case when the Kurdish leaders signed an agreement in principle with Baghdad on April 24, by which Saddam conceded the Kurdish demand for autonomy.

On April 9, the Secretary General announced the appointment of
Eric Suy as special representative to report on the situation in Iraq in
terms of Resolution 688. He said the permanent representative of Iraq
had expressed satisfaction with the appointment. A UN team, led by
Sadruddin Agha Khan, concluded an agreement with the government
of Iraq whereby Iraq agreed to extend full co-operation to the UN in
reaching relief to all those in need in the country.

Meanwhile, on April 11, the Council approved the text of a letter
that the President would send to Iraq in reply to its letter wherein it
expressed acceptance of 687 confirming that the ceasefire was in effect.
The President had circulated the draft of the letter four days in advance.
The British and the Americans kept proposing amendments. At the
meeting, I raised a basic point, more to have fun than in a serious mode.
I questioned the need for any reply to Iraq since 687 said that the
ceasefire would come into force once Iraq conveyed acceptance of 687.
I also kept asking other questions and seeking clarifications from the
Americans and British who had assumed that the draft reply would sail
through once the two of them had cleared it with the President, which
is what usually happened. Hannay explained that the reply was necessary since Iraq was notorious for writing ambiguous letters and the
Council had to be satisfied that Iraq's letter did in fact amount to an
unconditional acceptance of the resolution. My final question was:
when would the ceasefire come into effect? I suggested it should be
retroactive from the date of Iraq's acceptance of 687, but the Americans
and the British held that it would be effective from the date of the
President's reply. Eventually it was decided to leave this point vague.

The Council had to deal with an important matter arising out of
687, namely, the establishment of United Nations Iraq Kuwait Observation Mission (UNIKOM). The Five had worked out a draft among
themselves, which they brought to the Council on April 9. While the
other members had tried to keep themselves informed as best as they
could, none of them had been consulted. I strongly protested at the lack

of elementary courtesy of consulting non-permanent members. I also proposed an additional paragraph to make it clear that UNIKOM was being set up under Chapter VII of the Charter. This was important since it was to be set up without Iraq's consent and the principle of host country consent was extremely important for many. Pickering accepted my amendment on behalf of the Five. The resolution was then adopted unanimously in a formal meeting of the Council. After the meeting, the Chinese ambassador told me that he was very upset at Pickering whose role was only to convene meetings of the Five and not to speak or agree to anything in their name.

US, UK, and France pressed the Secretary General to send a police force to northern Iraq to replace their troops, in other words to bail them out. He refused to oblige them; he would only send police if Iraq made the request and if the Council authorised it. Iraq had made it clear that it would not agree to a police force. As far as the Council was concerned, the Soviets and the Chinese were holding out against the proposal. Since the US and its allies were anxious to pull out their forces, there was this curious phenomenon of the Americans wishing for a successful outcome of the negotiations between Iraqi government and the Kurds, so that they could withdraw without loss of face!

Under Paragraph 21 of Resolution 687, the Council was required to undertake a review, every 60 days, of Iraq's compliance with its obligations under the resolution so as to consider the question of revoking or reducing the sanctions. The first such review was carried out at an informal meeting on June 11, 1991. All members took part in the discussions, which went along predictable political lines. The US and its coalition partners argued that there was no basis to modify the sanctions regime in any manner whereas the non-aligned suggested that Iraq had indeed done a few things and deserved at least a partial relief. The 'coalition' members also referred to Iraq's massive acts of repression in the north and south as further grounds for absence of any justification for either lifting or reducing sanctions.

The more interesting debate was on how to reflect or record the lack of consensus on this question. Some, such as the US, were quite content to leave the matter without any further action. But many felt strongly that there must be a record of the fact that the Council had carried out the review under Paragraph 21 of 687 and that there was no consensus on lifting or reducing the sanctions. It was also argued by India and others that such a review could only be undertaken at an official meeting. Finally, it was decided that the President of the Council would write a letter to the Secretary General, informing him that a review had been carried out and that there was no consensus, and so on. The President's letter would be issued as an official document of the Council. This came to be known as the Ayala Lasso formula after the Ecuador ambassador who first proposed it. He was most unhappy that his name was linked to such a negative document.

Another provision of 687 on which action had to be taken was the setting up of a compensation fund to compensate all those who suffered losses due to Iraq's unlawful invasion of Kuwait. The Secretary General was required to submit proposals for the establishment and administration of the fund as well the percentage of the money earned from the sale of Iraqi oil which would be credited to the compensation fund. This last point proved controversial in the Council, with Britain and America pushing for 50 per cent and others, especially Cuba, Yemen, India, and Ecuador suggesting 10 or 15 per cent, with a maximum of 30 per cent, the figure proposed by the Secretary General. The subject first came up for discussion on June 13; it was settled only on August 7 when the Americans finally gave their consent to 30 per cent. The compensation fund eventually became a huge operation and paid scores of billions of dollars in compensation to individuals and corporations in many countries.

A subject which kept coming up before the Council every few days with tedious frequency was the friction between the United Nations Special Commission (UNSCOM) and Security Council on the one hand,

and Iraq on the other, as the weapons inspectors went about their job of destroying Iraq's Weapons of Mass Destruction (WMD) capability. This subject is dealt with in the next chapter.

Iraq's invasion of Kuwait was the first crisis which came before the Security Council after the end of the Cold War. Fortunately for the international community, it was the kind of conflict which the Council was ideally equipped to handle. It was an inter-state war in which one side was clearly the aggressor. There was no scope for members of the Council, the permanent members in particular, to indulge in politics regarding who was the aggressor and who the victim. Within hours of Saddam Hussein's army marching into Kuwait in the early hours of August 2, 1990, agreement was reached in the Council on demanding that Iraq immediately reverse its aggression. Again, when the Council adopted, within four days of its first resolution on Iraq, Resolution 661 imposing comprehensive sanctions against Iraq under Chapter VII, there was no negative vote; only Cuba and Yemen abstained. Even China supported the sanctions. The issue was clear-cut.

There was, at the United Nations, a fair amount of assessment at the time that the sanctions would work. However, from the very beginning, loopholes appeared, some legal such as oil sales to Jordan and others inevitable. In any case, the Council did not make a determination under Article 42 that the sanctions proved or would prove to be inadequate to achieve the desired result. In fact, the real issue was: what was the desired objective? This became apparent as the war progressed. It should have become clear to the discerning when the leaders of the coalition cleverly inserted the innocent-looking phrase 'to restore international peace and security in the area' in Resolution 678. Since the US and UK, as the leading permanent members on this subject, were the ones to decide when peace would be deemed to have been achieved and maintained, there was no way the sanctions would be lifted and the war stopped until Saddam Hussein was got rid of. They made this clear at the highest level and frequently during informal consultations. This explains the indiscriminate and disproportionate use of air power against military and non-military targets in Iraq. It is not clear why President Bush did not go all the way and topple Saddam Hussein; he badly wanted that to happen. He too miscalculated. He thought the Shias in the south and the Kurds in the north, with help from the disaffected elements in the army, would do the job for him. He could have completed the mission, since at least for him the war was legal and he could have accomplished it at no great expense, instead of leaving it for his son 12 years later, who had to embark on a highly controversial and unpopular war and who is still quagmired in it, suffering heavy losses in American-and Iraqi-lives and resources.

The Gulf War of 2003 has shown that the second-class, non-permanent members have it in their power to influence decision-making in the Security Council. During the 1991 war, the non-aligned did not acquit themselves well. They were divided and easily gave in to UK and USA who received vigorous support from the Soviets as also the French. In 2003, the non-permanent members showed some spine and refused to support the so-called second resolution. The situation was no doubt different, in the sense that two permanent members and one major western member of the Council were ready to cast a negative vote in 2003. The fact, nonetheless, remains that countries which were always expected to go along with the Americans refused to commit their support. The US and UK could not even muster a simple majority of nine. This saved the day for whatever is left of the international legal regime.

3

IRAQ, WMD AND OIL-FOR-FOOD

SECURITY COUNCIL RESOLUTION 687, passed in April 1991, technically ushered in the ceasefire between the 'coalition' and Iraq. Among other demands, it required Iraq to submit to the Security Council, *within fifteen days,* a declaration of the locations, amounts, and types of all the proscribed items and to agree to an inspection regime about the nature and extent of which Iraq had no idea at the time. Iraq had just been subjected to 43 days of intense bombing such as had not been witnessed since the Second World War as well as a ground offensive. Its leadership could not, even if it had wanted to, comply with this deadline. It was as if those who crafted Resolution 687 never intended Iraq to be in a position to comply with its terms. Iraq certainly deserved punishment for its unacceptable act of aggression against Kuwait, but its people did not deserve to be put in a situation wherein whatever the government did to satisfy the demands of the 'international community', they, the Iraqi people, would not get relief from the draconian sanctions regime put in place by the same international community.

Resolution 687 laid down in great detail Iraq's obligations in respect of destroying its existing stockpiles of weapons of mass destruction—nuclear, chemical and biological—as well as to forswear for all time to come any programme to develop and acquire such weapons. An elaborate mechanism was put in place to verify the destruction of existing weapons and to monitor ongoing and future programmes to ensure that Iraq did not engage in a clandestine programme to develop and manufacture these weapons. The IAEA, the nuclear watchdog agency based in Vienna, was entrusted with the responsibility in the nuclear field. A new mechanism was created called the United Nations Special Commission for Observation and Monitoring (UNSCOM) to deal with chemical and biological weapons as well as with the missile systems. It was the first such experiment, under Chapter VII of the Charter, designed to enforce disarmament of a member state. Some major powers that fashioned the establishment of UNSCOM seem to have envisaged it as a forerunner of an institutional mechanism, which could serve as a model to deal with similar cases in future.

The first head of UNSCOM was Rolf Ekeus, a Swede, who had spent many years in the field of disarmament negotiations. By coincidence, the director general of the IAEA was also a Swede, Hans Blix, who later became head of UNSCOM in its new incarnation under the name of United Nations Monitoring, Verification and Inspection Commission (UNMOVIC). Ekeus, with whom I had many conversations in New York soon after he took charge of UNSCOM, seemed to genuinely want to complete his assignment at the earliest; his family did not join him in New York and he was anxious to get back to his original post in Vienna. He insisted he could complete his task in a matter of months provided he received full co-operation from Iraq. Things did not develop as he might have wished.

For weeks and months after 687 was adopted, there was consensus, even unanimity, in the Council on the absolute need for Iraq to fulfil its requirements under the resolutions without excuses, and unconditionally. All the members were one in condemning what Iraq had done and punishing the nation for it. Gradually, however, some members came to the conclusion that the sanctions regime and the inspection mechanism were in reality a means to ensure that Iraq would never be able to satisfy the demands of the leading powers in the anti-Iraq coalition and would not be permitted to return to the international fold so long as Saddam Hussein remained in power. 'Regime change' was not just an unstated objective; it was frequently expressed by the leaders of the coalition countries. A vicious circle developed. Iraq, having come to the correct conclusion that the Anglo–American combine would never agree to lift or even reduce the sanctions, became less and less co-operative with UNSCOM. This played into the hands of the hardliners who could legitimately use Iraq's non-compliance to maintain undiluted the sanctions regime. Ekeus and company regularly complained about Iraq's attitude of defiance and non-compliance. Those members of the Council who were sympathetic to the sufferings of the Iraqi people had no option but to go along with the maintenance of the sanctions.

The Security Council witnessed, many a time, scenes of confrontation with Iraq. Tariq Aziz, the foreign minister of Iraq, made numerous trips to the United Nations to argue the case for lifting or diluting the sanctions. He complained about the arrogant behaviour of the UNSCOM inspectors. One of his major complaints was that nearly all the inspectors were from countries which had joined in the war against Iraq. He accused the inspectors of spying on behalf of the Americans and others and of their colonialist attitude. Ekeus, who had unrestricted access to the Council and who was acutely conscious of his responsibility for the safety of the inspectors, sought the help of the Security Council every time his inspectors were denied access to some site or were otherwise not treated in accordance with their status as UN personnel.

Ekeus came to the Security Council on February 27, 1992. He had been to Baghdad the previous week. The Iraqis had refused to submit

71

to all the demands of UNSCOM, claiming they had the right to convert some of the military facilities to civilian use. Ekeus and the western countries would not agree to such conversion. Iraq had refused to agree to the destruction of some facilities used for making missiles and missile components. When Ekeus presented this problem to the Council, the Russian delegate, who appeared to be resting for most of the time when Ekeus spoke, suddenly raised his hand and made a tough statement demanding Iraq had to be made to understand the seriousness of the situation. The following day, the President, who had been mandated the previous day to take up the matter with the Iraqi ambassador in New York, reported on his infructuous demarche with the ambassador. A deadline of 2:00 p.m. on February 28 had been fixed for Iraq to begin complying with the demand of the inspectors. Ekeus reported that Iraq had rejected the demand. The Russians outdid the Americans and British in using harsh language. Describing Iraq's attitude as intolerable, the Russian delegate reminded Iraq that it should have thought of the implications before committing its 'brazen aggression' against Kuwait. He said the Council should send a marble plaque to Saddam Hussein reminding him of Chapter VII action. He added Iraq was playing a cat and mouse game with the members of the Council, with Iraq acting as the big cat and treating the members of the Council as 15 little mice. The Council adopted a presidential statement condemning Iraq for its lack of co-operation.

In early March 1992, Ekeus came to the non-aligned caucus. He told them that his requirements were small and did not call for much sacrifice from the Iraqis unless they wanted to retain the capability to manufacture prohibited weapons. Iraq, he said, would continue to have the full right to acquire missiles of less than 150 km range, air force, tanks, and so on. Only those weapons that could be used to terrorise Iraq's neighbours were prohibited. As for conversion to civilian use, Iraq would have to accept control mechanisms to prevent possible conversion to military purposes. He thought Iraqi leadership was di-

72

vided, with Tariq Aziz favouring full compliance. Ekeus was concerned at the possible outcome of the meeting on March 11 when Aziz would be speaking to the Council. He referred to a Pentagon study, reported in the *New York Times* of March 9 which made no mention of the United Nations and which anticipated that the United States would rule the world one day all by itself. (What prescience!)

Ekeus shared with the caucus his assessment that much progress had been made but there was little or no political acceptance in Iraq of the need to comply fully with the demands of the Council. UNSCOM had accomplished close to everything in the field of chemical weapons but had not received information as to how Iraq had acquired them. Regarding biological weapons, there was no evidence of weaponisation; there was research activity but it had been substantially taken care of. Ballistic missiles were the main problem area. The super gun and large number of launchers had been destroyed but there was evidence of more launchers and undeclared missiles. It had been established from Russian sources that a total of 819 Scud missiles had been delivered to Iraq over the years. A number of them had been used in the Gulf War and 62 were destroyed. Iraq claimed that all the others had been used up in the war with Iran. Iraq was actively unco-operative in the missile area. The US and UK said Iraq still had 200 to 300 missiles.

Morocco asked Ekeus about Iraq's claim that it had complied with more than 90 per cent of its obligations. Ekeus said that it was even more than 90 per cent for chemical and biological weapons, but 0 per cent in respect of programmes and political willingness. Iraq had all the skills— engineering, scientific, and managerial—of high quality. Consequently, long-term monitoring was very important. Ekeus added Tariq Aziz gave the example of a prisoner under life sentence: if the prisoner was told to behave well, at the same time making it clear to him that good behaviour would not bring any relief to his life sentence, what incentive did he have to behave well?

The President of the Council, Diego Arria, the ambassador of Venezuela, had decided to make a statement at the beginning of the meeting on March 11 in which he would, in effect, read out a list of indictments against Iraq. He circulated the text of his proposed statement to all members a day earlier. It ran into 16 pages! Its tone was extremely tough and ended with an explicit threat of punishment.

Tariq Aziz again came to the caucus. The gist of his presentation was that Iraq was ready to comply with its obligations, but some members, whom he strangely felt shy to name, had their own political agenda which were not those of the Security Council nor of the non-aligned. The political orientation of some members was not endorsed by any Council resolution. Implementation of 687 was a very complicated task and called for goodwill and co-operation from the other side. He asked: did Iraq have to implement all the resolutions till the very last before the sanctions could be lifted or reduced? That might take years. What was the purpose of the Council reviewing the sanctions every two months if there was not going to be any change? It was unfair to punish 18 million people of Iraq if only 1 per cent of the commitments was left unimplemented.

A standoff developed between UNSCOM and Iraq in early July. UNSCOM designated the ministry of agriculture building for inspection on the ground that it had reason to believe that blueprints for the production of missiles were stored there. Iraq firmly rejected the demand, calling it provocative and an insult to Iraq's sovereignty and dignity. The inspectors were insistent and camped outside the agriculture ministry building. Many members of the Security Council felt that the demand for access to the ministry of agriculture was deliberately provocative. The discussion in the informal consultations went along usual lines, with the Russians talking the toughest.

The confrontation in Baghdad continued for a few days. Crates of fruit and vegetables were taken into the building and thrown at the inspectors. Four busloads of women were taken to the Sheraton hotel in Baghdad and demonstrated against the inspectors. At one point Ekeus suggested that a small team of two inspectors and an interpreter be allowed into the building during the night to avoid any media attention, but nothing came of it. On July 20, Ekeus briefed the Council on his failed mission to Baghdad. He had warned Iraq that denial of access to the building might have serious, even tragic consequences for them. Tariq Aziz indicated that they would be ready to receive inspectors from neutral and non-aligned countries, but they would have to come independently, not under any Security Council resolution. Ekeus could not agree to this. He told the Council the situation regarding the security of the inspectors was getting serious. Under the Secretary General's instructions, the inspectors stayed put in their place. The standoff ended on July 22, with the inspectors leaving their place in the face of dangerously provocative demonstrations.

There was jubilation in Iraq at the climb-down by the UN. Anbari, the Iraqi permanent representative, who was due to leave for Paris on his next posting, made tough statements on the TV and talked about the pride and self-respect of Iraqi people. On July 23, Anbari conveyed a proposal to Ekeus that he could nominate new inspectors from countries which had not taken part in the war against Iraq. Anbari mentioned China, India, Sweden, and other European countries. There were two more conditions. The inspectors should not have taken part in previous inspections and they would not inspect the offices of the ministers and permanent secretaries.

Ekeus finally worked out a deal with Anbari. A team of inspectors would be allowed into the building on 28th. The team would be led by a German and would consist of one more German, a Finn, a Swede, a Swiss, and a Russian, all from countries that had not taken part in Desert Storm. Two Americans and a Russian would wait outside the building and receive whatever material the inspectors brought with them. The Iraqis had won this round. Ekeus went to Baghdad. On his return, he told the Council that Iraq had been 100 per cent co-operative.

Nothing incriminating had been found. He had warned the Iraqis that another refusal of access would have severe consequences for them. At the same time, he assured Iraq that the inspectors would carry out their task with due regard for Iraq's dignity and sovereignty.

Ekeus told me on August 5 that he had gone to Washington to meet National Security Advisor Brent Scowcroft. The latter had told Ekeus that he had full confidence in him and that the question of inspections had a domestic aspect for US elections. Ekeus said that there was only one point of difference between UNSCOM and the Americans. The Commission believed that it had succeeded in destroying all launchable Scud missiles whereas CIA director Gates maintained that Iraq still had more than 200 of them. Ekeus said that even Israel was satisfied about the destruction of Iraqi missiles.

Van der Stoel,a former foreign minister of the Netherlands, had prepared a report on the human rights situation in Iraq. He was commissioned to write the report by the Human Rights Commission and his report was submitted to the Human Rights Commission in Geneva. Belgium proposed that his report should be circulated as a Council document and he should be invited to personally brief the Council. Only India had difficulty with the proposal for personal appearance of Stoel, but since all others agreed, the gentleman appeared before the Council in an official meeting on August 11, 1992. His report dealt almost exclusively with the situation of the marsh Arabs in southern Iraq. The Americans used the report to prepare their case to declare and enforce, unilaterally though with one or two allies, a no-fly zone below the 32nd parallel. US, UK, and France declared the no-fly zone on August 27. There was no juridical basis in any resolution for the no-fly zone.

Ekeus came to the Council on October 15 to brief members about the inspections. A 52-member team, led by a Russian, had left for Baghdad. Iraq had wanted Ekeus to delay the inspection since they feared that it would be exploited by George Bush for electoral purposes, but Ekeus would not agree. Saddam Hussein had described the inspectors as 'wolves and stray dogs who preyed on the flesh of Iraq'. Ekeus told me separately that the current mission had been sent following information provided by the Russians about the missile programme. He said if the mission was successful, he would be in a position to certify 'substantial compliance'. Iraq also had expectations of a quick relief from sanctions. They believed that Bill Clinton would be more reasonable since for him it was not a personal matter as it was for Bush.

Tariq Aziz addressed the Council on August 23 and 24. There was nothing unexpected either in his statements or in the statements of others. But his meeting with the non-aligned caucus on 24th was interesting. He said he was not seeking a confrontation with the Council as he realised it was futile. He complained that a very large number of inspectors were American, many of them serving officers in the army. The purely professional teams which came from IAEA did not experience any difficulty in Iraq. Iraq was not a colony and the people of Iraq were not barbarians. The sanctions committee of the Council was going to absurd lengths by rejecting items such as lipstick! Ayala Lasso of Ecuador asked Aziz about the boundary problem. Why had he not mentioned even once Kuwait's right to exist as a sovereign state? Aziz replied that the report of the Boundary Commission had inflamed the passions of the Iraqi people. The problem dated back to the Ottoman Empire. Iraq had never agreed to the borders drawn up by the British. While Iraq was a comparatively new state, it had existed as an entity for 6,000 years. Access to sea was of the greatest importance to Iraq. How could Sinbad the sailor have gone to China and India without access to sea? The Boundary Commission had squeezed Iraq's access to sea by giving away part of the port of Umm Qasr to Kuwait. I pointed out that Iraq was reclaiming the whole of Kuwait, not just of a part of Umm Qasr. Aziz said Iraq had always recognised Kuwait's right to exist. The emir of Kuwait had been given the highest Iraqi decoration in 1989. But Kuwait had not acted reasonably. 'This is not the way to talk to a big neighbour. Kuwait does not need that part of Umm Qasr since Kuwait already has a very big coastline. If Kuwait was reasonable, it could have gone to the Secretary General and said that Kuwait did not need any part of Umm Qasr. Instead, Kuwaitis were jubilant and celebrated the award of the Boundary Commission. This is not the way to behave towards a big neighbour of 18 million people.'

By the end of December 1992, those of the members who were completing their two-year term on the Council had come to have a nagging doubt whether in all matters involving Iraq, the tough demands made by the UN on Iraq were really justified by the realities on the ground. As far as UNSCOM and inspection teams were concerned, many members felt that UNSCOM often acted in a manner calculated to provoke Iraq into adopting defiant positions. There were occasions when Iraqi government's complaints against the behaviour of the inspectors appeared justified. Even though Iraq had co-operated, however reluctantly, with UNSCOM in the destruction not only of its WMD, but also of many priceless research laboratories, Ekeus was nowhere near giving the necessary clean chit to Iraq so that the sanctions regime could be at least alleviated. Ekeus frequently spoke of certifying 'substantial compliance' if Iraq co-operated fully, but never of 'full compliance' or even of 'compliance'. This did not make sense from Iraq's point of view. A certificate of 'substantial compliance' would not have won any relief from sanctions for Iraq. The reality was that so long as Saddam Hussein continued in office, the US and UK would continue to take an extremely harsh attitude towards Iraq. Justified or not, this was a definite impression among many in the Council as well as in the Secretariat.

In the first week of October 1994, observers in New York were wondering if Saddam Hussein was about to embark on another misadventure. Since October 7, CNN had been ceaselessly broadcasting news about substantial Iraqi troop movements towards the border with Kuwait. The elite Hammurabi division of the Republican Guards, which had escaped unscathed in Desert Storm, was reported to be moving south of Baghdad, along with another Republican Guards division.

These two, along with the three already in the south, constituted a force of about 50,000, with 700 tanks and 200 ACPs. The source for all these reports was the US.

Mrs. Albright reported the above in the Security Council on October 7. Hannay was the only one to confirm the information from his government sources. The French and the Russians said they did not have any such information. Mrs. Albright said her government was the only one with such satellite capability. Other members said they had no reason to doubt the reliability of the information given by the US but the more they said so the more dubious they sounded. The following day, October 8, the French and Russians redeemed their honour and reported they too had independent confirmation of Iraqi troop movements. The Russian delegate said their reports did not speak of such large numbers and hence were less alarming. Mrs. Albright brought a US army colonel who passed around satellite imagery; the members duly nodded their heads, showing their deep understanding of such photographs the likes of which they had not seen before. Russia held out for some time against an expression of deep concern of the Council in a presidential statement; but Hannay, enjoying his presidential functions, steamrolled his way through to a consensus.

The question was: what was Saddam Hussein up to this time? Public statements from Baghdad suggested that the regime was getting deeply frustrated at the delay in the lifting of the sanctions and that the move was a diversionary tactic to shift people's attention away from the economic difficulties. The most commonly accepted theory was that Saddam Hussein was once again engaged in a massive miscalculation. The Secretary General felt that Saddam Hussein was just being himself, namely, stupid. The UN Iraq Kuwait Observation Mission (UNIKOM) had reported the sprouting up of a large tent city about 3 km north of the border which could house about 6,000 people. The Iraqi explanation was that these people were Bedouins who had left or were thrown out of Kuwait after the Gulf War. Their aim was to stage a peaceful demonstration to draw the world's attention to their plight. Should they decide to cross the demilitarised zone into Kuwait, there was no way UNIKOM would be able to stop them without the use of force. In the meantime, the Americans were rushing troops and aircraft carriers to the region. By October 10, they had 30,000 troops and an impressive array of aircraft and aircraft carriers deployed in the area. In the shadow of American might, Kuwait rushed all its 18,000 soldiers and all its tanks to the north.

Saddam Hussein blinked. Hamdoon, his ambassador at the UN, confirmed that Iraq had decided to redeploy the troops away from Basra to further north. The crisis, though over, lingered on for a few more days because the temptation to benefit from it to the advantage of the Democratic Party in the November elections was too strong for Clinton to resist. The crisis helped push up the oil price. Saudi Arabia in particular could do with increased oil revenues since it still owed $ 21 billion to the US on the Desert Storm account! While Saddam Hussein did succeed in focusing attention on sanctions, he also made sure that they would remain in place for a long time. Even France, China, and Russia, who had started speaking up for Iraq for some time, would now not talk of easing the sanctions, let alone of lifting them. If Saddam Hussein had some concealed agenda, that agenda would remain concealed. What was likely to happen was that the US, UK, and others would propose a resolution demanding demilitarisation of southern Iraq, like the no-fly zone. In that case, Iraq would not be able to introduce even conventional forces such as tanks in the south. If Iraq introduced such weapons in the zone, the 'coalition' would have the right to 'take them out'. Secretary General, Boutros Ghali, was strongly in favour of such a move; in fact, he was in favour of demilitarisation of the whole of Iraq.

Sidorov, the deputy Russian permanent representative, warned other members of the Council on October 13 that they should not take Russian co-operative attitude for granted in future. He spoke in a bitter and angry tone. He had been trying for about ten days to obtain a condemnatory statement in respect of the blatant violations by the Bosnian forces of the demilitarised zone in Mount Igman in the Sarajevo region, but his efforts had been thwarted by US and the Muslim countries. He spoke of double standards. He attempted to slow down American rush to have a resolution on Iraq adopted by October 15, a Saturday. The draft had seen the light of the day only on the 14th. Specifically, he demanded that the Council should wait for his foreign minister, Kozyrev to brief the members about his accomplishments in Baghdad before taking action on the draft. Mrs. Albright dismissed the suggestion and said her instructions were to have the draft adopted by Saturday, and that was that!

Sidorov came to see me late on Friday the 14th, with a letter from Kozyrev to Secretary General, conveying information about the 'breakthrough' he had obtained in Baghdad. Sidorov said his instructions were to veto the resolution if it was voted upon on Saturday.

On Saturday, Mrs. Albright made it clear that the vote had to be taken before the end of the day. She dared the Russians to use their veto. The French and others objected to a paragraph which would require Iraq to notify the Secretary General about troop movements permitted under the resolution. US dropped that paragraph. In any case, US had prepared a draft which was milder than the previous one. For example, there was no provision for a demilitarised or exclusion zone. The draft demanded that Iraq not introduce troops and equipment in the south that it had tried to in recent days. There was no language threatening unspecified consequences.

Sidorov tried to introduce some elements to reflect the concessions Kozyrev claimed to have wrung out of Iraq. Most of all, he wanted a reference to Kozyrev's mission, but all he got was a generalised mention of 'all diplomatic efforts for a peaceful solution of the crisis'. He also managed to get a reference to Iraq's willingness, stated to Kozyrev, to consider positively the issue of Kuwait's sovereignty and territorial integrity in terms of Resolution 833. These concessions were enough for Russia to vote in favour (not even abstention) of the resolution which was put to vote on October 15, Saturday, minutes before midnight! China's position was interesting. During the consultations,

China objected only to the first preambular paragraph 'reaffirming' all previous relevant resolutions. Since China had abstained on some of them, including 678 and 687, they asked to replace 'reaffirming' by 'recalling'. However, it transpired that China had a problem with reaffirmation of only one particular resolution, and that was 688 which dealt with the problem of Kurds in northern Iraq. China finally accepted a compromise, recalling all previous resolutions and reaffirming 678, 687, and so on.

Kozyrev had his say in the official meeting of the Council. He entered the Council chamber after all the other 14 members had taken their seats. (A member of the British delegation observed that Kozyrev always did that.) He again complained about double standards and delivered a homily about the working procedures of the Council. He insisted that Iraq had agreed to recognise Kuwait's borders as defined in Resolution 833. But Tariq Aziz, who had specially come for the meeting, did not say anything that could be so construed. As Mrs. Albright curtly said, all that Tariq Aziz had done was to let slip the word 'Kuwait' out of his lips for the first time. Hannay in his statement asked a number of questions and ended by saying that finding answers to those questions would be very difficult so long as Saddam Hussein remained in power. Tariq Aziz bristled at this, grew all red in the face and shouted, leaving his customary cool demeanour: how did the British representative dare challenge the legitimacy of the Iraqi president? Hannay was much amused. He was equally amused when Kozyrev pointedly omitted mentioning Douglas Hurd's name when he referred to his colleagues with whom he had consulted about his Baghdad mission. Hurd had described the results of Kozyrev's visit as 'inadequate'.

Kozyrev came to see the Secretary General. It became evident that the Iraqis had led him up the garden path. It seemed that the Iraqis had promised him that they would send a letter to the Secretary General declaring their acceptance of Kuwait's borders as defined in 833. When the Secretary General told him, after checking with Goulding and me, that no such letter had been received, Kozyrev was visibly annoyed and felt betrayed. He asked his ambassador Lavrov to take up the matter with Iraq's permanent representative. Kozyrev himself was playing all these games for domestic considerations. Ever since becoming foreign minister, he had gone out of his way to please the US and the West. He was being attacked at home for his almost obsequious behaviour with his Western colleagues. Now, when Russian nationalism was trying to reassert itself, Kozyrev had to change his image or else he would lose his job. He was fighting for his political survival.

Perhaps the person most disappointed with Saturday's resolution was the Secretary General. He had wanted the Americans to use the opportunity presented by Iraq's stupidity to demand Iraq's complete demilitarisation. He could not have been happy with Kozyrev's initiative. Tariq Aziz saw the Secretary General on October 18. He told the Secretary General that he had in fact brought with him a letter from Baghdad in which Iraq would have recognised Kuwait's sovereignty and territorial integrity as per Resolution 833. He had decided against handing over the letter to the Secretary General after listening to Mrs. Albright's and others statements on the 15th, outlining what Aziz described as 'new conditions' for lifting of sanctions. These were: Iraq had to recognise Kuwait with the same constitutional procedures it had followed in 1990 annexing Kuwait as the 19th province. In other words, Iraq's decision on recognition had to be taken by the Revolutionary Command Council and had to be ratified by Parliament which must also rescind the 1990 decision. Tariq Aziz said he decided to take the letter back with him to Baghdad.

Iraq's Parliament formally recognised Kuwait's international borders as defined in Resolution 833 in early November. This was a big achievement for Kozyrev who was present in the Iraqi Parliament at the time.

A fascinating meeting took place between Tariq Aziz and the Secretary General on November 14. He had come to hand over copies of Iraqi Parliament's resolution on the independence and territorial integrity of Kuwait. It should have been a pleasant meeting and in the beginning it was. The Secretary General said Iraq's decision would be an important step in the difficult search for lifting the sanctions against Iraq. Sparks started to fly, however, when the Secretary General told him that he continued to believe that Resolutions 706 and 712 (dealing with oil-for-food) offered the most practical avenue towards partial lifting of sanctions. Iraq's acceptance of these resolutions would create a new attitude in the Council towards Iraq.

Aziz did not take this advice kindly but politely said that Iraq had not been against it and had not rejected it. However, Iraq had serious reservations about some elements of these resolutions since they infringed on Iraq's sovereignty. He also took strong exception to Mrs. Albright's references to Saddam Hussein's 'residences'—'she may call them palaces'—in the Council meeting where she had passed around photographs of these palaces, complete with swimming pools, artificial lakes, and so on. The Secretary General said: 'Don't have any illusions. Your sovereignty has already been restricted. Just look at the no-fly zones imposed on your country in the north and south. You also have so many other restrictions which have compromised your sovereignty.'

Aziz replied that these resolutions were not based on international law. The Secretary General said 'The resolutions were adopted by the Council by consensus and in accordance with the Charter. As far as I am concerned, they are valid. This is the law of the United Nations and I have to implement the law.'

Aziz replied 'You are totally wrong. Your facts are wrong. Get a copy of Resolution 687; it specifically respects Iraq's sovereignty. The no-fly zones are not based on any UN resolutions; they are unilaterally imposed on Iraq by major powers. As Secretary General, you are the custodian of the sanctity of the Charter, you have to uphold it.'

The Secretary General said 'You must re-read your Charter. I have taught the Charter for 30 years. You are trying to re-write the Charter. The Council, in any case, did not disapprove the no-fly zones.' (A bit disingenuous, this argument.) He went on: 'You may continue with all your illusions. All the mistakes that you have made in recent weeks show that you have not learnt anything and that you still have illusions.'

Aziz said, 'We will never agree to anything that will undermine our sovereignty. We will continue to fight to defend our honour for as long as necessary.'

The Secretary General said, 'Come on, Mr. Vice Prime Minister, you are not making a speech for public consumption here.' Aziz said 'I cannot accept such advice.' The Secretary General said 'It is not an advice; it is my personal point of view. I know my responsibility.' Aziz said 'Iraq will continue to co-operate with the UN but we will never accept infringement of our sovereignty.'

In the meeting of the Council the same afternoon, Iraq's act of recognition of Kuwait's borders hardly attracted any attention. If this had happened six months earlier, before Saddam Hussein embarked on the demonstration of the Republican Guards' strength on the borders with Kuwait, the sentiment in favour of lifting the sanctions might have been more evident.

OIL-FOR-FOOD

The Security Council adopted Resolution 986 in October 1995. It was basically a political exercise meant to deal with the humanitarian situation in Iraq. Iraq had been under the most severe sanctions regime ever devised and rigidly monitored by the Council for over five years by that time. This had had a devastating effect on the civilian population, though the Iraqi leadership, party, and army did not lack in anything. Mrs. Albright even showed to Council members photographs of dozens of what she called 'palaces' built by Saddam Hussein during the previous few years. There was an outcry of public opinion about the miserable conditions in which the people of Iraq were living, with women, the aged, and children being the worst hit.

An earlier attempt by the Council to provide temporary relief was flatly rejected by Iraq as incompatible with its sovereignty. Resolutions 706 and 712 had worked out an oil-for-food formula. The idea was that it was absurd for the international community to fund relief effort for the Iraqi people when Iraq was such a rich country. So, why not let Iraq sell a part of its oil and use the proceeds for its people's food and other urgent needs? But this had to be done under strict monitoring; otherwise the money would end up fattening the regime as well as for the weapons programmes. Resolution 986 imposed a somewhat less intrusive regime, more sensitive to Iraq's sovereignty concerns. Emilio Cardenas, the able and amiable Argentinean ambassador, was its principal architect. I am sure he was genuine in his sympathy for Iraqi people, but he also wanted to help his American friends escape some of the opprobrium. It was negotiated with Tariq Aziz personally by the Secretary General. Aziz had proposed amendments and generally taken a great deal of personal interest in the matter. Left to himself, he would have embraced it. However, at the last minute, he was disowned by his boss. Resolution 986 nevertheless was passed unanimously. Nothing came of it, since Iraq rejected it. That would have been the end of the matter.

However, Boutros Ghali took it upon himself to persuade the Iraqis to at least give a chance to Resolution 986, to agree to its implementation on a trial basis for six months. The basic idea in 986 was that Iraq would be allowed to sell oil worth $2 billion over a six-month period which would be used to buy food, medicines, and other necessities for the Iraqi people. Iraq was very reluctant but the Secretary General kept at them. Finally, a formula was worked out by which Secretary General would write a letter to Tariq Aziz who would reply agreeing to his invitation to start talks about the implementation of 986 without explicitly accepting it. The issue was difficult enough with Iraq. It became many times more complicated because of American and British sensitivities. For the Americans, Saddam Hussein was the biggest foreign policy issue. The administration simply could not afford to agree to any arrangement which would be used by its opponents to portray it as being soft on him. The two delegations badgered the Secretary General endlessly to make sure he was going to implement 986 very strictly, not letting Iraq off the hook by leaving it any loophole. It was a difficult, tightrope-walking exercise, but finally it worked out without causing adverse political fallout for the Secretary General or the other two parties.

The Secretary General maintained that he was moved by humanitarian considerations. He was particularly touched, he said, when he read World Food Programme and World Health Organisation reports on the conditions in Iraq. The Secretary General said he also had in mind the poor workers from several developing countries, including Egypt, India, and others, who deserved to receive compensation. This was no doubt the case, but from what little I understood of him, he was too much of a politician and his actions were guided also by political considerations, but never by monetary considerations. He probably enjoyed the challenge which was to implement Resolution 986 without upsetting the Americans. Cynics in the Council believed that the US and others had supported Resolution 986 since they counted on Iraq never agreeing to its implementation.

Resolution 986 left all the modalities to the Secretary General but the Americans were breathing down his neck all the time. The first step was to conclude the memorandum of understanding (MoU) between Iraq and the Secretariat. The Secretary General gave this task to Hans

Corell, the legal counsel. Corell negotiated the MoU with Anbari for four months. His task became almost impossible when the Secretary General thought it prudent to bring the US and UK into the picture. He would have preferred not to give them a copy of the draft MoU, but the two said they would not react on the basis of a few extracts of the MoU; they asked for the whole text. Mrs. Albright and Weston, Hannay's successor, met the Secretary General many times and he kept refusing to share the whole text with them. He forbade Corell also from giving them the text. But he did not want to risk producing a text which would later be rejected by these two countries. He did something which must have made Corell extremely unhappy. He asked his chief of staff to give a copy of the MoU to 'Skip' Gneim, Mrs. Albright's deputy.

Sure enough, the Americans came up with a series of amendments. The Secretary General got into the act and started directly negotiating with Anbari. The MoU was finally signed on May 22 but only after it was duly vetted by the British and Americans. This was supposed to be confidential but nothing remains secret in this the leakiest of organisations. There was uproar in the Council. Even members other-wise friendly to the SG criticised him for the discrimination.

Following the signing of the MoU, many things still needed to be done. The most important of these was the preparation of the 'distribution plan'. This plan would describe in great detail the items Iraq would be allowed to import and how they would be distributed. Akashi and Goulding came up with a proposal to set up a 'steering committee' for the implementation of 986. Their idea was that they should co-chair it. The Secretary General, on his own, decided that I should chair it. I had nothing to do with the Secretary General's decision though my other two colleagues might have thought that I had managed to get the Secretary General to take this decision. Chairing the steering commit-tee was an interesting though difficult experience. Nothing about Iraq was easy because of the tremendous interest of the Americans in every aspect of Iraq. And there was also the huge interest of the oil market.

Oil prices went up or down depending on the work of the steering committee. The Anglo–American duo visited me many times. Every little thing acquired political meaning. We had to decide in which bank to open the escrow account. The Deutche Bank had the best credit rating but it was ruled out because the Americans said Saddam Hussein had an account there. Swiss banks were out, since the US objected to Swiss banking practices of secrecy and maintained that Saddam Hussein had dealings with them. We could not have American banks because Iraq would obviously not agree. Finally, we selected BNP which was on the list of acceptable banks, even though its credit rating was inferior to that of other banks. The French were thrilled. Then, we had to appoint three or four oil overseers. Four of the P-5 claimed their right to these positions and got them; only China did not press.

I agreed to talk to the Americans whenever they asked to see me. Many of their concerns were legitimate. There was a tendency to regard everything coming from them as tainted or motivated or bad. But the fact was that the Iraqis were past masters at hiding, fabricating, and distorting things. Time and again, the Iraqis had affirmed positions which subsequently were found to be lies and deceptions. But I had to be firm with the US. I once had to tell Gneim that I would not listen to any offensive or rude remarks from him. I had to say the same kind of thing to Sahaf, the foreign minister of Iraq when he tried to bully me. I told him I would not let him say impolite things about the Secretary General or the UN.

Most people thought the Secretary General and I were dragging the whole process because we did not want to create a problem for the former which might affect his re-election chances. This factor did play a part, certainly with me. I had even spoken to the Secretary General about it. I wanted to send the Secretary General's report on the implementation of 986 only in November. This having been said, the actual circumstances on the ground in fact dictated the pace of our work. Numerous new issues regarding Iraq kept coming up and Iraqis

themselves raised a number of objections. Iraqis thought we were playing the American game though the Americans never once suggested that
they would like the report to be delayed.

Iraq had an excellent public distribution system, with outlets all
over the country, through which essential foodstuff and other items
were made available to citizens at subsidised prices. The Americans
insisted on an adequate number of UN personnel to supervise the actual
distribution to make sure that there was no abuse of the oil-for-food
programme. They were particularly insistent that the actual distribution in the north of the country, the Kurdish area, would be run by
Kurdish authorities with help from the UN; the government in Baghdad
was to have absolutely no role in the distribution system in the north.
This was a difficult one for Iraq to swallow since it would mean a de
facto autonomous region for the Kurds.

On November 25, Ambassador Hamdoon, Anbari's successor,
came to me with a letter from Iraq informing me that it was agreeing
to all the modalities that I had been insisting upon. He confirmed that
Iraq now wanted the speediest possible implementation of 986 and
agreed to everything. This story made big headlines in the media. But
the issue of the pricing mechanism was still left unresolved. Iraq had
insisted that the 661 sanctions committee must approve the pricing
formula before implementation could start. Technically, this was not
required but Iraq took this position to be on the safe side. The US had
put the pricing formula on hold. With Iraq now agreeing to drop all its
demands, the onus shifted to US. I called Gneim to my office. He was
not upset at the turn of events. The US removed the hold and the
formula was approved on November 27. We were now in the happy
position when implementation of 986 could start in a few weeks. I did
not understand the reason for the change in Iraqi position. My colleague in the Secretariat Ismat Kittani, the brilliant and much liked
former Iraqi diplomat, a Kurd, felt that Saddam Hussein was probably
close to arriving at a deal with the Kurdish leader Barzani and 986 had

a part in it. As for the US, the state of the oil market might have had something to do with their position.

The oil-for-food programme got off the ground soon thereafter. Initially, Iraq was permitted to sell up to $2 billion worth of oil for six months. The limit was raised to $5.26 billion in December 1999 and was done away with altogether later. Over its lifetime, it generated funds to the extent of $64.2 billion. The United Nations was simply not equipped to handle such huge amounts or to supervise such a highly politically charged rationing system. Mistakes were inevitable.

4

FORMER YUGOSLAVIA

TITO'S YUGOSLAVIA, A country which wielded influence far beyond its inherent strength for nearly three decades, started disintegrating within ten years of his death in 1980. What had held the country together was Tito's charisma combined with ruthlessness, the communist party which was pan-Yugoslav in its ideology, and the Yugoslav National Army (JNA) that was genuinely and passionately committed to the concept of a unified Yugoslavia. There was one more, crucial factor. Tito had always realised the strength of nationalist sentiments among the constituent republics and had evolved a political and constitutional arrangement which conferred an extraordinary amount of autonomy to the various 'nations' constituting the republic. His successors lacked Tito's charisma and sagacity as well as his deep understanding of the nationalistic urges of the peoples and his readiness to accommodate them.

Towards the end of 1980s and early 1990s, Slobodan Milosevic, the President of Yugoslavia, started whipping up Serb nationalist sentiments in Kosovo, Croatia, and elsewhere, and reneged on the

constitutional arrangements, thereby provoking strong secessionist feelings in the other republics. In June 1991, Croatia and Slovenia declared
independence. Slovenia, being a more or less homogeneous nation,
achieved its independence without much fighting. But Croatia had a
significant Serb minority which, additionally, was concentrated in a few
areas. The Serbs in Croatia strongly opposed independence for Croatia
and received active support from the JNA which was dominated by Serbs.

The Yugoslav question first came in the informal consultations of
the Security Council on September 20, 1991. Since early September,
several members of the UN had written letters to the President of the
Council expressing grave concern at the situation in Yugoslavia and
asking for an urgent meeting of the Council to consider the situation.
Before the meeting on September 20, which had been convened to
discuss procedures for the election of the Secretary General, the President consulted me, since I was to assume presidency in October, about
Yugoslavia. I told him India could not agree to any action by the
Council in the absence of a request from the Yugoslav government. I
would not even agree to his having bilateral consultations with members since it would amount to the Council taking action on the domestic
situation in a member state. However, I added, if all the 13 other
members agreed, India would not block his having bilateral consultations. He said no other member had raised an objection. On checking
later, I found this not to be the case. Romania and Ecuador had not even
been consulted by the President. The same no doubt was true of Cuba,
Yemen, Zimbabwe, and others.

At the meeting, Hohenfellner, the Austrian ambassador, spoke
firmly in favour of the Council lending its political and moral authority
to the efforts of the European Community (EC) in dealing with the
Yugoslav crisis. He suggested that the Council should adopt a resolution calling upon all the armed units in Yugoslavia to observe the ceasefire
of September 17 arranged by the EC. UK was more restrained and said
it was not clear how to involve the Yugoslav parties; it was obvious that

there could be no question of acting against or in defiance of the will of the parties. The Soviet position was that everyone should support the efforts of the EC; it suggested that the Secretary General might be asked to go to Yugoslavia and talk to the parties there. The US was cautious; at that early stage, it was in favour of maintaining the territorial integrity of Yugoslavia. It strongly supported the President having intensive consultations with members and others. Thereafter all the non-aligned members spoke, expressing in varying degrees a common sentiment— the Council should not get involved unless Yugoslavia asked for its help. Nearly every one of them said that the Council could not go beyond the limitations imposed by the Charter. Romania's intervention was the strongest. The President said he would undertake further consultations. On September 22, the President informed members that the foreign minister of Yugoslavia, Budimir Loncar, wanted the Council to be seized of the matter and quickly adopt a resolution UK, Belgium, and Austria were preparing a draft resolution proposing, inter alia, arms embargo against the whole of Yugoslavia under Chapter VII.

The Yugoslav situation obviously had touched a raw nerve among the non-aligned members; they were almost emotional about Yugoslavia, one of the three founding members, along with India and Egypt, of their movement. Even Zaire and Cote d'Ivoire were very firm in opposing any action in the absence of a written request from Yugoslavia. For once, the non-aligned caucus took a common position and told the President that they insisted on a formal request from the Yugoslav government. In its absence, the non-aligned nations would not support any action, not even a presidential statement.

The non-aligned caucus met with the Yugoslav permanent representative, Darko Silovic, on the 24th at the latter's request. He said the Yugoslavs needed help from others since they could not solve their problems by themselves. Yugoslavia expected help and understanding from the non-aligned countries. Zaire asked him whether the situation in his country posed a threat to international peace and security or merely to regional peace. Silovic responded that the Balkans, especially Yugoslavia, had always been an explosive region and were responsible for two world wars. He said no negative precedent would be set since the Council would be acting with the consent of Yugoslavia. Once Silovic withdrew, Zimbabwe said that his foreign minister felt that we could not be insensitive to Yugoslavia's request. Some others also felt the same way.

Yugoslavia decided to send a letter, to everyone's relief. During an informal meeting, Munteanu said that Romania had extremely strong reservations on the draft resolution proposed by Austria and others. He emphasised that Romania would never agree to even a hint of arbitration for the next five centuries! He did not want any reference to any part of past history. The non-aligned nations prepared a series of amendments to the draft on the 25th many of which were accepted by the sponsors. The Council unanimously adopted Resolution 713 on the 25th, imposing arms embargo under Chapter VII against Yugoslavia, which automatically included all the constituent units of the country. (No one gave importance to this fact at the time but it would play a vital role later when some countries proposed lifting the arms embargo only against Bosnia.) It also supported the efforts of the EC to find a peaceful solution to the crisis. This was significant; it thereby confirmed the responsibility of the regional forum to deal with the political aspects of the problem. Throughout the Yugoslav crisis, there was a conscious and consistent division of labour between the UN and the regional organisation, namely, the EC. The former would handle peacekeeping while the latter would promote peace-making.

Secretary General Perez de Cuellar appointed Cyrus Vance as his Special Envoy for Yugoslavia on October 8 to liaise with the EC. On November 12, UK, France, and Belgium presented a draft resolution proposing oil embargo against Yugoslavia. The Yugoslav permanent representative told the non-aligned that he had strong objection to the idea which would further punish innocent civilians who had already suffered enough. Oil embargo would completely cripple Yugoslav economy. Silovic said there was a new element; both sides were now talking about a peacekeeping force. In the light of what Silovic said, the non-aligned members took a strong and common position against the oil embargo. Cyrus Vance briefed members on Yugoslavia. On the 15th, the Secretary General informed Security Council members of his decision to send Vance and Under Secretary General Goulding to Yugoslavia in response to an indication from the EC mediator Lord Carrington that the Croatian parties were favourably disposed towards receiving a UN peacekeeping presence. One advantage of this mission, which seems to have been intended by the Secretary General, was that the Europeans would have to delay presenting their draft resolution on the oil embargo.

On November 25, the Secretary General presented an interim report on Yugoslavia. Vance had managed to get the leaders of Croatia and Serbia together with the defence minister of Yugoslavia to sign a ceasefire agreement in Geneva on the 23rd. France, Britain, and Belgium immediately came up with a draft resolution which they said should be adopted by the Council the following day, the 26th. The non-aligned nations, demoralised by the Gulf crisis, did not react negatively, but India proposed that a presidential statement, rather than a resolution, could be considered. Regarding the proposal for a peacekeeping force contained in the European draft, India said it was not enough to obtain the agreement of the governments of Serbia and Croatia; the formal request of the Government of Yugoslavia was indispensable. China, Zaire, and Ecuador supported India. The non-aligned nations agreed to the idea of a resolution but decided to present amendments to the draft. During a meeting with the non-aligned nations, the representative of one of the sponsors was so offensive that he managed to upset even a mild person like Ayala Lasso, the ambassador of Ecuador. After protracted negotiations, agreement was reached on the text.

When all the members were ready to move to the official chamber for a vote on the Yugoslav draft, an interesting technical point came up.

The Secretariat pointed out that it would need at least an hour and a half to make the draft available in all the six official languages as was required under the rules. Tom Pickering and others invoked Rule 31 to establish that the Council had the authority to adopt a resolution even if it was not available in all the languages. India suggested that the President might read out the entire text of the resolution so that later there would be no argument regarding the wording. But Saffronchuk, the Director in charge of Security Council affairs, was adamant; he said the responsibility would remain with members in case the texts in different languages did not conform to what the members had in mind. But he added that India's suggestion would take care of this concern. Merimee, the French ambassador, wanted the English and French texts read out, but he accepted Pickering's amendment to the Indian suggestion that the President could read out the French text. Interestingly, no one was prepared to wait for an hour and a half! Resolution 721 was adopted on November 27. While endorsing the principle of a peacekeeping presence, it clarified that the deployment would not happen without full compliance by parties with the terms of the ceasefire agreement.

In December, the same three European members proposed another draft on Yugoslavia. The non-aligned members proposed a set of amendments which, according to what the co-ordinator of the caucus was told by the President of the Council, the sponsors rejected in toto. This incensed the non-aligned members, not that their anger meant much in practical terms. After the caucus meeting, India was informed by the British delegate that the sponsors were in fact prepared to accept several amendments of the non-aligned members. At the informal consultations, the President reported that the amendments proposed by different delegations had met with opposition from the sponsors, whereupon the latter stated that they were quite happy to accept most of them! On December 15, the Council adopted Resolution 724, endorsing the Secretary General's view that conditions still did not exist for establishing the peace operation.

On December 10, 1991, Perez de Cuellar wrote what turned out to be a most significant and prophetic letter to the President of the EC Council of Ministers, which happened to be Germany. In his letter, the Secretary General expressed his deep worry that any early, selective recognition of declarations of independence by individual constituent units of Yugoslavia could fuel an explosive situation, especially in Bosnia and Herzegovina (BiH), and Macedonia, and serious consequences for the entire Balkan region could ensue.

An awkward and unprecedented situation came up when the Council met in informal consultations at 9:30 p.m. on December 14. The Zaire delegation was absent. Even informal consultations had never been held unless all 15 members were present. Frantic efforts were made to locate the Zairians but to no avail. Finally, Vorontsov suggested, and everybody agreed, that we could continue our informal consultations in an absolutely informal manner!

The Council adopted Resolution 727 on January 8, 1992, authorising the new Secretary General, Boutros Ghali, to send 50 military liaison officers to promote respect for the ceasefire. What started innocuously with 50 personnel mushroomed into a huge operation which, by March 1995, had a force of 38,599 military from 39 countries, 803 civil police, and 2,017 other civilian staff!

On January 15, 1992, all the twelve members of the EC announced from Lisbon, since Portugal had the presidency of the EC, their decision to recognise Slovenia and Croatia as independent countries. With this, the state of Yugoslavia as had existed since 1919 ceased to exist. Later in the month, Vice President Jovic of 'Yugoslavia' came to New York to plead for early deployment of UN PeaceKeeping Force (PKF). He said the ceasefire had been holding at a tolerable level. He admitted candidly that Yugoslavia had ceased to exist and added that the one outstanding problem related to the situation of Serbs in Croatia. He said there was no point in trying to keep the republics together by force and that his government was ready to recognise Slovenia and other republics as soon as the remaining moot problems were negotiated. He demanded that the PKF be deployed and be kept until the fate of the Serbs in Croatia and in BiH had been assured. In an oral report to the Council on January 28, Boutros Ghali said that there were still some problems in deploying the PKF. France and others urged the Secretary General to deploy the PKF but the Secretary General held his ground, saying the obstacles must not be underestimated.

On February 6, the Secretary General informed members that there were two major obstacles to the deployment of UNPKF. Firstly, Croatian President Tudjman, following Croatia's recognition by many countries, had taken the position that Croatia, a sovereign country, could not accept the plan in its entirety since it infringed on its sovereignty. The second obstacle was Babic, leader of Krajina Serbs in Croatia. Following a strong approach by Cyrus Vance, Tudjman sent a letter unconditionally accepting the plan; the problem of Babic, however, remained. Nevertheless, on February 15, the Secretary General presented a report, recommending deployment of 13,000-strong PKF. But even a cursory reading of the report left no one in any doubt that the Secretary General was not fully convinced of the wisdom of his own recommendation. He continued to harbour doubts which he mentioned in his report. Many members were certain that Boutros Ghali had made his recommendations so as not to alienate France and other influential members. Even before he took charge of his office, the western permanent members in particular had exerted efforts to project themselves as the sole defender of his position and interests. They were extremely sweet to him and portrayed the January 31, 1992, summit meeting of the Security Council as designed primarily to express support for him.

The Council adopted Resolution 743 on February 21, setting up the United Nations Protection Force (UNPROFOR) for Yugoslavia for a period of 12 months, instead of six months which had been the normal period for which peacekeeping forces had been established till then. The

British wanted the force to be set up under Chapter VII; the implication was that the consent of the country concerned was not required. However, the fiction of consent of the host country was maintained, at least for the time being. The Secretariat was keen on having a contingent of troops or at least police from India but this was firmly and repeatedly turned down by India. The Secretariat then asked India to provide a general to command UNPROFOR. At my suggestion, the Secretary General rang up Prime Minister Narasimha Rao who responded: 'You leave me no choice in the matter'. General Satish Nambiar became the first head, civil as well as military, of UNPROFOR.

By April 1992, the situation in BiH, had fast deteriorated. The Bosnian Serbs had captured two villages near the border with Serbia. The JNA had, reportedly, actively helped the Bosnian Serbs. UNPROFOR was not then, nor ever proposed to be deployed in BiH though its headquarters were in Sarajevo. By May, the situation had become tragic and desperate. The Serbs and JNA were pounding Mostar as well as Sarajevo. More than 1,000 people had been reported killed during a single fortnight. The Serbs had captured nearly 60 per cent of the territory. The question that arose was whether to extend the mandate of UNPROFOR and deploy it in Bosnia also. The French and Austrians were asking for it whereas the Americans were not enthusiastic about it. The Secretary General and Vance were not ready to recommend it since the indispensable condition for deploying UN peacekeeping force, namely, cessation of fighting and a ceasefire in place was far from being met. The UN was simply not willing to deploy troops to engage in combat with the rival fighting forces. Even the Europeans, who could relatively easily send a contingent under the Western European Union, were unwilling to do so. A compromise was agreed upon in the form of sending Under Secretary General Goulding to make an on-the-spot assessment and report back to the Council.

An interesting facet of the Yugoslav problem arose when Serbia and Montenegro announced the formation of the Federal Republic of

Yugoslavia (FRY) in the last week of April 1992. The new FRY claimed to be the successor state to the previous Socialist Federal Republic of Yugoslavia (SFRY). The acting permanent representative of SFRY wrote a letter to the President of the Council, enclosing the text of the declaration on the establishment of the FRY and asking for the circulation of the letter as an official document. The letter was typed on the stationery of the new FRY. The Secretariat advised him to withdraw the letter and send another one on the stationery of the old SFRY which alone was recognised as a member of the UN. This the Yugoslav mission did. The President of the Council authorised the circulation of the letter. However, just before the letter was being sent out, he stopped the circulation. The President for May authorised circulation following prolonged negotiations, after agreement was reached on issuing a presidential statement to the effect that the circulation of the letter did not prejudge the position of the Organisation or of member states regarding the status of FRY.

The Secretary General continued to be under pressure from the Europeans to extend UNPROFOR's mandate to Bosnia. However, things were so bad that the Secretary General simply could not oblige them. He submitted a report saying that the UN was in no position to deploy PKF in Bosnia. He reminded members that the headquarters of UNPROFOR were in Sarajevo only for the sake of convenience and since Sarajevo offered a neutral venue vis-à-vis Zagreb and Belgrade. UNPROFOR's main, indeed, only mandate was to preserve peace in the UN-protected areas (UNPAs) in Croatia. Given the state of affairs in Bosnia, the Secretary General informed members that he had accepted General Nambiar's recommendation to move the bulk of UNPROFOR headquarters personnel to Belgrade. Thus, far from agreeing to deploy peacekeeping force in Bosnia, the Secretary General had to reduce UN presence there. However, the Council adopted Resolution 752 on May 15, deliberately ignoring the Secretary General's views on deployment of PKF in Bosnia. Instead it asked him to keep the situation under review and present another report on May 26. Morocco and some others wanted to impose Chapter VII sanctions against Serbia, or FRY, but most others, including UK, reacted in a lukewarm fashion towards the idea.

On May 18, the Council held two consecutive meetings to recommend the admission of Slovenia and Croatia to UN membership. Hannay asked the President when he intended to take up Bosnia's request for membership. The latter replied that Bosnia's application had been received by the Secretary General but he, the President, had not yet received it. The Legal Counsel of the UN had taken the view that since Bosnia had been recognised only by about 40 states, it might not be prudent to circulate the request as an official document. The Secretariat preferred that the President carry out bilateral consultations to reach consensus on circulation to avoid controversy. The following day, the President conveyed to the members that there was no objection from anyone to the circulation of Bosnia's application. He proposed that action on Bosnia's application should be taken up in the General Assembly at the same time as Slovenia and Croatia's applications. In fact, the President of the Assembly, Ambassador Shihabi of Saudi Arabia had let it be known that he would not convene the Assembly unless Bosnia's application was considered simultaneously with the other two applications.

Slovenia, Croatia, and Bosnia were admitted to UN membership on May 22. Such rapid-fire admission of Bosnia was a victory for the Islamic states. Islam had clearly emerged as a dominant factor in international life. It was the Islamic pressure which compelled America to recognise Bosnia. The same Islamic pressure would propel the Security Council into imposing sanctions against Serbia on May 30 through Resolution 757. There was also the factor that Milosevic and Karadzic, the Bosnian Serb leader, were hell-bent on capturing as much territory as possible. Already, the Serbs controlled 70 per cent of Bosnia's territory.

In the last week of May, Secretary James Baker admonished his European colleagues at a meeting in Lisbon for hesitating to act against the Serbs. It was characteristic of the US that having taken a back seat for the previous few weeks, it pushed the Europeans for tough action once it decided to take the front seat again. This 'on again, off again' approach of the US and the school masterly and even arrogant attitude of Baker irritated the Europeans. France in particular was very resentful of the US. France was convinced that the immediate imposition of oil embargo and severance of air links would only harden Serb position and might endanger UNPROFOR personnel. The Russian position was similar to the French. Foreign Minister Kozirev did succeed in persuading Milosevic to reopen the Sarajevo airport to permit food and other necessities to flow into Bosnia. The Islamic countries were getting impatient for strikes against the Serbs. The Americans felt obliged to play up to the Islamic sentiment because of the IOU that the Arabs had collected from them on the Gulf crisis and because of what the Americans had done to Libya, an Islamic country.

Around the first week of May, Serbia and Croatia held a secret meeting in Graz, Austria, and concluded a deal whereby the whole of BiH would be divided between the two of them. A few days later, the Croats and Muslims signed an agreement in Split. These manoeuvres indicated how much the leaders of the various communities cared for their peoples or for principles.

As has happened time and again, the Europeans fell in line with the Americans. On May 29, US, UK, France, and Belgium presented a draft resolution in which the American view had clearly prevailed proposing sanctions against FRY. France wanted to delete one paragraph recommending derecognition of FRY to the Assembly. Following extended negotiations over two days, this particular paragraph was deleted. The French tried to exclude sports and air links from the scope of the sanctions but gave in to American pressure. On India's initiative, food was excluded from sanctions. The Russians at one stage had expressed reservations about sanctions, but in the end voted in favour. Hannay said privately that Russia could not afford even to abstain. Resolution

757 was adopted on May 31 by 13 in favour with only China and Zimbabwe abstaining.

On June 2, the Secretary General reported that the Serbian forces in Bosnia were not under the control of the Belgrade authorities and there were elements of Croatian army in Bosnia which were under the control of Zagreb. The implication was that it would not be correct to hold Belgrade alone responsible for the situation in Bosnia. In the light of this report, it appeared that Resolution 757 was a mistake, though US and UK ignored the Secretary General's report and insisted that Belgrade alone was responsible. On June 5, the Secretary General sent a letter reporting an agreement among the three parties in Bosnia, reaffirming their commitment to the ceasefire and requesting deployment of UNPROFOR so as to secure Sarajevo airport. The Secretary General's letter said that the Serbs had not yet signed the agreement though they had agreed to it. Goulding informed the Council orally that the Serb failure to sign was purely technical. He gave the Council the important bit of information that the JNA troops which were allowed to withdraw from the Marshall Tito barracks in Sarajevo would leave their heavy weapons behind under the control of the territorial defence forces of the Bosnian government.

On June 8, the Secretary General confirmed that the Serbs had signed the June 5 agreement and submitted recommendations regarding the enlargement of UNPROFOR. The same day the Council adopted Resolution 758, authorising the Secretary General to deploy military observers to Sarajevo to supervise withdrawal of anti-aircraft weapons and the concentration of heavy weapons at agreed locations in the city. But Goulding reported orally that the fighting in Sarajevo had intensified and that the city was being slowly destroyed. Conditions for deployment of UNPROFOR did not exist. The Bosnian forces had been using the artillery left behind by the JNA. Goulding also raised the question whether the enlargement of UNPROFOR should be under Chapter VI or VII. Most western members proposed that, in the light of Goulding's report, the Council should adopt a resolution authorising deployment when the conditions for it were met. The other view, articulated by UK was that the Secretary General would have to come back to the Council and that the deployment must not be automatic or self-executing.

By the end of the day, the President circulated a draft resolution, the essence of which was that the Secretary General would have to get back to the Council before deploying anything. NATO was looking for a new doctrine which would permit use of NATO forces for purposes other than those for which it was established. Bosnia's President Izetbegovic was bombarding Bush for the use of force against the Serbs. It was not clear if the Russians would support military action against Serbia or against Bosnian Serbs. A telegram from Vorontsov to Kozirev was published in Izvestia according to which the former had recommended voting in favour of 757, given Russia's dependence for economic assistance on the West.

George Bush, however, was reported saying that the US was not the policeman of the world. The Pentagon was totally opposed to American military involvement in Bosnia. US lives could not be put at risk where its national interests were not at stake. But the media in America had mounted pressure on the administration to bomb Serb positions around Sarajevo.

Within days, the latest ceasefire in Bosnia had broken down completely. An all-out war had broken out there on June 17. The internal assessment in the UN Secretariat was that the Bosnian Muslim side was responsible for the outbreak of fighting this time. The Bosniak calculation was to create a situation which would make American intervention inevitable. More and more was being heard about the right of humanitarian intervention. In the meanwhile, on June 15, Bosnia and Croatia concluded a military alliance regularising Croat military presence in Bosnia. The foreign minister of Serbia told the Indian ambassador in

Belgrade that Izetbegovic had a plan to import 3–4 million Turks of Bosnian origin to decisively change the demography of Bosnia.

The efforts of General Mackenzie of Canada to arrange a ceasefire in Sarajevo did not succeed. The military option was being discussed openly. Bush met with Baker, Cheney, Scowcroft and others on June 26 to discuss options. Kofi Annan, head of DPKO, read out the Secretary General's statement to the Council members on the same day in which the Secretary General, for the first time, held the Serb side as primarily responsible for the bloodshed. He categorically condemned the Serb attacks on Sarajevo. He added that if the Serb attacks did not stop within the next 48 hours, the Security Council would have to decide what other means would be required to bring relief to the suffering people of Sarajevo. Separately, the Organisation of Islamic Conference (OIC) was lobbying for military intervention in Bosnia.

On June 28, 1992, President Mitterrand took off in a dramatic flight from Lisbon, where he was participating in an EC meeting, for Sarajevo. He was intending to fly directly to Sarajevo but deferred to local UN advice and spent the night in Split from where he took a helicopter to Sarajevo. He spent six hours in Sarajevo, walked its streets, visited hospitals, and met with Izetbegovic as well as Serb officials. Mitterrand's courageous trip electrified European capitals and earned him tremendous popularity at home and jealousy and bitterness among his allies. The visit was kept a secret even from German Chancellor Helmut Kohl with whom he had breakfast just a few hours earlier. This was instant success for the French theatre. The Secretary General reported on June 29 'with pleasure' that progress had been made in the assumption of responsibility by the UN for Sarajevo airport; Serb forces had begun withdrawing from the airport area and both sides had begun the process of concentrating their heavy weapons under UNPROFOR supervision. The Secretary General decided to accept General Nambiar's recommendation to deploy additional units of UNPROFOR foreseen in Resolution 758. However, the internal Secretariat feeling was that the

Bosniaks were not interested in ceasefire; they wanted outside military intervention on their side.

Meanwhile, in Croatia, the Secretary General reported that the Croatian army had launched an offensive on June 21, seriously threatening UNPROFOR's operations. The President suggested a draft resolution on the 30th. The debate on the draft was interesting for the time spent on whether the Croat government should be asked to accept 'the general course of action' or 'the course of action'. The compromise was 'to follow the general course of action'!

Lord Carrington briefed the members of the Council on July 9. This in itself was an unprecedented event since Carrington was neither a UN official nor a UN representative; in fact, he worked for the EC. Carrington gave a candid and comprehensive analysis of the origins and present state of the Yugoslav crisis. He said the crisis started with the death of Tito. Nationalism was reborn with the death of Tito and Marxism. Badinter (previous negotiator for EC) had said that Croatia did not satisfy conditions for recognition, but the EC had gone ahead and recognised it. Macedonia, on the other hand, satisfied all the conditions for recognition but the EC refused to recognise it, because Greece would not agree to any name of the new country containing the word 'Macedonia'. Bosnia did not respect its own constitution but the EC recognised it after the referendum. EC recognition had unravelled the EC peace conference on Bosnia. The peace conference became a series of bilateral and trilateral negotiations. The three parties had agreed on March 18 on the principles for a constitution for the country the gist of which was autonomy, not on the basis of geography but on the basis of nationality. As soon as the EC recognised Bosnia, the Serbs started to fight. In Croatia also, the Serbs started to fight as soon as EC recognised Croatia, even though Croatia did not satisfy the Badinter criteria. The Cuteleiro process on Bosnia had made good progress but the Bosniaks broke off their participation after the attack on the bread line in Sarajevo on May 28. Carrington's assessment was that Izetbegovic

Consulting in the Council Chamber. From left: Author,
David Hannay, Boutros Ghali, Emilio Cardenas.

was unwilling to negotiate because he felt that the balance of forces had turned in his favour and because he hoped for large-scale UN military intervention. Milosevic, he said, had much more influence on Bosnian Serbs that he cared to admit. Tudjman had total control over the Croats in Bosnia. Carrington said that Kosovo could be even more dangerous than Bosnia, since the Serbs would never grant independence to Kosovo whose Albanian majority had already held a referendum and declared independence.

On July 17, news was received about the London agreement among the parties on ceasefire and on placing of heavy weapons under UN supervision and protection. Hannay said at the consultations that the London agreement had changed the situation and suggested that the Secretary General should be asked how he intended to respond to the request contained in it. But on the 20th, the Council received a bombshell in the form of a letter from the Secretary General, in which he protested against the Council 'setting peremptory dates' for submission of reports and against the manner in which the Council took its decisions. He did not mince words in saying that he would not submit the report asked for by the Council on July 17. 'I find myself in the invidious position of having to advise the Council on the implementation of a mandate behind which the Council has already thrown its political support. I must express my considered opinion that it would have been preferable if the Security Council had requested and awaited a technically grounded opinion by UNPROFOR and me, given our responsibility for the operation of UNPROFOR, before taking any decision. I very much hope that it would be possible for the Security Council and the Secretary General to work in greater co-ordination. I would hope my views would be ascertained in areas which are clearly within my competence; otherwise, an unfortunate gap may arise between political desiderata and the technical realities on the ground.'

Such open confrontation had never been seen before. Even during the 1960s, during the Congo crisis, there was tension between the

Soviets and the Secretary General, but never between the Secretary General and the Council as a whole. In the circumstances, Hannay handled the matter very well. He dismissed the Secretary General's letter in one sentence. He said that there was a saying in his country: 'Less said soonest mended'. No one else referred to the letter.

Boutros Ghali's letter made big news in the media. On the morning of July 21, the Council members heard that the Secretary General had decided to tell the Council that he would not agree to comply with the request made in the London agreement. Hannay felt that it would be most unwise of the Secretary General to take such a decision. The Secretary General, whom I met before the meeting, was very angry and asked me: 'How can you, the Council, take a decision like that? In London, they conclude a quasi agreement and simply call upon the Council to comply with their demand without even consulting the Council about it. I will never agree to it.'

I asked him how he proposed saying no. 'You will see in my report how I will say no,' was his response. He added that Austria and Hungary had their interests in the Yugoslav question and the Security Council should not allow itself to be used in that game. Hannay, upon being told of my talk with Ghali, reacted that the success of the UN depended upon co-operation with European countries and the resources made available by them; failure to meet their expectations on Yugoslavia could hurt that support.

In his report, made available on July 22, the Secretary General stated conditions did not exist for him to recommend that the Council accept the request of the three parties in Bosnia about the UN supervising the heavy weapons. He raised what he called two questions of principle. Firstly, he talked about the relationship between the UN and regional organisations in the field of peace and security. According to him, under Chapter VIII, the Council could 'utilise' regional organisations in certain circumstances. 'There is no provision for the reverse to occur. In other words, the tail of the regional organisations cannot wag the

UN's dog!' The second principle was that the UN did not participate in the negotiations of the London agreement. Experienced UN staff ought to have been involved in the negotiations which would result in the UN being entrusted with a peacekeeping task. He was gracious enough to state at the end that he was not questioning the Council's right to decide what its response should be to the London agreement.

Boutros Ghali came to the informals the following morning 'to remove two misunderstandings'. There was no question of a confrontation between the Secretary General and the Council. Without the Council's co-operation the Secretary General could not do anything and, he pointedly added, vice versa. Secondly, there was no confrontation between him and Carrington. 'But I have told him that it is impossible to implement the London agreement. I cannot agree that the UN should become merely the executing agency for regional organisations.'

Ghali told the P-5 members the same morning that the UN was getting more deeply involved in Yugoslavia without being provided the necessary resources and that Yugoslavia could become UN's Vietnam. The Europeans must ask for UN help before undertaking any agreements, not after. Concluding his remarks, he said: 'I am at the service of the Security Council; indeed it is my raison d'etre. But it is my duty to defend this organisation which, in the last analysis, is your organisation. But this organisation represents more than the totality of the interests of the member states.'

The above confrontation seemed academic since the ceasefire agreement of July 17 was not being observed at all. Carrington told the media in Belgrade that the Muslims were as much, if not more, guilty of violating the ceasefire. Ghali's senior aides started protecting their boss more actively and said that one of the main problems was Carrington's ego and vanity. Boutros Ghali scored a success in his disputation with the British the next day. One paragraph in a draft resolution under discussion would ask the EC to examine the possibility of expanding the scope of the London conference. India proposed an addition: 'in association with the Secretary General'. The British suggested 'in consultation with the Secretary General'. The Secretary General said loudly he could not agree. We settled on 'in cooperation with the Secretary General'. During this whole exercise, Boutros Ghali had in mind UN's experience with the Middle East peace conference. At the Madrid conference, UN was invited only as an observer. Ghali's predecessor had agreed to it, but Ghali felt it was insulting to the organisation. He refused the status of an observer and won his point and got an invitation as a full participant for the UN.

On July 25, Prime Minister John Major announced the convening of a broadened conference on Yugoslavia in the second half of August. UN was mentioned as many as four times in the official announcement. The Security Council itself was paralysed because of the failure of all the parties to abide by the July 17 ceasefire. Boutros Ghali would co-chair the conference on Yugoslavia along with John Major in August. Aime, the able chief of staff of the Secretary General, told me that Hannay had called him and proposed a 'truce'. But there was another bolt from Boutros Ghali on August 3 in the form of an interview with *New York Times* in which he accused the Security Council of being 'Eurocentric'. He suggested that the British media was perhaps not happy with him 'because I am a WOG'. Brian Urquhart, a former Under Secretary General and widely regarded as the father of the concept of peacekeeping operations, on being told of the reference to WOG, was reported to have exclaimed: 'My, my, dear, dear'! Ghali was attempting to project himself as the champion of the third world, but it was the third world which was more unhappy with him than the first. In those early days, he remained the favourite of only the Americans, and even they would not be pleased with him when he described Yugoslavia as UN's Vietnam.

Ambassador Diego Aria of Venezuela was very indignant with the Secretary General's interview. 'There are times when you have to be a diplomat and times when you have not to be a diplomat,' he said. He added that aggrandizement of an individual could not be permitted at the expense of the institution. He proposed that the caucus should meet Boutros Ghali and register its unhappiness at parts of his interview. India advised caution, pointing out that 'By now we know our Secretary General and could not be certain how he would react'. Far from expressing contrition, the Secretary General might accuse the non-aligned nations of playing the European game. The caucus agreed to seek instructions from respective governments. That was the end of the matter.

For the first time, on July 30, the Austrian ambassador raised the desperate situation facing the town of Gorazde in Bosnia. He proposed that the UN should airdrop relief supplies to the beleaguered population in Gorazde. Many members expressed sympathy but no action was taken. One of the main reasons for lack of action was the fact that the initiative had come from Austria which was regarded as very much an interested party on the side opposite to that of the Serbs.

On August 5, the President, Ambassador Li of China, informed members about a letter he had received from the Serbian Republic of Bosnia and Herzegovina—Republika Srpska—announcing his intention of informally circulating the letter among members. India objected, pointing out that the entity of the republic had not been recognised by anybody; consequently the communication could not be circulated even informally. India added that such letters ought not to even be brought to the notice of members and should be consigned to the wastepaper basket or to the files of the Secretariat. It was so agreed by everybody!

Boutros Ghali reluctantly admitted on August 10 that the original division of labour between the UN and EC with the former responsible for peacekeeping and the latter for peacemaking had been eroded in recent months. He said he had proposed, and Prime Minister Major had agreed, that the two of them co-chair the forthcoming conference on Yugoslavia. He clarified that the co-chairmanship did not entitle him to engage the Security Council into any commitment.

The uproar over the concentration camps in Yugoslavia intensified by many decibels. Margaret Thatcher added her powerful voice to the demand for urgent and effective action. She did not miss an opportunity to embarrass her successor in office but also criticised Bush. The harrowing pictures on the TV screens of the emaciated bodies of Muslims in the camps and the firing upon the mourners at the funeral in Sarajevo of the two infants killed by sniper fire made it impossible for Bush and Major not to act. Bush had made no secret of his extreme reluctance to get involved in what he described as a 'quagmire'. In any case, he was determined not to use American ground forces. His people in New York produced a draft resolution, somewhat similar to 678 on Iraq. It would authorise use of all necessary means but only to ensure humanitarian assistance and not to restore peace and security as was the case with 678.

The draft ran into difficulty with the British and the French. Major was even more reluctant than Bush to involve UK in this operation. The French wanted to avoid any language which would authorise NATO to undertake the operation since France did not participate in the military processes of NATO. The three of them sorted out their differences and produced a draft, the crucial paragraph of which called upon, instead of authorised, countries and regional organisations to take measures necessary to enable concerned UN agencies and other organisations to distribute relief assistance to the needy. This would have to be done 'in co-ordination' with the UN. Resolution 770 under Chapter VII was adopted on August 13, 1992, with India, China, and Zimbabwe abstaining.

Just prior to the vote, the Secretary General, in another unprecedented move, wrote to the President to put on record his concern at the adverse security implications for UNPROFOR personnel. He further brought to the attention of the Council the fact that many troop-contributing countries expressed similar concern at the safety of their troops. The sponsors of the resolution studiously avoided commenting on the Secretary General's letter. In some respects, Resolution 770 was more ominous than 678 on Iraq since it roped in the UN in a co-ordinating role, even though action would be taken without the UN exercising any control whatsoever. Almost the sole purpose of the sponsors of 770 was to satisfy domestic public opinion and to blunt the pressure of Islamic countries. For Bush, he was getting hurt from Bill Clinton in the one area, namely foreign policy, where he, Bush, claimed special expertise. In the Council, however, it was Hannay who assumed leadership because, among other factors, the American ambassador, Pickering had left. Resolution 770 would also help Major; he was president of EC and was under criticism for receiving very small number of refugees from the Balkans and for even expelling some.

The Secretary General made an oral presentation, as usual, on a number of issues before the Council. On Bosnia, he seemed proud of the fact that he had co-chaired the London conference. He described the situation in Bosnia as extremely serious. The UNHCR had abandoned the airlift of humanitarian assistance following the death of two French peacekeepers. Cyrus Vance had fixed September 12 as the deadline for the Serbs to place all their heavy weapons under UN supervision. Additional troops would be required by UNPROFOR to carry out its enhanced mandate. The expenditure on additional troops would be borne by the troop-contributing countries. The Secretary General's written report was made available after he had left the room. From the comments of the British and French delegates, it became obvious that they had seen the report before it was given to the rest. India expressed strong objection to this practice. The British delegate admitted that he and some others had seen the report in advance and justified it on the ground that they would be providing additional troops at their own expense for UNPROFOR activities in Bosnia.

At informal consultations on September 13, Vance and David Owen, the new EC negotiator in the place of Carrington, came out strongly and categorically against lifting the arms embargo against Bosnia. Owen said the Muslims were getting practically everything.

They were not doing well, not because they lacked munitions but because they did not have a well-organised, professional, and disciplined army like the Serbs. Ambassador Snoussi of Morocco persistently questioned Vance and Owen about this. Owen said the Bosnian Serb superiority, if it existed at one time, had greatly dwindled. The reality was that the Muslims had all the arms they needed. He said no Yugoslav faction was likely to run out of arms. The Bosnian government was beginning to get more modern weapons not available to the Serbs. The Islamic countries were giving money for humanitarian purposes but the money was being used for buying arms and nobody could or wanted to do anything about it. The gun running in small ships was unstoppable. Owen informed members that the two French soldiers killed a few weeks ago were in fact killed in a deliberate ambush by Muslims. At least some of the shelling on Sarajevo from the surrounding hills was being done by the Muslims. All in all, Vance and Owen demolished the case for lifting the arms embargo against Bosnia.

The two of them also spoke about Kosovo. Vance made it clear there was no question of independence for Kosovo. Yugoslav President Cosic wanted to redraw the borders of Kosovo. The fertile plane areas would be merged with Serbia, the hilly areas would be joined with the Albanian portion of Macedonia, and the rest would be merged with FRY.

By the middle of September, the OIC had built up strong pressure to expel Yugoslavia from the UN. During the Jakarta non-aligned summit, Malaysia led the campaign to throw Yugoslavia out of NAM, but the Africans blocked the move. The Americans for their own reasons did not want the General Assembly to take the lead in the matter. Any action that the General Assembly would take would be in the form of rejecting the credentials of the Yugoslav delegation. The US did not favour that approach since it could set a precedent which could be used against Israel at some stage. The Americans prepared a 'non-paper' whereby the Security Council would declare Yugoslavia's membership 'extinguished'. The Europeans and the US conducted negotiations on the text of a draft resolution. A text was worked out which Hannay presented to the caucus on September 15. He explained that the question of Yugoslavia's status had reached a stage where it could not be handled any more by mere statements. Europe ruled out of court Yugoslavia's claim to continuity of former SFRY. Belgrade's tactics to 'grab first and negotiate later' was no longer acceptable. The draft resolution reflected a political and not a juridical approach which would be more draconian leading to Yugoslavia's extinction from the UN. The draft prepared by them would recommend to the General Assembly that it should decide that Yugoslavia would not be allowed to participate in any body of the UN. Hannay had expected that it would be difficult to obtain clear majority for the draft and was pleasantly surprised at the positive reaction from a majority of caucus members. He had somehow managed to arrive at a wrong assessment or was deliberately being cautious.

The Russians had been negotiating the text of the draft resolution with Hannay. They told Djokic, the Yugoslav Charge d'affairs that they would veto any resolution seeking to suspend Yugoslavia, but Djokic gave no credence to Russian assurances. The Yugoslav Prime Minister Panic publicly announced that FRY was ready to apply for fresh membership provided there was gentlemen's agreement that its application would be approved as smoothly as those of other former Yugoslav republics. But Djokic was experienced enough to realise that there was no such thing as gentleman in the UN and that FRY's application would run into considerable difficulty. Vorontsov's efforts produced an amended draft which would recommend to the General Assembly to decide that Yugoslavia not be allowed to take part in the Assembly and its bodies instead of all UN bodies. The Council would further decide to consider Yugoslavia's application before the end of the fall session of the General Assembly.

The next question was whether Yugoslavia should be allowed to sit at the Council table when its fate was being decided. The usual suspects were opposed to the idea but relented when most others argued in favour. Zimbabwe in particular asked whether the Council should function merely as executioner without giving an elementary opportunity to the victim to present its case. The final compromise was that Yugoslavia would sit at the table but the President would declare that it was without prejudice to the position of member states on the status of Yugoslavia. Yet another point of disagreement arose on whether Yugoslavia should be permitted to speak in the Council, as they wanted to. UK said its difficulty was that Yugoslavia was not a state in terms of Rule 37 of the Rules of Procedure of the Council. The President was also not in favour of disturbing the delicate political balance reached by members. The resolution was adopted as Resolution 777.

The General Assembly adopted the resolution on Yugoslavia on September 22 by a vote of 127 in favour, 6 against, and 26 abstentions. There was widespread unhappiness at the way the Security Council had handled the matter. Most of those abstaining or voting against the resolution based themselves on India's statement of abstention in the Council. Basically, two points were made. Firstly, the Charter had three articles dealing with membership. Article 4 dealt with admission and Articles 5 and 6 dealt with suspension and expulsion. Resolution 777 was not based on either of these two articles. Hannay admitted as much and explained that had the framers of the Charter envisaged such a possibility they would have incorporated a suitable provision. The second concern was about the safety of the UNPROFOR personnel and its functioning. The main reason for African abstentions was their sentimental attachment to Yugoslavia. The resolution was extremely shaky on legal grounds. Yugoslavia was not expelled. Its nameplate would be retained in the General Assembly and its permanent mission would continue to function with all the privileges of circulating and receiving documents, and so on. The resolution affected Yugoslavia's participation only in the General Assembly and not in other organs such as ECOSOC. At the same time, the resolution talked of a fresh application by Yugoslavia. If it was not expelled, why should it apply afresh?

In early October, US, UK, and France introduced a draft resolution on no-fly zone in Bosnia. Bush had personally announced a week earlier that the US would seek Council authorisation for use of force to enforce no-fly zone. The British and French were not enthusiastic since they had troops on the ground. But, inevitably, they gave in. The US in turn made a concession. In the first instance, the Council would not act under Chapter VII. In case the Bosnian Serbs did not respect the London agreement which was the basis for the no-fly zone, the Council would meet immediately to consider enforcement measures. Resolution 781 was adopted on October 9. The Americans lost no time in announcing that the no-fly zone became effective from the moment Resolution 781 was adopted. In the next few days, one of two things could happen. Either the Serbs would be foolish enough to disregard the no-fly injunction and use their aircraft or the Bosnians might put out a story of Serbs having violated the restriction or provoking them hard enough to disregard it. In either case, the US might reactivate the Council to obtain authorisation to use force to enforce the no-fly zone.

Vance briefed the Council on October 14 and painted a very grim picture of the situation in Bosnia. The situation had appalling human dimensions and there could be a catastrophe of untold suffering during the winter months ahead. He quoted the UN High Commissioner for Refugees Mrs. Ogata's phrase 'the edge of human nightmare' to emphasise the seriousness of the impending tragedy. He and Owen had managed to persuade Karadzic to move the Serb aircraft to Serbia. He was opposed to lifting of the arms embargo against Bosnia. He also strongly reaffirmed the need to maintain the sanctions against Yugoslavia.

Talking about arms embargo, there was an interesting development. A few weeks earlier, an Iranian Boeing 747 plane landed in Zagreb, ostensibly carrying humanitarian cargo. On inspection, the cargo was found to contain large amount of arms and ammunition. There was also a contingent of 'freedom fighters' in the guise of relief workers. The Croatian government reported the incident to the sanctions committee of the Security Council. The Iranian government was given seven days to explain. The Iranians disowned the incident and promised to investigate it. That was the end of the matter. Such was the clout of the Islamic countries.

The OIC continued to press for lifting the arms embargo against Bosnia. Lawrence Eagleburger, the Acting Secretary of State told the foreign ministers of the South Asian Association for Regional Cooperation at a breakfast meeting in New York that the US was opposed to the lifting of the embargo; there were already too many weapons in the area and even the Bosnian Muslims had enough to defend themselves. Jajce fell to the Serbs in late October. Nearly 30,000 Muslim refugees fleeing Jajce were attacked by the Serbs. This caused an uproar but once again the Council felt impotent and could do no better than issue a 'strong' statement to which the Serbs were totally immune. UNPROFOR was getting a bad name. It was in no position to offer protection to the refugees from Jajce or from any other place. It could not even monitor what was happening in Bosnia. Hungary alleged that UNPROFOR personnel were engaged in contraband activities such as selling arms.

The Marti Ahtissari group of the International Conference worked out a possible arrangement for Bosnia which could involve dividing the country into seven to ten autonomous regions, but not on ethnic or religious basis. The Bosnian government accepted the proposals but the Croats and the Serbs rejected them. The President of the Council, Hungary, tried to encourage members to promote negotiations among the parties on the basis of Ahtissari ideas, but China made it clear that it was not within the Security Council's jurisdiction to discuss constitutional arrangements within a country.

In an unusual outburst, Vorontsov, during informal consultations on November 3, 1992, said the Council was being challenged in Bosnia, Angola, Cambodia, and Somalia. The Council was not acting with sufficient firmness. 'Here we have 15 countries with big military machines, but not a single military machine is available for use by Security Council. The UN should have its own military force. In today's world, a big war is not likely; there will be no third world war. There are big military forces around Bosnia, like big tigers just lazing around. It is time that those tigers are put to use.' Vorontsov was disappointed that no other member took his bait, though some eyebrows were raised as he was speaking.

Here is an example of how the Security Council spends or wastes time on what would certainly be regarded by outsiders as trifling matters. On November 12, Erdos, the Hungarian president of the Council, suggested that Vance and Owen should speak in the morning session of the official meeting of the Security Council and Ogata and Mazowiescki, special human rights investigator, should speak in the afternoon. Belgium insisted that all four, who would be invited to address the Council under Rule 39, should speak in the morning. The President continued to press for the sequence suggested by him. He said there was logic in separating the four persons into two groups, but offered no explanation of the logic. He even brought in the Secretariat, saying they too preferred his idea. He pleaded with members not to prolong the debate on this point and not to waste time, but not a single member, not even a close ally like Austria, would support him. The President had to relent. The President then proposed that the Council should sit through late at night so that the list of speakers would be exhausted; or, as an alternative, the Council should resume only on the following Tuesday so as to permit some OIC countries to visit Bosnia over the weekend at the invitation of the Bosnian government. There was vocal opposition to both these absurd proposals. It was agreed that after listening to as many speakers as could be done, the Council would resume on Monday since there was no crisis situation.

At the same meeting, Austria proposed an amendment, which was to play a big part in subsequent events in Bosnia, calling upon the

Secretary General to examine the possibility of establishing 'safe havens' in Bosnia and submit a report on it in due course.

In the last week of November, the Secretary General sent a letter to the Council about the situation in Macedonia. President Gligorov of Macedonia asked the Secretary General to send a peacekeeping force to his country to monitor its borders with its neighbours. Vance and Owen proposed that the Secretary General should send a group of military and police personnel to Macedonia to study the situation there and make recommendations regarding peacekeeping force. In his letter, the Secretary General said he intended to send a group of such observers and, in the light of their report, would make recommendations regarding the deployment of a peacekeeping contingent. He added that the deployment, in response to a specific request of the competent authorities of Macedonia would be the first example of 'preventive deployment' which he had recommended in his Agenda for Peace. The President circulated the usual reply to the Secretary General, saying that the Council agreed with his proposal.

In this case, however, the traditional reply created difficulties for China and India as well as for European members. The Europeans could not agree to the term Macedonia since the name was not acceptable to Greece. China and India had a problem with the very concept of preventive deployment. The reply consequently was modified. The word 'Macedonia' disappeared. Instead of supporting the Secretary General's proposal as such, the reply supported the specific proposal to send a group of military and police observers. The following phrase was added at India's instance: 'As recommended by the co-chairmen of the Steering Committee of the International Conference on Former Yugoslavia and as requested by the concerned competent authorities'.

In Resolution 777, the Council had decided, inter alia, to consider the question of the status of Yugoslavia before the end of the fall session of the General Assembly. The British had made it clear that they did not consider it opportune to review FRY's status at least until the elections in FRY on December 20. There was no enthusiasm on the part of any member to open this question at that stage. The Legal Counsel in the Secretariat opined that there was no need for the Council to take a formal decision in the form of a resolution in case it wished to postpone consideration of the matter until a later date. As advised by the Legal Counsel, India, President for December, proposed a letter to the President of the General Assembly, merely stating that the members of the Council would keep the matter under continuous review and had decided to defer consideration till a later date. 'It was so agreed'.

In a letter dated December 9, the Secretary General proposed deployment of one battalion from UNPROFOR to Macedonia in order to forestall the deterioration of the situation there. He had not spelt it out in those terms, but the deployment would amount to 'preventive deployment' and 'preventive diplomacy'. Everybody supported the proposal. The following day, the Council adopted a resolution, authorising the Secretary General to proceed as proposed. US inserted some amendments which were so close to the traditional Indian thinking that many members thought they were really Indian amendments. For instance, one amendment noted the request of the Macedonian authorities for the deployment of UN troops. This resolution was a watershed. The fact that it was adopted without any discussion of its historic nature was a testimony to the changed international situation. The Council adopted one historic resolution almost every week!

Vance briefed me, in my capacity as President, on December 17 on Bosnia. He remained firmly opposed to lifting the arms embargo against Bosnia. An enlarged meeting of the Steering Group was meeting in Geneva. Of the 33 ministers attending, only three or four supported lifting the embargo. Regarding the no-fly zone, Vance had informed the Geneva meeting that more investigations were needed to determine whether air combat activity had taken place. There were allegations that helicopters had been used for combat, but UNPROFOR could not confirm them. There was also confusion whether training flights were permitted; this had now been clarified by a new regulation that two training flights per month were allowed. Vance felt strongly that the Security Council must take into account all such inaccuracies before considering enforcement action. General Nambiar and General Morillon had very strong views on the compatibility of such military action with UNPROFOR's humanitarian assistance activities. Use of force could endanger UNPROFOR and other humanitarian relief personnel working in Bosnia and elsewhere. Vance said the existing sanctions against Serbia should be strengthened. Pressure should be exercised on Belgrade to permit UN presence in Kosovo. The co-chairmen of the Steering Committee had met with Izetbegovic and Tudjman for five hours in Geneva on December 16, as a result of which some progress had been made towards achieving a greater degree of commonality between the Croats and Muslims on the constitutional arrangements. Some maps had been handed over. If the two parties could agree on a map, it would be a major breakthrough and could serve as a basis for agreement among all the three parties in Geneva on January 3. Vance said he would convey his views to the Council in a letter but the letter never came.

The Council adopted a resolution on December 18 condemning the mass rape of Muslim women in Bosnia and supporting the European Council's decision to send a fact-finding mission to investigate the matter. The Secretary General was requested to extend all possible help to the EC mission.

The Secretary General repeated his strong reservation on the proposal to enforce the no-fly zone since it would jeopardise the safety of UNPROFOR personnel. General Morillon, commander of the UN forces in Sarajevo, publicly accused Bosnian Muslims of attacking his residence with mortar fire in an attempt to kill him, his son, and General Nambiar. He said he had no doubt whatsoever that it was the Muslims who were involved in the incident.

The Yugoslav story would get more complex and tragic in the months ahead, as the following chapter would reveal.

5

BOSNIA AND HERZEGOVINA

THREE OF THE CONSTITUENT units of the Socialist Federal Republic of Yugoslavia—Tito's Yugoslavia—which started breaking away as independent states in 1991 were ethnically homogenous or 'pure' and did not experience any upheaval. Slovenia was almost wholly Slovene. Serbia and Montenegro were wholly Serb and in fact joined together to form the new Federal Republic of Yugoslavia and claimed to be the successor state to former Yugoslavia. The other three republics—Croatia, Macedonia, and Bosnia-Herzegovina—had mixed populations, with a majority group and significant minorities from other groups. Bosnia was the most complex case since it had three 'national' groups, with the Muslims constituting about 42 per cent of the population, Serbs about 35 per cent and Croats nearly 20 per cent (Strangely, Muslims were considered a 'nation'.)

The problem arose because the seceding states claimed the right to secede on the basis that they were separate 'nations'. A logical extension of this principle of separate nations should entitle the minority nations within these 'nations' to either claim their own independence or to merge with their 'mother' nations. Thus, the Serbs in Croatia wanted to merge with Serbia, the Serbs in Bosnia demanded their own separate state with the right to eventually join with Serbia, and the Croats in Bosnia insisted on a seperate mini-state of their own, with the right to unite with Croatia. Understandably, neither the seceding states nor the international community supported such further disintegration which would have led to endless complications of drawing up new boundaries and perhaps to large-scale suffering and 'ethnic cleansing'. Equally understandably, the 'mother' nations felt it their duty and right to go to the rescue of their kith and kin. The situation was readymade for conflict. Bosnia had the most complex population mix and consequently was the most difficult problem to resolve.

The situation in Bosnia became even more complicated because of the religious factor. The Serbs were Orthodox Christians and the Croats were Catholics. The competing Christian affiliations did contribute to making the problem more difficult, particularly since the Orthodox faith had become resurgent in Russia after the demise of the Soviet Union and played an important domestic role in Russia. But the most active factor was Islam which had emerged as a major actor in international relations in the post-Cold War era. The Muslim countries of the world perceived Islam to be in danger, with the UN imposing sanctions against Muslim countries such as Iraq and Libya. They intervened, diplomati-cally and even militarily—in the form of sending military material—on the side of Bosnian Muslims. Images of emaciated bodies of Muslims held in concentration camps by Serbs inflamed public opinion in the Muslim world, as elsewhere. The US, on the other hand, did not cherish the prospect of the emergence of a 'Muslim' state in the heart of Europe. The British and the French were somewhat sympathetic to the Serbs. All these prejudices played their part as the Bosnian crisis unfolded.

In September 1991, the Security Council had imposed an arms embargo against Yugoslavia, meaning all the constituent units of the former undivided Yugoslavia. As time went by, the sentiment among Muslim countries, as also in the United States, grew against Serbia and Serbs, and, correspondingly, in favour of the Bosnian Muslims—also known as Bosniaks. 'Lift and strike' became the incessant demand of the OIC, suggesting lifting of the arms embargo against Bosnia and striking the Serbs by air power. David Owen, the EU negotiator, and Cyrus Vance, the UN special envoy for Yugoslavia, were both categorically opposed to lifting the arms embargo against Bosnia. They said that the Muslims were lacking not in arms but in trained military forces. As for strikes against the Serbs, they maintained that it was not as if the Serbs alone were the guilty party; the Muslims and the Croats were equally unco-operative with the efforts to find a political solution to the problem.

In March 1993, there was heavy fighting in and around Srebrenica, a Muslim pocket surrounded by Serb-held territory. The Serbs occupied vantage points surrounding Srebrenica, threatening its occupation. On April 16, 1993, the Security Council passed Resolution 819, declaring the pocket as a 'safe area', demanded withdrawal of Serb forces and condemned 'ethnic cleansing'. The following day, the commander of UNPROFOR in Bosnia succeeded in getting the commanders of Serb and Muslim forces to sign an agreement on the demilitarisation of Srebrenica. The Council adopted Resolution 824 on May 16, 1993, declaring additional towns—Sarajevo, Tuzla, Zepa, Gorazde, and Bihac—as safe areas. Resolution 824 did not empower the UN to take any enforcement action against the Serbs, but it was felt, overoptimistically, that the mere designation of these places as 'safe areas' would be enough to ensure their protection. The Serb onslaught, however, continued.

On June 4, Resolution 836 expanded UNPROFOR's mandate to 'protect' the safe areas, including to deter attacks against them, and to occupy some key points on the ground. It authorised UNPROFOR to use force in reply to bombardments against safe areas and deter armed incursions. It further decided that member states, acting nationally or through regional organisations—euphemism for NATO—could take all necessary measures, including the use of air power, to support UNPROFOR. It soon became evident that merely designating some places as 'safe areas' would not ensure the safety of the Muslim populations there and that the UNPROFOR would have to be provided additional troops and equipment if it was to make the areas reasonably safe.

The Secretary General was asked for his views on what it would take to give teeth to the concept of safe areas. On June 14, 1993, the Secretary General submitted a report in which he pitched the requirement for additional troops at 34,000 if the pockets were to be made safe. However, he was well aware that troops of this order would simply not be available. Perhaps because he did not want to be accused of deliberately inflating the figure and of being anti-Muslim, and certainly under pressure from some members, especially Britain, the Secretary General allowed himself to put forward a light option of 7,600 troops. With the benefit of hindsight, offering the light option was perhaps not well-advised. But he did make it clear that the light option presumed the consent and co-operation of the parties without which the safety of the areas could not be ensured. Regarding the use of air power or air strikes, he said that the first time air power was to be used, he would take the decision in consultation with the Security Council members. The reference to 'consultation' would later prove contentious. Air strikes would be carried out by NATO, since the UN did not have, nor did it wish to have, its own strike aircraft. This meant that NATO would have to go through its own procedures for obtaining the required authorisation from its competent organ.

The Security Council naturally embraced the light option in Resolution 844 on June 18. However, the additional troops were not made available at least for six more months. As far as the Council was concerned, they had discharged their responsibility by authorising the troops; they did not believe it was their duty to help obtain the troops!

The ambassadors of Britain, USA, and France came to see the Secretary General on January 25, 1994, in connection with the issue of air strikes on the Serbs in Bosnia. The Council had adopted a resolution laying down a procedure for authorising air strikes but there was some ambiguity about who on the Secretariat side could authorise the strikes. The Secretariat and NATO, which would actually carry out the strikes at the request of the UN, had made a distinction between close air support (CAS) and air strikes. The former was meant to provide protection to humanitarian agencies in their work whereas the objective of the latter was punitive.

The British ambassador asked the Secretary General how he intended to proceed once he received the recommendation of Akashi, his special representative in Zagreb. The Secretary General replied that the resolution itself did not differentiate between close air support and air strikes. He thought he should ask the Council for guidance. The British ambassador said that air strikes encompassed both forms of air operations. The UK saw no need for the Secretary General to go to the Council for guidance; it would be better for him to speak to individual members rather than approach the Council as a whole. (The reason for this advice was to keep the Russians out of the picture since they were most likely to oppose any air operations against the Serbs.)

France and US strongly supported the British advice against referring the issue to the Council. The Secretary General said, in that case, he might write a letter to the Council after giving the green light for CAS. He suggested that 'consultations' mentioned in the resolution could mean 'inform' and not consent. US felt that the Secretary General might delegate the CAS authority to Akashi; the Secretary General said he had no objection but in that case also, he would send a letter to the Council. The ambassadors, seeing that the Secretary General was not falling for their line, said that they were asking him to delegate the power to Akashi only for Tuzla and Srebrenica. The Secretary General said he agreed, but would do so after receiving Akashi's report and recommendations. In case Akashi felt that it would be counter-productive to bomb those two places, he would report to the Council. It was evident that the three permanent members wanted to convey only one message to the Secretary General: do not ask the Council for clarification or decision; you have the mandate to take decisions. In other words, the Secretary General must take the responsibility. It was also strange that the three of them should have taken so much trouble to emphasise that they were talking of CAS and not air strikes. The NATO summit declaration clearly spoke of 'air strikes'!

In the third week of February, there was suspense and excitement in New York about the NATO ultimatum to the Serbs regarding Sarajevo. Mrs. Madelene Albright was perceived as being particularly concerned whether or not the Secretary General would authorise the air strikes. The French Ambassador Merimee observed, with a tinge of condescension, that Mrs. Albright was perhaps nervous because that was her first crisis. The Secretary General's explanation was that Mrs. Albright had protective instincts towards Bill Clinton; she did not want him to suffer another foreign policy set back after Somalia and Haiti. On February 28, NATO at last had the opportunity to use force, though outside its 'area'. Two NATO F-16s shot down four Galeb aircraft in Bosnia at about 6:50 p.m. local time. The identity of the aircraft was not established; they were in all probability Serb—Bosnian Serb or Krajina (Croatia) Serb.

The UN force in Bosnia was short of troops. Turkey, Greece, and Italy were prepared to provide contingents, but the UN had a firm practice of not inducting troops from neighbouring countries. John Major, the British Prime Minister, tried to persuade the Secretary General on March 1, 1994, to accept troops from at least Italy. The Secretary General promised to consider and added that Iran was ready to send 10,000 troops. This was deliberately provocative to Major since the Americans would never agree to Iran. Eventually, after a few weeks, the Secretary General relented on Turkey. The British lobbied actively for

Turkey's inclusion. Turkey also mounted a big campaign. The OIC wrote to the Secretary General on Turkey's behalf. The decisive factor was that UNPROFOR needed additional troops which were simply not available from other countries. Greece protested strongly as did the Bosnian Serbs, but the Russians welcomed Turkey's participation in UNPROFOR.

Bosnia's Muslims and Croats signed an agreement among themselves and between them and the Croatian government in Washington on March 1, 1994, for a federation and confederation respectively. Granic, the foreign minister of Croatia, told the Secretary General the following day in New York that it had been a painful decision for his government but they had signed it in the interest of peace. The Serbs would be invited to join the federation on an equal basis. He informed the Secretary General that Serbia would open an office in Zagreb and Croatia would open an office in Belgrade on the same day. The Americans had of course worked out the agreement on the federation and confederation with only one objective: to prevent the emergence of a Muslim state in Europe.

The Russians, for some time, had been chafing at being ignored or taken for granted by their fellow permanent members, whether on Middle East or on Bosnia. So they seemed to have decided to make a show of their independence by adopting tough positions on some issues. This produced the desired effect on the others. The French put forward a draft resolution proposing the appointment of a civilian expert to assist the Bosnian government to restore utilities in Sarajevo. The Russians had no objection to that but they firmly rejected other provisions which would have had the effect of adding more 'safe areas'. Vorontsov's views were taken seriously by the French. Merimee told me that the Russians were not bluffing this time and that his draft was 'dead' at least for the present.

Russia had its own success on March 1. Karadzic, the Bosnian Serb leader, on a visit to Moscow agreed to open Tuzla airport to humanitarian flights on condition that Russian observers be stationed there. The Americans welcomed Russia's co-operation but in fact there was nothing but competition between the two. The Russian attempt at independence lasted precisely two weeks. On March 16, Russia ended up co-sponsoring the French draft!

On March 18, the *New York Times* published an article by Kozyrev, the Russian foreign minister, entitled 'Don't threaten us'. The title said it all. During the Cold War years, the Soviets were reluctant to be described as a superpower; they thought it was not an apt adjective for a country which was keen to be perceived as a friend of the third world countries. In his article, Kozyrev referred to Russia as a superpower in almost every alternate paragraph.

Hannay suggested to the Secretary General on March 22 that General Rose, the British, UNPROFOR commander in Bosnia, should be sent to the US Congress to persuade them to agree to American participation in the Bosnian operation. US did not want to send troops to Bosnia because it did not wish to get involved in the mess there. Boutros Ghali was always opposed, as a matter of principle, to his special representatives being asked to be present at meetings even in New York, let alone elsewhere. He politely but firmly discouraged Hannay from pursuing his request. He told me later Rose would have had to go to Washington, 'over my dead body'. His response was an equally strong 'no' when the DPKO made a similar proposal of General Rose coming to New York. He almost always reacted vehemently, nega-tively, every time someone requested the presence of a special represen-tative in the Council for the purpose of briefing members on a given peacekeeping operation.

The first CAS strikes were ordered on April 10, 1994, around Gorazde. The situation there had deteriorated over the previous few days. General Rose and Akashi had been downplaying the seriousness of the Serb offensive. Rose and Akashi did not want to do anything that would upset the Serbs and consequently jeopardise the talks for a 'global ceasefire' which the Serbs had proposed. The Serbs however continued to play for time and pressed on with their offensive. They occupied much of the high ground around Gorazde and shelled the town. The UNHCR staff was in a panic and the UN Military Observers (UNMOs) were confined to their barracks. One UNMO was wounded. Even at 3:30 p.m. the previous day, the force commander did not indicate a need for air strikes. In fact, he said air strikes would not serve any purpose. However, at 4.45 p.m., Rose made the request for CAS. The force commander called Akashi in Paris who immediately gave the authorisation. Akashi called me at 5.25 p.m. and I informed the Secretary General. The actual air strikes were launched at 6.25 p.m. and 6.29 p.m. Two F-16s attacked the Serb command position. Until the following morning, we had not received the damage assessment report because of bad weather over Gorazde. But we knew that the Serbs lobbed two shells in the centre of Gorazde half an hour after the air strike.

We in the Secretariat called the operation CAS but it was more in the nature of an air strike. To describe it as an air strike would have given rise to a host of avoidable legal and political issues. The Secretary General was happy. This brought him positive mention in the media. He asked his spokesperson to tell the media that Akashi had authorised the air strikes in consultation with him. Understandable.

The CAS operation over Gorazde was the crossing of an important threshold in Bosnia. The US Defence Secretary Perry and the Chairman of the Joint Chiefs of Staff General Shalikashvili had declared only the previous week that the US was not in favour of air strikes over Gorazde since the situation was significantly different from that in Sarajevo. Both of them were much criticised for that statement. I myself wondered if it was not a ruse to put the Serbs offguard and encourage them to persevere in their push towards Gorazde so that it became easier for the UN to call for an air strike. This is precisely what happened.

The Russians, however, were not pleased. The Russian Charge d'affaires in Geneva called on the Secretary General on April 11, and demanded to know why Russia had not been informed of the air strike in advance. Boris Yeltsin had called Bill Clinton and told him that such action and decision could not be taken without Russian participation. The Secretary General explained to the Charge d'affaires that the operation was one of CAS, not an air strike. He said the Russian role was very important to de-escalate the situation. The previous day's operation was very limited and was in response to Serb escalation. The Russian charge d'affaires said that the distinction between CAS and an air strike was a difficult one. Escalation had already taken place. If fresh air strikes were to happen, it would be difficult for Russia to help de-escalate the situation. Russia must be informed in advance of any such plans in future. Russia felt ignored. The Secretary General was not the one not to have the last word. He said the resolution was adopted by all 15 members including Russia; it allowed states to take action even unilaterally, but we in the UN had managed to give it a different interpretation. The resolution referred to 'air power' but we had made the distinction between CAS and air strikes. The charge d'affaires left, saying that the whole affair had generated very strong reaction in Moscow. The Russians were seriously worried about the impact of this development on their domestic politics. Zhirinovsky, the nationalist leader, was likely to benefit the most from it.

The next 36 to 48 hours would be critical. If we did not get the Serbs to talk about a ceasefire and if they and we in the UN kept making tough statements, there would be a real danger of UNPROFOR becoming a party to the conflict, as had happened in Somalia. The Deputy Force Commander General McGinnes told me over the phone that a settling of scores was going on between General Mladic and Karadzic. Mladic seemed to be gaining the upper hand, which was bad news for peace prospects.

The subject of Russian sensitivity came up in the Secretary General's talks with all the German leaders during the following days. Foreign Minister Kinkel told the Secretary General in Bonn on April 12 that

Kozyrev had told him two days ago: please consult us, include us in any decision-making. Kinkel offered to speak to Kozyrev if the Secretary General thought it might help, to which Boutros Ghali replied that he was ready to do the same if Kinkel thought it would help! Professor Rita Sussmuth, President of Bundestag, told the Secretary General the same day that the prestige of the UN was very low in Russia because of the events of the previous two days in former Yugoslavia. In another meeting with Kinkel on April 13, he said the Baltic States and the Russians were both getting hysterical about each other. Out of three and a half hours of his talks with Kozyrev, he had devoted one and a half hours on the Baltics. 'Even when I played tennis with Kozyrev in the morning he talked about the Baltics,' said Kinkel to the Secretary General. Kozyrev said that an enemy image was developing about Russia in all those countries. A dangerous mood was developing, especially after Zhirinovsky's success. 'I am a friend of Kozyrev, but he is becoming harder and harder, and not just for home consumption,' added Kinkel. 'We Germans try to help the Russians when we can. Europe cannot do well unless Russia does well.'

In a talk with Chancellor Helmut Kohl on the same day, the Secretary General suggested that Russia had to be persuaded to return to an active diplomatic role. Kohl promised to speak to Yeltsin about it the following week. He said: 'I keep telling Clinton that Russians had to be brought in.' The Secretary General said he was trying his best to help Russia overcome its feeling of isolation or unimportance. Kohl agreed that this was the most important point. 'Russians are a great and proud people, with great history, a superpower. They had got used to 50 per cent of the world falling at their feet. I shall never forget the three funerals in the Kremlin. They feel they are not being respected,' said Kohl. He went on: 'Between us here, last December, around a table of 12 EU leaders, Yeltsin was also sitting. Frankly, the behaviour of some of my colleagues was not at all polite. Yeltsin was sitting next to me. He took my hand in his hand under the table and whispered to me: 'People here do not like me!'. I am accused in Germany of helping the Russians too much, but there is no alternative. If reforms fail, things will go back to the old ways; this will be even more expensive.'

The same theme was repeated by the foreign minister of Spain on April 14. He told the Secretary General that during his visit to Spain the day after the air strikes over Gorazde Yeltsin was really upset and angry. The Secretary General said that what had happened over Gorazde had exacerbated the internal situation in Russia. Lukin was a hardliner whereas Kozyrev was pro-dialogue.

The Bosnian Serbs had launched their offensive on Gorazde on March 29. By the third week of April they were effectively in control of the town though they had not yet entered it. There were 65,000 civilians in the town and their lives were in danger. The UN had hardly any presence in the town. Gorazde had been declared a 'safe area' by the Security Council in June 1993, along with five other places, but the concept of 'safe areas' was flawed from the beginning. Until Gorazde happened, it was believed that the mere designation of a place as safe area would do the trick.

The reports from UNPROFOR consistently downplayed the seriousness of the situation. This was true of both the military and the civil authorities. Their concern was not to provoke the Serbs to such an extent that they would refuse to negotiate. On April 10, CAS was provided by NATO at Akashi's request. On the 11th, another CAS operation was carried out. US NATO planes bombed a Serbian tank—a single tank—and a command post. According to the *New York Times* of April 19, two of the six bombs turned out to be duds! (The ineptness and capacity to make blunders can at times be high in the US armed forces. In the second week of April, US planes shot down two of its own Cobra helicopters over the so-called air exclusion zone in northern Iraq in clear weather and broad daylight, thinking they were Iraqi helicopters. Twenty-six American, British, French, Turkish, and Kurdish people were killed in this 'friendly fire'.)

We in the Secretariat had been warning of dire consequences of the use of air power and they all came true! Nearly 150 UN, UNHCR, and other personnel were taken hostage by the Serbs. The humanitarian convoys were stopped. The Serbs continued with their relentless shelling of Sarajevo. They even shot down a British sea harrier jet with a ground to air missile. Through all this difficult period, Akashi persevered with his extremely difficult negotiations with Karadzic. Finally he got so frustrated that he said in a public statement that it was meaningless for UNPROFOR to continue its activities. On April 18, Ganic, the vice-president of Bosnia, told the Secretary General in no uncertain terms that he held the latter personally responsible for the tragedy of Gorazde. The Secretary General and I reminded him of the lack of adequate resources. His point was that in that case, we should have said so publicly and called upon those with resources to save Gorazde. He insisted that the Secretary General was not making full use of the authority of CAS. According to him, Akashi was saying he had authority to call for CAS involving only two aircraft, the Secretary General having reserved to himself the authority if more aircraft were required. (The Secretary General told us later that Ganic was lying.)

After Ganic left, we discussed the matter among ourselves. I suggested that whatever Ganic might have said, the Secretary General should go to the Council and tell them that the UN could not do any more with its present resources; let us leave it to the Council to decide what to do; the Secretary General was being unfairly blamed. During our meeting, a cable arrived from Akashi, recommending that the Secretary General should propose to the Council that it should issue an ultimatum to the Serbs to stop attacking Gorazde and decide to set up a weapons exclusion zone of 30 km along the Sarajevo model. We agreed that the Secretary General should go the Council in the afternoon and tell the Council (a) that he supported Akashi's recommendation and (b) that he would write to the NATO Secretary General, asking him to obtain the NATO Council's authorisation to respond to UNPROFOR

137

requests for *air strikes*—as opposed to CAS—to defend Gorazde. Once Boutros Ghali decided on something, he raced far ahead of his advisers. During lunch time he decided that he would ask for NATO decision in respect of all the safe areas, not just Gorazde. He wanted the letter to NATO to be signed before even he went to the Council. In the event, he signed the letter during the meeting. He felt proud when he announced the decision to the media near the Council chamber. The ball was now in NATO's court and that was *the* point. No one was shedding too many tears for the people of Gorazde or elsewhere. The important point was that each side should try and toss the ball out of its court.

The Secretary General was not sure that NATO would agree to the air strikes. Goulding was so sceptical that he wanted us to have another meeting with the Secretary General to discuss what to do in case NATO said 'no'. I had no doubt that NATO would say 'yes'; the Secretary General had put them in a spot and they had no choice. In the Security Council, only Vorontsov had expressed reservation regarding the Secretary General's initiative and said that the Council needed to take a fresh decision before air strikes could be invoked, but his was the lone voice of dissent. He also said, with some credibility, that air strikes would solve nothing, make matters worse, lead to even more UN people being taken hostage, and adversely affect the negotiation prospects.

Most observers believed that the air strikes would not solve anything, but every one was equally committed to it. The Bosnian Muslims were masterminding a brilliant public relations campaign. They succeeded to a large extent because of Serb intransigence and stupidity. The Americans would have liked to expand the scope of air strikes beyond safe areas. They also articulated the view that NATO did not need UN request to launch air strikes. There was potential for conflict and misunderstanding between UN and US–NATO.

A big diplomatic battle was going on between USA, France, Russia, and UN. Each of them had proposed an international conference. Yeltsin had proposed a summit of the USA, Russia, UN and EU. Clinton called for a conference to be prepared by foreign ministers. Mitterrand wrote to the Secretary General asking him to take the initiative of convening another international conference on former Yugoslavia. The Secretary General was pleased with this approach. He wrote to Clinton, Yeltsin, and the Greek Prime Minister Papandreou (chairman of EU) proposing a working group of the four actors to prepare the conference.

Warren Christopher wrote a letter to his NATO colleagues—a 'very badly drafted letter' in the words of Hannay—calling for a wide-ranging list of air strike targets throughout BiH. The letter generated very negative reactions among many of its recipients as a result of which the Americans backed down and confirmed the air strikes would be in conformity with Resolution 836. The other point about obtaining UN request was settled in Washington on April 21, following Anglo–French demarche. US agreed to the concept of double key or two fingers on the trigger of air strikes—UN and NATO.

NATO took its decisions on April 22 in two instalments on the Secretary General's requests for air strike preparedness to protect the safe areas. The Secretary General forwarded them to the Security Council. The decisions contained an ultimatum on Gorazde to expire at 20:01 hrs on Saturday April 23 and 72 hours later for other safe areas. The Council met at Russian request. Vorontsov asked me for the Secretary General's reaction. I told him that the Secretary General was en route to Barbados to attend the world conference on development of island developing countries but he supported, in general, NATO decisions. I added that it was for the Council to take a decision in the matter. Vorontsov said Moscow was relaxed about the ultimatum on Gorazde but felt that the decisions went beyond the Secretary General's request and UN resolutions. He read out to me a message from Moscow saying that they would hold the Secretary General personally responsible in case of an allout war against the Serbs.

Saturday, April 22, was a day of confrontation between the UN and US–NATO. The latter was anxious to strike well ahead of the expiry of the ultimatum. But Akashi had worked out an agreement with Milosevic, Karadzic, and Mladic in Belgrade on April 22–23 according to which the Serbs should have stopped firing and shelling as of noon on April 23. The shelling, however, continued, at times heavy, on Saturday. The NATO Secretary General Worner pressed Akashi to agree to immediate strikes but Akashi did not agree; he wanted to give time to Serbs to comply with the agreement. Worner felt very frustrated and angry. He wanted to speak to the Secretary General but the latter was incommunicado since he was airborne. Mrs. Albright called Kofi Annan several times from Washington pressing for air strikes 'since it would soon get dark over Gorazde'. But Akashi was supported by his generals and held his ground.

The ultimatum expired and there were no strikes. The Serbs largely pulled out but they burnt down many houses as they left. NATO–UNPROFOR differences became public. CNN lost no time in quoting US sources that UN had blocked NATO calls for air strikes. We in the Secretariat did worry about this for some time but we had confidence in Akashi taking the correct decisions in consultation with his military. Akashi did well. By resisting NATO pressure, he restored UN credibility with the Serbs, Russians, as well as the non-aligned nations. The Bosnian government was very unhappy with him. The other side of the coin was that the Bosnian Serbs got the measure of Akashi as someone extremely reluctant to use force; after all Karadzic was a psychiatrist! The Secretary General issued a statement on April 23 that he would issue instructions to launch air strikes if the Serbs violated the ultimatum or the agreement. But even Christopher acknowledged that the Serbs were largely in compliance.

The deadline for the Bosnian Serbs to pull out their heavy weapons from the 20 km exclusion zone from the centre of Gorazde was 8 p.m. on April 26. After the confrontation between NATO and UNPROFOR three days earlier, the general expectation was that Akashi would lean in the direction of asking for air strikes. But Akashi pulled out another rabbit from his hat. He called me to 'give you good news'. He said there had been substantial withdrawal of Serb heavy weapons from the exclusion zone and he had decided, in consultation with his force commander, that there was no need for air strikes. Most importantly, his media statement made it clear that NATO, in the person of Admiral Smith, fully concurred with this decision.

In the Security Council consultations on the 26th, Mrs. Albright lashed out at Akashi for the remarks attributed to him in the *New York Times*. She said it was 'totally unacceptable for an international civil servant, whose salary for the most part we pay' to publicly criticise President Clinton or any other government leader. The reference to 'paying' the salary was a bit of tongue in cheek. She went public and made the same remark at the stake out near the Council chamber. It was going too far since she had personally complained to the Secretary General about Akashi and the Secretary General had asked Aime to ask Akashi to check himself.

When I told Akashi about all this, he was quite cool. 'I thought she was my friend. Do the Americans pay?' This was a reference to the fact that the US at the time was heavily in arrears in the payment of its dues to the UN budget. The Secretary General told us a couple of days later that he had spoken to Mrs. Albright about her remarks on Akashi, especially the salary bit. 'We have always been taught from our childhood not to talk about money in public,' Secretary General told her. Apparently, she was not impressed.

The Council held an official meeting on April 27 to give an opportunity to ministers from a few Islamic countries to outdo one another in condemning the 'UN impotence' in defending Bosnia. The three clear winners were the foreign ministers of Pakistan, Iran, and Malaysia. Pakistan accused the Council of being anti-Islam and Malaysia held the Secretary General personally responsible. Of course, nothing came out of the debate, nothing was expected to. The Secretary General left the meeting just as the Bosnian minister was to begin his statement and returned soon after he finished it. He told me later that he had intentionally left the room at that time and hoped the Bosnians had noticed it!

Izetbegovic, the president of Bosnia, asked for Akashi's scalp in early May. He said publicly that his government would not deal with him. The Secretary General promptly issued a statement reiterating full confidence in Akashi. The immediate provocation was Akashi's decision to permit Bosnian Serb tanks to transit the Sarajevo exclusion zone under UNPROFOR escort. The sight of Serb tanks being escorted by UNPROFOR would surely be too much for the Bosniaks to swallow. Akashi's explanation was that in return for this gesture he had obtained a lot of concessions from Karadzic such as stationing of observers in Brcko, arrival of British troops in Gorazde, and so on. The US Senate passed a resolution on May 12 by a vote of 50 in favour and 49 against calling for the lifting of the arms embargo against Bosnia. The resolution was non-binding.

In Kuala Lumpur, 40,000 people demonstrated against Boutros Ghali (and Akashi), calling for his resignation for his perceived anti-Muslim bias. Bosnia was the decisive factor for Malaysia's strong opposition to Boutros Ghali's bid for a second term in 1996.

The foreign ministers of US, UK, Russia, France, Germany, and Belgium, the EU Commissioner Hans Van den Broek, as well as David Owen and Stoltenberg, the co-chair of International Conference on Former Yugoslavia (ICFY), met in Geneva on May 13 to discuss Bosnia. The meeting was convened to harmonise the positions of the main actors who often spoke with differing voices. They issued a communiqué in which for the first time they agreed collectively that the territorial compromise should be on the basis of 51 per cent for the Muslim-Croat entity and 49 per cent for the Serb entity. This was a major advance since the Americans thus far had firmly resisted agreeing to such percentages. The 51:49 percentages were almost the same as those worked out by the ICFY co-chair. The Bosnian government was demanding 58 per cent. The idea of a phased reduction of sanctions against Serbia parri pasu with the implementation of the overall agreement was accepted by the Americans. Christopher did not want to include the two co-chairs in the meeting mainly because of the Americans' dislike of Owen. At best he was prepared to invite them to the dinner. The compromise was to ask them to join the meeting from 4:30 p.m. Kozyrev was miffed because Christopher assumed the role of self-appointed convener of the meeting. So, he was given the honour of hosting the dinner.

The Geneva communiqué only created a façade of unity. The Bosnian government by now felt confident, militarily, to roll back the Serbs. The Muslim-Croat side was getting enough arms from outside and was convinced that diplomatically it would always manage to get the US to support it. The Muslims were following a consistent line; they wanted the West, US, and NATO to intervene on their behalf. Anything which would have the effect of diminishing the prospects of this involvement would be rejected by them. This was why they did not accept the Geneva communiqué's call for a four-month ceasefire; they would agree to two months. The Serbs wanted an indefinite or unlimited ceasefire.

Cracks soon appeared in the Geneva 7 group. The French, British, and Russians started saying that the 51:49 formula had a better chance of being accepted by the Muslims if they were asked to do so 'in an American accent'. Douglass Hogg, Britain's Minister of State said that the Muslims must realise that they had been defeated. Juppé, the French minister, announced on May 19, apparently without consulting his colleagues, that the seven ministers would meet again in Geneva on June 13. If that meeting was not successful, he added that France would withdraw its troops.

We in the Secretariat had several problems. Firstly, UNPROFOR, especially Akashi, tended to give too much benefit of doubt to the Serbs. He was not wrong in trying to keep his lines open with the Serbs. He was justified in not letting the Serbs perceive him as being hostile to them. But, at the same time, he had to be firm and not allow himself to be taken for granted by them. And then there was the problem of dealing with the Council, all of whose members, minus Russia, had zero tolerance for anything critical of the Muslims. They did not receive reports of Bosniak attacks, even substantiated with credulity or enthusiasm. Within the Secretariat, there was no desire or willingness to question UNPROFOR or Akashi. Whatever explanation he gave was accepted, or at least not challenged. I, as the one responsible to keep the Council briefed as accurately as possible, had started sending notes to DPKO, with my queries and doubts, but they routinely conveyed them to UNPROFOR. For my part, and this was the Secretary General's approach too as far as I could tell, I wanted to be transparent and truthful without worrying about their politics. And there was no doubt that everything about the former Yugoslavia was political.

Silajdzic, the foreign minister of Bosnia, complained to Vieira de Mello of UNPROFOR about the blackmail of Britain, France, and Spain to pull out their troops from Bosnia unless the government agreed to the 51: 49 formula. He added that the final percentage for Muslims would have to be between 51 and 58. The Secretary General returned from Paris on May 22. He told us at a 'prayer meeting' that in Paris, Prime Minister Balladur was very upset with him for having appointed an American by the name of Eagleton as special coordinator for Sarajevo. 'How can you appoint an American when the US has done nothing in Bosnia?' The French had their own candidate for the job. Akashi had convened a meeting in Geneva on June 2 and 3 to discuss and conclude an agreement on the cessation of hostilities in Bosnia. He had shot off letters to Izetbegovic and Karadzic and had also invited Owen, Stoltenberg, Churkin, the Russian negotiator, and Redman, the American negotiator. But the Bosnians had consistently maintained that they would not attend unless the Serbs withdrew their militia from Gorazde. Akashi gambled that since the Serbs were keener than the Muslims for a long-term ceasefire, he could pressurise Karadzic into accepting the Bosnian demand. Akashi might also have calculated that, when the chips were down, the Muslims would not refuse to attend. He proved wrong on both counts. Karadzic ignored his 'ultimatum', as Akashi described his letter to Karadzic internally in the Secretariat, and the Muslims stuck to their position. Akashi did, however, manage to get the talks underway in Geneva on June 6. The Bosnian government obtained full satisfaction regarding the withdrawal of all Serb militias from the 3 km exclusion zone around Gorazde; they did not accept UNPROFOR's word for it but insisted on a joint UNPROFOR-Bosnian government's report on withdrawal.

July 19 was the deadline for the Bosnian parties to respond to the contact group proposals regarding the map. The Bosnian Muslim parliament and the Muslim-Croat federation voted overwhelmingly in favour of accepting the map. The Bosnian Serb parliament in Pale deliberated for two days and took a decision, the details of which were not made public immediately. They decided to send a delegation to Geneva with their response. It was believed that their response was 'generally' positive, but they wanted clarifications particularly regarding constitutional provisions. The Serbs demanded international recognition for their entity and the right to join with Serbia. They also demanded access to sea and better arrangements at the Brcko corridor. The Serbs seemed to have heeded Douglas Hurd's advice: do not say 'yes, but'; rather, say 'yes, and'. The UNPROFOR started making contingency plans in case the contact group's package was accepted by both sides.

The Serb reply was delivered in a sealed pink envelope on July 20 by Karadzic in Geneva. It said that the proposals could serve as the basis for further negotiations. The Serbs asked for three clarifications: constitutional provisions, Sarajevo, and access to sea. Charles Redman described the Serb response as rejection but the press statement of the contact group was somewhat more cautious: the federation side accepted the proposal and the Serb side did not. The contact group ministers would meet on July 30 to discuss specific measures of disincentives against Serbs. Milosevic was widely believed to want his Bosnian brethren to accept the map so that his life would be made a bit easier.

Would the Russians go along with more sanctions against the Serbs, particularly since they had not rejected the map? Izetbegovic had declared on the very first day that he would accept the proposals since he was confident that the Serbs would not.

The Secretary General wrote a letter to the President of the Council, an eight page missive on the future of UNPROFOR in the light of the fate of the contact group proposals. The draft of the letter was discussed in the Secretariat over three days. Boutros Ghali almost always held internal discussions on important issues. It was a very good way to involve all senior aides concerned. Often, the dealing officers or desk officers would also be asked to join in these sessions. Stoltenberg was called from Geneva. Annan first produced an 'elements' paper which Goulding converted into a letter. The Secretary General took the lead in the whole matter. His thesis was that if the package was accepted by the parties, the scale of operations to implement it would simply be beyond UN's capability. There was no way the UN could plan, deploy, and run an operation involving 50 to 60 thousand troops under Chapter VII. The Americans would never agree to place their contingent of 25 to 30 thousand under UN command. On the other hand, the Russians had clearly expressed opposition to entrusting the job to NATO. The only solution, under the circumstances, would be to ask the contact group countries consisting of USA, UK, France, Russia and Germany to take over the entire operation, including its financing.

All the Secretary General's aides agreed with and supported this approach. But there were differences among us on some aspects. I said the UN should try to retain political control. The Secretary General agreed, but effectively countered it by saying that no one had a precise idea on how this was to be done. Annan was not happy with the approach. He suggested it would be a good idea if we were to first sound out the Americans since they would be the key players. The Secretary General did not think it was a good idea. Annan was also concerned about the timing of the letter; he thought it would make good sense to wait until July 30 for the contact group ministerial meeting's determination on the Serb response. The Secretary General thought we did not always have to react to things; it was essential for the Secretariat to put forward its view point before others. Stoltenberg and Goulding agreed with the Secretary General. The other side of the coin was that in case the Serbs rejected the plan, the contact group would activate the Security Council to adopt enforcement measures against the Serbs. In that scenario, UNPROFOR would have to be withdrawn. There was unanimity on this point.

So the letter was sent off on July 24. It was decided that I would hand over copies of the letter to the ambassadors of the contact group on Monday, the 25th. I did that and explained to them the gist of the letter. None of them had any idea of the letter until that moment. The Germans did not say a word, but the other four were visibly upset and in a state of shock. Alvaro De Soto was to have briefed the press about the letter the same day but this was not done at the request of the contact group who wanted to keep the letter confidential. But the French were observed handing copies of the letter to journalists at noon near the stake out! All the contact group members were unhappy with the timing and contents of the letter. The Secretary General called me from Oyster Bay, where he had gone for a few days rest, and told me: 'Believe me, Ambassador Gharekhan, within two weeks all of them will agree with me.'

In the meantime, Akashi and his commanders were having a series of meetings with NATO on the modalities of NATO and UNPROFOR working together to implement the package. It was suggested that we should send the letter to Akashi for his comments. This was summarily turned down. 'Akashi should be given the party line which he must follow.'

The contact group ministers met in Geneva on July 30. They issued a communiqué calling for enhanced and better enforced sanctions against the Serbs. The Serbs wanted to reopen a couple of issues, but the

Americans in particular said nothing doing. Milosevic, in an attempt to distance himself from the Bosnian Serbs, urged them to accept the package and negotiate later. He said, on August 2, that the Bosnian Serbs would be committing 'treason' and 'crimes against their own people' if they continued to reject the plan. He threatened and actually cut off all relations with them. In a strong, forthright statement, FRY reminded the Serbs in Pale of the tremendous sacrifices made by the mother Serbs so that the Pale Serbs would achieve their dream of Republika Srpska. When the international community was offering them a republic on half the territory of Bosnia, how could they reject the offer?

The Bosnian Serbs managed to take away some heavy weapons from the weapons collection point in Sarajevo on August 2 at 4 a.m. The site was guarded by a Ukrainian unit of UNPROFOR. It was quite an embarrassment for UNPROFOR. NATO was called in to strike Serb targets which it did. NATO struck one non-functional Serb tank on August 5. It worked. The Serbs returned all the weapons. The contact group ambassadors began drafting a resolution tightening the sanctions against FRY. But Milosevic's complete breaking off of all relations with Bosnian Serbs put a spoke in their plans. Russia argued that it would be paradoxical to impose additional sanctions against FRY at a time when it was acting so strongly in support of the contact group's own efforts to force the Bosnian Serbs to fall in line.

Clinton wrote a letter to the Congress on August 11, giving the Serbs an ultimatum to agree to the contact group's plan by October 15, failing which he would canvass and support a resolution in the Security Council by October 30 lifting the arms embargo against Bosnia. Ambassador Keating of New Zealand remarked that the dates were obviously related to the Congressional elections in November—'only an apology for policy', he added. Vorontsov passed a note to the Secretary General on August 11, suggesting he send Stoltenberg to Pale in a last-ditch effort to convince Karadzic to accept the map. The Secretary

148

General liked the idea so much that he adopted it as his own and that was how I presented it to the Council.

Stoltenberg, Goulding and I went to see the Secretary General in Oyster Bay—a beautiful retreat in the Piping Rock Country Club property. Stoltenberg reported on his mission to Pale. He said that the Pale leadership categorically rejected the map, which they found not viable for security and economic reasons. They offered to give up all their territory in Sarajevo in return for the eastern enclaves. They wanted access to sea for which they were ready to negotiate with the Muslims but the latter were not interested. Stoltenberg said secret negotiations were going on between Milosevic and Tudjman who might meet in Athens. Milosevic told Stoltenberg that he had been fooled long enough by Pale Serbs, but now he had decided to cut them off completely. He did not agree to international monitoring of his borders with Serb entity in Bosnia, since it would strengthen his internal opposition which was already accusing him of succumbing to external pressure. He had no objection to journalists or diplomats visiting the border.

The Secretary General and the three of us discussed the next steps. The Secretary General wanted Stoltenberg to go back and negotiate with Pale and Belgrade. He suggested Stoltenberg should try and work out a deal involving Sarajevo and the eastern enclaves. Stoltenberg felt distinctly uncomfortable and I agreed with him. I pointed out that Stoltenberg had no authority to negotiate anything, to offer any deal, unless the contact group gave him the necessary mandate. Goulding pointed out that any such approach could further divide the contact group. The Secretary General saw no problem with that. However, he was persuaded to drop his idea. We agreed that Stoltenberg would tell the contact group and the Security Council that he would be ready to try again to persuade Milosevic to agree to international monitoring. Stoltenberg said that the church in FRY was very supportive of Bosnian Serbs and strongly opposed Milosevic's policies.

In a referendum on August 27–28, the Bosnian Serbs rejected the contact group map by over 90 per cent. US General Clark met Mladic, the Bosnian Serb general, in Banja Luka on August 27 in an effort to get a promise out of him not to attack UNPROFOR in case the arms embargo against Bosnia was lifted. Mladic's response was a categorical 'no' to this suggestion. What General Clark did get from Mladic was a pistol as a gesture of peace! Kozyrev called for easing of sanctions against FRY as a reward for closing its borders to Bosnian Serbs. The contact group insisted on Milosevic agreeing to the stationing of monitors. If Milosevic agreed, some of the sanctions might be eased.

President Chirac came calling on the Secretary General around September 19. He looked fit and very much presidential timbre. He spent about 45 minutes tête-à-tête with the Secretary General. He clearly enjoyed talking and listening to the Secretary General. Chirac expressed serious concern at Clinton's threat to lift the arms embargo against Bosnian Muslims. His view was that such a step would have exactly the contrary effect to the one desired by the Bosnian government; it might lead to the disappearance of Bosnia! That, in turn, would inflame the Islamic world, with all-round increase in global tensions. He hoped the US would find some way to avoid lifting the embargo. (Holbrooke, the new US assistant secretary of state for Europe, told Akashi in Zagreb that the US would like UNPROFOR to take more 'robust' action against the Serbs; such robustness might help the administration in at least delaying having to act on Clinton's pledge to move by October 15 in the Security Council to lift the embargo.)

[Chirac asked several times about the situation in Sri Lanka, but the Secretary General told him the UN was not involved. At one stage, the Secretary General mentioned China and Japan as the major powers of the next century. 'And India,' Chirac added. (He had no idea there was an Indian in the room.) Talking about Cambodia, particularly about the Khmer Rouge army along the Thai-Cambodian border, Chirac said the Thais always wanted a well-equipped army, anti-Vietnamese, between them and Vietnam. Consequently, they would never let the Khmer Rouge disappear as a well-organised armed force. When Zaire came up during the talks, Chirac opined that the Americans were following an 'idiotic' policy towards Mobutu; he was the only person who could keep the country together. Chirac was also highly critical of the US policy towards Haiti.]

Clinton addressed the General Assembly on September 26, 1994. He made no mention of his earlier, premature threat to lift the embargo against Bosnia by October 15. It seemed that the pressure was acting in a direction contrary to the one expected by the Americans—from UK, France, and Russia to US not to lift the embargo. Bosnia was a fascinating diplomatic story. US, having got Izetbegovic off its back for the time being, was trying hard to save its face and credibility with the Muslim countries by pushing UNPROFOR to be more robust in employing air strikes against the Serbs. They pressurised the British and French to fall in line with this approach but these two so far had been opposed to more air strikes for fear of endangering the lives of their troops. (There were no American troops in Bosnia.) The French and British did not really want UNPROFOR to be more aggressive in the use of air strikes. They were banking on the Secretary General to bail them out by taking the responsibility for not acting in a more robust way. They all knew that Akashi, de la Presle, and Rose were strongly opposed to air strikes as a weapon to punish the Serbs indiscriminately. The Secretary General and all of us in the Secretariat fully supported Akashi and his generals. We did not want UNPROFOR to become one of the warring parties or to serve the interests of only one side. In spite of many grievances, the Serbs still had some confidence in UNPROFOR's neutrality. As recently as on October 5, Akashi had succeeded in Pale in persuading Karadzic to agree to reopen the Sarajevo airport. A day later, 200 Serb and Muslim prisoners were released. This usefulness of UNPROFOR would be lost if the Americans had their way. In all this political game, the UN would end up taking the rap, with the US,

France and UK being in the happy position of justifying their views to their constituencies.

But the Secretary General was not going to oblige them easily. He told Merimee that he would have to transmit NATO's decisions, when received, to the Security Council. The NATO council had been meeting for three days; some of its members, especially Canada, were not enthusiastic about robust air strikes. The NATO proposal was that the Secretary General should first agree with them; the other troop-contributing countries would be informed thereafter. In other words, other troop-contributing countries would have no say in a decision which would affect their troops. The Secretary General told the French that whereas the NATO decision would be taken by its political body, they expected him to take the decision by himself. Kozyrev also protested strongly to the Secretary General about the projected NATO move. The Secretary General asked him to send him a letter, which arrived on October 6, by which date NATO had still not been able to reach a consensus.

In all this exercise, de la Presle, the French general and Rose, the British general, had been very loyal to their international duties. De la Presle even threatened to resign if NATO insisted on its position. Sure enough, an anti-Rose campaign started in the American media. The Americans asked the British to withdraw Rose and at one time the British agreed to replace him.

By about October 20, the Bosnian conundrum had almost reached the point of no solution. The BiH government felt entitled to adopt an intransigent attitude in any negotiations because it had been magnanimous by not insisting that Clinton respect his pledge of lifting the arms embargo if the Serbs did not accept the contact group proposal by October 15. The Serbs were getting isolated and the closing of all political and economic contacts with them by Milosevic had had a devastating impact on them. But, on the surface at least, the Bosnian Serb leadership became only more determined to face the whole world alone.

A kind of Massada complex seemed to have gripped them. Akashi had an extremely difficult two hours of talks with Karadzic on October 6 in Pale. He managed to get him to agree to reopen Sarajevo airport the following day. But Karadzic told him that the Bosnian Serbs would decide within a week whether they wanted UNPROFOR to stay or not. In case they decided to opt for a military solution, they would ask UNPROFOR to leave. Their reasoning was that if they had to fight, they would rather do so sooner than later, before the Muslims managed to get all the heavy weapons. The Serbs simply would not accept the map in its present form. Interestingly, Karadzic told Akashi that Belgrade should not suffer sanctions because 'we never took orders from them'.

About NATO, Mladic said: 'We are not afraid of NATO, they are not that powerful. The Haitians threw rocks at them.' Karadzic said that Republika Srpska would insist on a special relationship with FRY but the Bosnion Serbs would never give up their state. 'The Serbs would never accept BiH as a state. Come to Zenica and you will see Teheran— it is worse than Turkey which is at least a secular state. We will not accept to live under the Muslims. The war did not make them funda-mentalists; it is in the nature of Islam to become so. Ask the French about Algeria. In Islam, they are allowed to kill. Do you know of any other religion which allows this? We have suffered for 500 years and are sensitive to the dangers, just as those confronted with dangers of Islam are in Cyprus, India, and Lebanon.'

On Friday, October 28, Mrs. Albright introduced a draft resolu-tion on lifting the arms embargo against the Muslims. According to the draft, the embargo would be lifted six months from the date of the adoption of the resolution, unless the Serbs accepted the contact group plan before that. The British, French, Russian, and Spanish ambassa-dors objected to the automaticity of the end of the embargo. They said the contact group had agreed that they would consider lifting the embargo as a last resort. They did not believe that the time for last resort had come. The peace process, according to them, had not ended and they could not agree to the logic of peace being converted into the logic of war, which would be the inevitable consequence of the American proposal. None of them said they opposed the draft, but they all said they would not support it.

The position of the Czech Republic was similar. Only Pakistan and Oman said they would support the resolution. The Americans had put forward the draft to satisfy the Congress. The draft almost certainly would undergo changes, primarily to remove the automaticity. Recent successes of the Bosnian army around Bihac in fact militated against the argument for lifting the embargo. The Bosnian Serbs had suffered a major defeat. They would certainly try to score a victory somewhere but their capability to move their heavy weapons seemed to have been seriously impaired due to the blockade imposed by Milosevic, especially in respect of fuel.

Clinton had been prone to commit faux pas about Bosnia. Twice in a few weeks, he described the conflict as a 'civil war' whereas the entire case against the Serbs was that BiH was the victim of their aggression. When I represented India in the Council, I had once said it was a case of civil war and Tom Pickering had immediately joined issue with me.

The Secretary General's publicly stated position was that he would have to withdraw UNPROFOR in the event the arms embargo was lifted. But I saw the reports of a press interview with him in London which quoted him as saying that he would maintain UNPROFOR with troops from Muslim countries.

Early in November 1994, the Muslims and Croats mounted a joint offensive to capture the town of Kupres from the Bosnian Serbs. This was the first co-ordinated attack by the Muslims and Croats. The morale among the Muslims was high. They had never been short of weapons and ammunition, but during recent months they had received substantial deliveries of arms from Iran, perhaps also Pakistan, and from some western arms suppliers. All the stuff had to pass through Croatia which retained its share, perhaps 25 per cent before releasing it for BiH. The

Croat armed forces were much better equipped, with more MiG fighters and helicopters than before. The Muslims were still inferior in respect of heavy artillery, but the Serb advantage in this was fast being eroded because of fuel shortage.

The Russians did nothing to discourage the BiH government from pressing ahead with its military advantage. Karadzic declared a state of emergency and ordered general mobilisation. It was doubtful if he could mobilise a significant number of additional troops. The Serb morale would have to be low and would sink lower if they suffered another defeat or if they were unable to inflict a defeat on the Muslims in the near future.

Ganic, vice-president of BiH, told Akashi in early November that he had no faith in the contact group. In fact, he had a very low opinion of the contact group. The Bosnians were convinced that the military operations would compel the Serbs to accept the map and come to the negotiating table. But if the Muslim-Croat side could regain all the territory through war, they would prefer to do so rather than give the Serbs the escape route of accepting the map. We in the Secretariat, as well many others, were convinced that UNPROFOR's presence would become untenable if the arms embargo were lifted. But I was not so sure about it any longer. The Serbs might take a few hostages but they would not engage in generalised hostilities against UNPROFOR, provided the UN was ready to resort more readily and more often to NATO's air support.

The war in Bosnia heated up as November progressed. Both sides violated all the agreements with impunity. The Muslims were keen to get rid of UNPROFOR whom they perceived as a nuisance, an interfering factor, an obstacle. They launched a major campaign against General Rose who was behaving as a true UN general and refused to let UNPROFOR behave as if its mandate was to fight on the side of the Bosnian government and against the Serbs.

Stoltenberg and Owen met with Milosevic for two and a half hours in Belgrade. The latter assured them that he was not at all worried about the negative—for him—fallout from the Bosnian Serb reverses in Bihac and Kupres. He said he had been in touch with about 20 members of the Serb parliament in Pale and predicted a change in leadership there in the near future, and acceptance of the contact group map.

On November 10 USA announced that it would no longer take part in monitoring and enforcing the arms embargo against Bosnia. The administration was anticipating the mind of the new Congress and taking pre-emptive action since the Republicans had captured both Houses, the electorate having dealt a resounding defeat to Clinton.

The hostilities in BiH threatened to spread to other parts of former Yugoslavia. The use of NATO airpower became more frequent, almost a habit. On November 21, 38 NATO aircraft from US, UK, France, and Netherlands struck the Udbina airfield in sector south on UNPAs of Croatia, which were under the control of Krajina Serbs in Croatia. On November 23, NATO carried out two air strikes in the Bihac area in BiH against surface-to-air missile sites of the Bosnian Serbs. This strike was sought to be justified as self defence since two NATO British sea harrier jets were attacked on the 22nd by Bosnian Serbs, but without damage. The attack on Udbina raised the war to a qualitatively new level as it took place on Croatian territory and against Krajina Serbs who, technically, were not a party to the war in Bosnia.

The Security Council met on November 19 to consider the situation in Bihac which, for the most part, was of the Muslims' own making. The BiH government captured some territory previously occupied by the Bosnian Serbs. The Bosnian Serbs regained most of the lost ground and were reported to be on the verge of taking Bihac which had been in Muslim hands since the fall of Abdic. Abdic, with his followers, had taken shelter in the UNPA and had rearmed his soldiers with the help of the Krajina Serbs and was leading the offensive towards Bihac, in conjunction with Bosnian Serbs. The reason for striking Udbina was that the Krajina Serbs had taken off from there and bombed planes in Bihac area. This had happened three times. The last time, on November

19, they dropped napalm and cluster bombs. Since Udbina was in Croatian territory, Tudjman was persuaded to urgently agree to NATO carrying out the strikes.

The Bosnians had almost achieved their objective they had been working for, for over two years. They had got the Americans not only fully supporting them politically; the US, through NATO, was pushing actively and successfully for punitive strikes against the Bosnian Serbs. The US was reported to have sent military personnel to help the BiH government in its military operations. There were even reports, denied by the US, of their having given military equipment. In anticipation of the Republican-dominated Congress lifting the embargo, the administration had proposed a package for the Bosnian government worth between $500 million to $5 billion. Persuasion certainly paid.

Tudjman was claiming that Republika Srpska Krajina (RSK) was taking part in the offensive against Bihac, which RSK denied. Sacerbey, the BiH ambassador in New York, said in a letter that RSK had fired 10,000 shells in Bihac on a single day on the 22nd. Tudjman was said to be getting impatient to get involved in the conflict since, he said, the Croat territory was being used to commit aggression against a neighbour. The US claimed to have restrained Tudjman. If Tudjman joined in, Milosevic would find it impossible not to go to the help of his fellow Serbs in Bosnia. And then what would the Russians do?

Towards the end of November, the Serbs had regained practically all the lost ground in Bihac area. The couple of air strikes against them had been like pinpricks. On November 26, NATO wanted to carry out a strike against a missile site which had fired at NATO aircraft the previous evening, but Akashi and his generals refused to turn the key, to the great annoyance of US and Willy Claes, the new Secretary General of NATO. The factual position on the ground was that the Serb anti-air defence system was so thick that NATO was unwilling to undertake such operations. The US wanted NATO to carry out more generalised strikes, not confined to Bihac. This would have meant a ground war which, in turn, would have led to the pulling out of UNPROFOR.

Defence secretary Perry stated on November 27 that it was not possible for the Muslims to defeat the Serbs. He said air operations by themselves could not defeat the Serbs and the US was not prepared to send in to Bosnia the hundreds of thousands of ground forces it would take to roll back the Serbs. Perry's statement was a good example of the disarray in Washington on the Bosnian question.

There was a lot of talk about lack of unity in NATO because of trans-Atlantic differences regarding Bosnia. For the second time within a year, the US had had to suffer humiliation. The half-hearted attempt to lift the embargo had to be abandoned. Bihac was about to fall, but UK, France, Canada, and Spain would not support the US demand for indiscriminate air strikes. The ultimate humiliation would probably come in Brussels when the contact group countries would offer, in however disguised a form, the possibility for the Bosnian Serbs to unite with Serbia through constitutional arrangements.

Croatia announced that if Bihac fell, it would enter the war.

The Secretary General announced suddenly that he would go to Sarajevo on November 30 for separate talks with Karadzic and Izetbegovic. This dramatic announcement came as a surprise to me and everyone else at the headquarters including Aime and Annan. The Secretary General took the decision during a telephone conversation with Akashi on the 28th morning. The idea came from Akashi. I did not think it was such a wise idea.

The Secretary General's mission to Sarajevo turned out to be a big disappointment. He had hoped that he would be able to get the parties to agree to at least a few days ceasefire and to resume discussions. He was snubbed by Karadzic who insisted that the Secretary General should treat him on par with Izetbegovic and should go to the Serb-held area near Sarajevo airport to meet him. The Secretary General insisted that the meeting take place at Sarajevo airport as had been agreed, it seems, between Akashi and Karadzic. In the event the Secretary General did not meet Karadzic. The Secretary General did meet Izetbegovic for two hours. The first hour was okay in the sense that Izetbegovic listened to what the Secretary General had to say. But in the second half of the meeting, Izetbegovic became emotional and accused the UN of not protecting the civilians, and so on. The Secretary General told him that UNPROFOR would have to be pulled out if the parties did not co-operate with it. The Secretary General returned to Paris without obtaining even a limited ceasefire. Worse, he read out a prepared statement which was a minor disaster for him. He said he had gone to Sarajevo at the express request of Izetbegovic and Karadzic. This simply was not the case. Then he said if the parties did not co-operate with UNPROFOR, it would be impossible for him to persuade the Security Council to maintain UNPROFOR in BiH. This was an unfortunate formulation. The statement was widely interpreted as an ultimatum by the Secretary General to the parties. Also, it put things upside down, or rather backside first. There was absolutely no pressure or demand in the Council to close down UNPROFOR that the Secretary General needed to counter. If anything, the Council wanted to maintain UNPROFOR and it was the Secretary General who had been threatening to withdraw it.

I had a long conversation with the Secretary General on the phone in his suite in the Crillon hotel in Paris on the basis of which I briefed the Council on the 30th afternoon. I told him about the furore regarding his 'ultimatum'. He explained how he had not given any ultimatum to anyone. In fact, during the press conference, following his prepared statement, he said he was in favour of keeping UNPROFOR and would try to persuade the Council to maintain it. General Rose told the Secretary General, very clearly, that he just could not implement his mandate, that he was prevented from doing anything at all, that UNPROFOR was completely paralysed, and that even air strikes or close air support were not possible because of the very thick network of anti-missile sites.

It transpired that the idea of the Secretary General going to Sarajevo came from Mrs. Albright. She suggested to Annan that the Secretary General should go to Bihac. The Secretary General did not agree to that but modified the idea to visit Sarajevo as his own.

For several weeks, Akashi and his generals were worried about NATO plans to send a large number of aircraft over Bosnian airspace on reconnaissance missions in connection with enforcing the no-fly mandate. NATO was worried at the massive anti-aircraft missile systems deployed by the Serbs. Willy Claes told Goulding on December 1 that 80 per cent of BiH territory was covered by Serb anti-aircraft missile systems. UNPROFOR was concerned that the use of a large number of aircraft by NATO would almost certainly lead to 'lock-on's. UNPROFOR's presence in BiH would become untenable. Akashi wanted the Secretary General to speak to Claes about it. This was a politically sensitive matter at a time when UNPROFOR was criticised as being pro-Serb. Annan and I were not in favour of approaching NATO. But since Akashi was keen, the Secretary General asked Goulding to speak to Claes in Brussels. Claes told Goulding very clearly that he could not and would not accept any restrictions on NATO's no-fly recce missions. He respected the dual key for close air support and air strike missions and would not blame UNPROFOR if it refused to turn the key. If the Secretary General wanted to prevent NATO from undertaking such missions, he, Claes, would need a letter from the Secretary General and the North Atlantic Council would have to take a decision. The Secretary General wisely decided not to do any such thing.

Akashi went to Sarajevo and Pale on December 3. In Pale, Karadzic was unrepentant. He did not apologise for snubbing the Secretary General. All he said was he regretted not having met the Secretary General. He offered to lift the restrictions on the freedom of movement of UNPROFOR, nearly 500 of whose personnel were kept in varying degrees of captivity for several days. In one blatant incident, Bosnian Serbs penetrated into sector north of UNPAs and captured seven

Ukrainian soldiers with their equipment and APC. Lavrov could not believe that the Serbs would take *Ukrainian* soldiers as hostages. Karadzic flatly refused to help in the matter of restoring gas supply to Sarajevo. He said he had not yet decided whether or not to ask for the withdrawal of UNPROFOR. He wanted permanent ceasefire throughout Bosnia, followed promptly by political negotiations in Geneva on the map.

Jimmy Carter did it again. Karadzic invited him to take a hand in the Bosnian crisis. Carter did not hesitate and flew to Zagreb, shuttled between Pale and Sarajevo and got the parties to agree to a ceasefire starting December 23 and to negotiate a four month cessation of hostilities throughout BiH starting January 1. He also got them to agree to commence negotiations on a comprehensive settlement but ran into difficulties regarding reference to contact group plan. Karadzic insisted that the contact group plan should only be the basis for negotiations but Izetvegovic demanded that negotiations should be held with the acceptance of the contact group plan. Carter dismissed this difference, regarded as fundamental by experts, as 'semantic'.

Some people including Akashi and the Secretary General were not inclined to take Carter's mission seriously. But Carter in fact had the advantage of not being an expert. He tried essentially the same approach as with Cedras in Haiti. People like Cedras and Karadzic (and Saddam Hussein) crave for recognition and equal treatment. Carter spent nine hours with Karadzic; he took his wife, Rosalyn, with him and said publicly that the American people had not been exposed to the Serb side of the story. But Karadzic, the psychiatrist, also used Carter's goodness and craving for recognition (and the Nobel) effectively for his side. He scored a big success by getting everyone, including the contact group, to agree that the contact group plan was only the basis for negotiations. In other words, the contact group had to abandon its position that its plan had to be treated on a take-it-or-leave-it basis. Fearing that Carter would offer such a significant concession to the

Serbs, Galbraith, the American ambassador in Zagreb, urged Akashi to suggest to Carter that he need not go to Pale, but Akashi did not fall for it. In fact, Carter told Galbraith that Warren Christopher had personally told him that the contact group plan was only a basis for negotiations. The Bosnian government once again felt let down by the US. Izetbegovic was a disillusioned man by now. But the Americans, despite considerable clout, could not push their allies to fall in line with their views on 'lift and strike'.

Karadzic also used Carter in his principal battle with Milosevic which was for the political leadership of all Serbs. Both Karadzic and Milosevic were ruthless politicians. The latter had liquidated many rivals and claimed to have won over more than 35 members of the Pale parliament. But Karadizc had the upper hand. If he managed to have the contact group plan modified according to his demands, it would be Milosevic who would have cause to worry. Akashi signed the ceasefire agreement with Karadzic and Izetbegovic on December 23. The agreement signed by Karadzic had six paragraphs whereas the agreement signed by Izetbegovic had one paragraph less. The latter refused to include the paragraph relating to the release of prisoners and detainees. In one of his cables, Akashi had mentioned, with a bit of sarcasm, that Carter did not know the difference between ceasefire and cessation of hostilities. Not many people did. Ceasefire stopped fighting but left the opposing forces where they stood. Cessation of hostilities called for the withdrawal of forces to an agreed distance from the ceasefire line and the interposition of neutral, or, in the present case, UN forces.

Akashi succeeded in getting Izetbegovic and Karadzic to sign the agreement on complete cessation of hostilities for a period of four months on December 31, 1994. It was not a bad note on which to end the year.

The situation remained tolerable in the New Year, except in Bihac. The one cloud from the UN point of view was the decision of the Croatian government to terminate the mandate of UNPROFOR in Croatia.

Tudjman had threatened this in the fall of 1994, but had been persuaded by the Americans to agree to an extension of six months. This time the Zagreb government seemed serious and determined. In a meeting with Akashi on January 11, Sarinic, the foreign minister, said: we know you are peacekeepers, not peace-makers. We are not blaming you, but the fact remains that none of Croatia's concerns has been met by UNPROFOR. Tudjman was reported to have replied 'sorry' to Clinton when the latter wrote to him to reconsider his decision. Sarinic offered to Akashi that UNPROFOR could maintain its headquarters in Zagreb if it wished. The Croats were concerned, with good reason, that the continued presence of UN would create a Cyprus-type situation in their country.

Ambassador Nobilo of Croatia delivered to me a letter from his president on January 13, 1995, conveying the decision to terminate UNPROFOR's mandate with effect from March 31. In his oral presentation, Nobilo referred to the danger of 'Cyprusisation'. I was sympathetic to Croatia's concern. Bringing and keeping a dispute to the UN was a sure way to preserve the status quo for a very long time which meant for ever. Nobilo felt that this decision would exert pressure in Belgrade to move forward in the political area, perhaps forcing them to recognise Croatia within its present international borders. The prospects of war breaking out in Croatia were very real. The Croatian government was militarily much stronger than it was two years earlier. They had even started making fighter planes and helicopters. The Croatian, or Krajina Serbs, on the other hand, would have difficulty in obtaining fuel for their military needs.

The contact group visited Belgrade, Pale, and Sarajevo to revive the negotiating process following the Carter visit. The very fact that the contact group visited Pale was a victory for Karadzic. He continued to regard the contact group plan as anything but a basis for negotiations. He offered a new formulation to the contact group: 'We accept the basis for negotiations as proposed by the contact group.' The contact group liked the idea and took it to the other side. It said a lot for the changed environment that they expressed disappointment when Sarajevo did not react favourably to Pale's formulation. According to Stoltenberg, Pale's claim to federate with Belgrade at some stage in future was no longer contested by the contact group in principle. The Bosnian Serbs also conveyed to the contact group that they would prefer the future union between them and the federation not to be composed of the federation and the Republika Srpska, but formed by these two entities. In Sarajevo, Izetbegovic was by now a moderate; his prime minister, Silajdzic, was the hardliner.

France proposed a summit meeting of the contact group to which Milosevic, Izetbegovic, and Tudjman would be invited. The idea was that these three should announce mutual recognition of one another within the existing international borders. Milosevic would be offered lifting of sanctions. The French and British were inclined to be more reasonable, but the Americans were ready to consider only a partial lifting of sanctions. Milosevic demanded full lifting of sanctions as well as recognition as a successor state to former Yugoslavia; this was a non-starter for the Americans.

Tudjman was under pressure from his friends to reconsider his decision on UNPROFOR. The Germans told him bluntly that if he persisted in his position, the situation might turn unfavourable for him: 'Don't come rushing to your friends at that time'. But Tudjman knew that the friends would have to help, whether they liked it or not. He wanted to go down in history as the man who united all Croat territories. The Krajina Serbs wanted the UN to stay. The weak depend on and need the UN.

The cessation of hostilities agreement in Bosnia expired on May 1. Akashi's efforts to have it extended even for one more month did not succeed. The Bosnians insisted on their pre-conditions, namely, that the Serbs would have to accept the contact group plan or Milosevic must recognise Bosnia with its international borders. The Americans obviously did not think it necessary to exert pressure on the Bosnians or the latter simply did not yield to the pressure.

The Croat government launched a well-planned offensive on May 1 to take control of the highway and integrate sector west into Croatia. The offensive was successful. By the end of the day, the highway was firmly in government hands and the Serbs had capitulated without a fight. The Serbs fled in thousands towards Banja Luka in Bosnia. The Croats repeatedly bombed the Sava Bridge to prevent supplies and reinforcements from Karadzic reaching his Croatian brethren.

When the first reports of the events in Croatia reached New York, Russia called for an immediate meeting of the Council, but Merimee did not want to be rushed into it on the first day of his presidency. We asked Akashi, who was trying to negotiate something with the parties, whether a statement from the Council would help. He replied: 'Yes, definitely'.

The principal players indulged in their usual shadow boxing game. Russia made a half-hearted attempt to get the Council to call for a return to previous positions and the Americans attempted, feebly, to change the word 'offensive' to 'operation', but neither insisted. In any case, the Croats had already achieved their objectives. The Knin Serbs retaliated by lobbying missiles into the populated areas of Zagreb, killing half a dozen and wounding many more civilians. The Germans and Americans would surely have known in advance about the Croat design and told Tudjman that so long as he made it a swift and surgical operation, they would live with it. They in fact helped Tudjman by rejecting all calls for a return to status quo ante.

The UN, by its very presence, enabled the Croats to arm and train for the military solution of the problem. If the UNPROFOR had not been deployed in Croatia, the Krajina Serbs would have been in a much stronger position. Earlier, in March, Tudjman in what was described as a constructive gesture, agreed to let UNPROFOR stay, but on his terms. He negotiated well. The overall UN operation, UNPROFOR, was split into three separate but co-ordinated missions for Croatia, Bosnia, and

Macedonia. The operation in Croatia would be called UN Confidence Restoration Operation (UNCRO). The Croats were happy since 'CRO' sounded very much an abbreviation of Croatia. The mission in Bosnia would continue to be called UNPROFOR. The mission in Macedonia would be called UN Preventive Deployment Force (UNPREDEP). All these names were suggested by Shashi Tharoor, the great Indian novelist, and the most able deputy of Kofi Annan.

The Secretary General briefed the Council on May 16 when he presented four options about the future of UNPROFOR: status quo; withdrawal; status quo with substantial air strikes; and reduction, redeployment, and modified mandate. In a major exception to his strongly held and consistent position, the Secretary General announced that General Janvier and General Smith would come to the Council to present the military's point of view. This became necessary after the refusal by Akashi to authorise NATO air strikes on May 7 in response to a mortar attack the same day which killed 10 and wounded many more in Butmir. Smith asked for air strikes but Akashi and Janvier overruled him. That decision came in for tremendous criticism particularly in the US. Bosnian Serbs were presumed to be responsible for the mortar attack although UNPROFOR could not categorically confirm it. Mrs. Albright was furious. She asked: What is the logic in this decision? I pointed out that the Secretary General had delegated the authority to Akashi and that was that.

Defence secretary Perry came to see the Secretary General on May 19. The Secretary General liked him, respected him. Perry told the Secretary General that there was no truth in the perception that the US favoured air strikes since it did not have troops on the ground. On the contrary, if the US had ground troops in Bosnia, he would have been even more in favour of air strikes as the only way to effectively protect the troops. His judgment was that the Bosnian Serbs treated UNPROFOR with disdain because they knew that it would almost never ask for air strikes. The Secretary General told him that his own generals, who took their orders not from him but from elsewhere—meaning their own governments—did not favour air strikes. After Perry left, the Secretary General told Kofi and me that Perry's talk about US favouring air strikes even if they had ground troops there was not convincing.

I was quite exercised about the beating the UN took in the media over Bosnia and Rwanda, but the old hands in the 'House' were very cool about it. In a note to the Secretary General, I suggested that we should tell the Council clearly that the mandate regarding safe areas simply could not be implemented. Similarly, in Croatia, after the swift and successful military operation in sector west, we should have no illusion that UNCRO, with its limited staff, would deter the Croats from attempting similar undertakings in other sectors. Consequently, we should reduce the strength of UNPROFOR. The Secretary General agreed with me, but Akashi and his generals resisted, mainly for reasons of prestige. Is there a general in the world anywhere who wants fewer troops? The Secretary General had told Perry that the generals and Akashi were convinced that both sides in Bosnia were preparing for war in summer. Perry agreed.

Sacerbey, the Bosnian ambassador, came to see the Secretary General to protest about what the latter had said about both sides being responsible for starting hostilities in Bosnia. The Secretary General was most curt with him. He said: 'I have taken note of what you have said. If you have nothing more to say, I have to go to the Security Council now'. He got up and left. Sacerbey felt hurt and insulted. He wrote a letter to the Secretary General saying: 'You even missed the customary hand shake'. The Secretary General could not care less.

By the middle of May there was a strong expectation that the efforts of the contact group would bear fruit. Milosevic would recognise Bosnia's borders though not necessarily its government in return for relief in sanctions. The US member of the group, Bob Frasure, was the interlocutor with Milosevic. Even Izetbegovic was in touch with Milosevic through his special envoy Filipovic and there were reports that Iran was indirectly involved on behalf of the BiH government. Milosevic also kept in touch with Tudjman; his reaction to the take over of sector west was hardly audible!

UN was going through difficult times. The Croat offensive of May 1 brought out starkly UN's impotence and the events in Bosnia destroyed whatever credibility UNPROFOR might have had. The cause of all this lay in giving unrealistic mandates and inadequate resources to the UN. As for Akashi's and Janvier's refusal to authorise air strikes, General Smith himself later admitted that it was a mistake on his part to have asked for them in the first place.

Janvier's presentation in the Security Council was certainly robust. He told some home truths to members about the unsustainability of the present mandate, the uselessness of UN troops in the safe areas, and the urgent need for a modified, or at least a redefined, mandate with consequent redeployment of troops. Mrs. Albright was particularly upset with his views on the eastern safe area enclaves. She asked with some passion and satire: 'What will you do with the civilians in the enclaves? Will you take them with you when you withdraw?' Janvier was cool. He replied that there was no way the UN, with its grossly inadequate level of troops, could either protect the civilians or deter attacks; the Bosnian forces in the enclaves were strong enough to defend them; the Bosnians were in fact using the enclaves to launch offensives against the Serbs, and that what the UN troops were now doing could easily and as well be done by a few military observers, namely, to alert the authorities in UN about impending offensives by any party. He added that the safe areas had to be demilitarised through agreement between parties; if such a mutually agreed demilitarised regime was violated, air strikes could be called in.

At Merimee's monthly lunch for the Security Council in May, the Secretary General asked Mrs. Albright: 'Will you permit air strikes if the Bosnian government was guilty of serious violations?' She replied in the negative. Her position was at variance with that of others who maintained that the UN resolutions did not make such a distinction. She tried to explain by saying her government would be willing to consider air strikes against the Bosniaks if the UN had not been partial to the Serbs. This provoked a most strong reaction from the Secretary General: 'I protest most energetically against the accusation of bias on the part of UNPROFOR. It is not UNPROFOR which is biased but your government which is biased'. The vehemence with which he spoke shook everyone. However, after the lunch, he hugged her!

The last week of May was extremely difficult. Akashi and his generals issued an ultimatum to the 'warring parties', but effectively aimed at the Serbs, to cease firing heavy weapons by noon on May 26, and return the heavy weapons to the weapons collection points, or clear them out of the exclusion zone by noon of 27th. Both sides stopped fighting by the deadline on 26th, but the Serbs did not return their weapons. Four hours after the ultimatum expired, NATO aircraft hit two ammunition dumps near Pale. The Serb response was heavy shelling of other safe areas, especially Tuzla where a rocket killed 71 and wounded over 100, mostly children. Next morning, Akashi ordered another strike. There was a temporary jubilation. Akashi issued some tough statements, warning the Serbs of unspecified consequences. Mrs. Albright made no effort to conceal her satisfaction and even Clinton did not miss the opportunity to thump his chest. But the euphoria soon gave way to gloom.

The Serbs retaliated the only way they could and precisely as the Secretary General and the rest of us had anticipated. They took UN 'blue helmets' hostages. More dramatically, they tied up three of them to ammunition dumps. For the first time in UN history, peacekeepers were used as 'human shields'. The air strikes were effectively neutralised. Chirac asked the Secretary General to convey his message to the Council: either authorise UNPROFOR all necessary support to protect its personnel or France will pull out. The Secretary General asked for the advice of the Council. For a while there was silence. Then Mrs. Albright said that the Council had entrusted the responsibility to the Secretary General who alone must decide. The situation deteriorated further. The Serbs took nearly 325 hostages. The French and Americans in a futile and symbolic gesture ordered aircraft carriers to the Adriatic and the British announced the dispatch of 6,000 additional troops to Bosnia.

General Smith spoke a number of times to General Mladic and appealed to his professional ethics. Mladic kept telling Smith that he, Smith, had behaved most stupidly. 'We had always told you that we will treat you as our enemies if you use air strikes against us, now look what you have done.' Mladic asked Smith to take tranquilisers so that he could take decisions when his nerves were steady. Mladic kept taunting Smith to consult his masters Ganic and Izetbegovic and act according to their instructions. The Croatian Serbs, in a separate action, brought down a BiH government helicopter, killing the Bosnian foreign minister. Sacerbey became the new foreign minister. The Secretary General decided there would be no more air strikes. He told us in an internal meeting that he had withdrawn the authority from Akashi. In a cable received on May 30, Akashi came as close as possible to implying that the decision on air strikes was influenced by the criticism of his decision on May 7 against allowing air strikes.

The contact group urged the Serbs to accept their plan as a starting point for negotiations. The bankruptcy of the contact group in dealing with the complex issues was evident to all by now. Their initial blunder was to present their plan as a take-it-or-leave-it proposition. They were now looking for an elegant way to get out of it without angering the Bosnian side. The western powers were looking to Yeltsin to help them out.

We finalised the Secretary General's report on Bosnia late on May 30. It had been a difficult report to draft. The Secretary General had insisted that there should be no attempt to tailor the report to suit the convenience of any power or powers. He absolutely rejected all suggestions of expediency. He said that the credibility of the UN, about which the Council members did not care since they all had short-term interests to worry about, was of paramount importance and had to be defended. We all agreed with the Secretary General that it was not possible to ask a peacekeeping operation to combine enforcement action in its mandate.

The Secretary General asked me to go to Zagreb to be seen to be doing something about the hostage crisis. My name was proposed by Goulding. At about the same time there was a meeting in Paris of the defence ministers of NATO. The Secretary General suggested I attend that meeting as well but I pointed out that Annan was the right person to take care of that meeting. The Secretary General did not agree and decided that Stoltenberg should go to Paris.

In Zagreb, Akashi and I thought we would both go to Pale. We got a message from Karadzic that he would be happy to meet me but not Akashi. My reaction was to say 'no, thanks', but Akashi said it was understandable that Karadzic did not wish to see him since his hands were bloodied with Serb blood, he having ordered the May 25–26 air strikes. The Secretary General approved my going alone. We asked for clearance for our aircraft to land at Sarajevo which had been closed to all traffic for over a month. The alternative was to go to Split, from there to Kiseljak by helicopter, and then by road in an APC over Mt. Igman. I ruled out the alternative not because of the risks involved, which were not high, but because it would show that the UN was too anxious to talk to the Serbs. I assumed that Karadzic should be equally keen to talk to me. I insisted on landing at Sarajevo. We got the clearance.

Before leaving Zagreb, we checked three times about the landing clearance at Sarajevo. The captain of the Yak-40, a Norwegian, insisted on and obtained a fax message confirming the clearance. When we were overhead Sarajevo, we were told that the Serbs could not guarantee our security since there had been fighting overnight and they did not want to be blamed in case some harm came to us. We were asked to proceed to Belgrade from where we would be escorted by helicopter to Pale.

Much as I would have liked to meet Karadzic professionally—as well as the resultant publicity—I had no hesitation to decline the Serb proposal and return to Zagreb. I was convinced that the Serbs had deliberately planned the whole thing to snub me and the UN. Subsequently, every one—Akashi, all his generals, and theSecretary General—agreed with me. I learnt that Karadzic had indeed been most anxious to meet me, but it was Mladic who refused the clearance. Janvier had met Mladic the previous day somewhere in Bosnia—the meeting was never made public—when the latter told him that I would have to go via Belgrade. If I had been informed about this in time, I would have altered my travel plans. Mladic was categorical with Janvier that hostages would not be released unless the Serbs received guarantees of no more air strikes.

The Serbs had shot down a NATO F-16 over northern Bosnia. Mladic insisted to Janvier that he would talk about it only to an American general. Janvier asked to meet or at least to see the pilot, but Mladic could not or would not arrange that nor would he provide some evidence about the pilot being alive.

During this visit, I learnt that all was not well between Janvier and Smith. Janvier's meeting with Mladic was arranged by the French authorities. Janvier did not want to take Smith into confidence about the meeting but was persuaded by Akashi to do so. Smith told me on a secure line that with the air strikes of May 25–26, the UN had crossed the line from peacekeeping to peace enforcement and that it would be impossible for the UN to win back Serb confidence. Janvier reminded me that it was Smith who had asked for the strikes. In fact, Smith had wanted a third strike on May 27 but Janvier had advised Akashi against it.

The NATO defence ministers decided in their Paris meeting to establish a multinational brigade to provide rapid deployment to UNPROFOR. These troops would not wear blue helmets nor would their vehicles be painted white, but they would carry UN insignia on their sleeves. Their precise relationship with UNPROFOR was left vague. Stoltenberg, who was present at the meeting, told me in Zagreb, that the defence ministers were more realistic than the contact group. David Owen, who was in Zagreb for his farewell visit, believed that it was not yet too late for UN to regain its neutrality. One way to do so would be to supply some fuel to the Serbs. He too thought the air strikes of May 25–26 were a major mistake. Owen said Smith should quit if he thought that with the strikes UN had crossed the line.

During this visit, I was struck by the 'sympathetic understanding' which all UN staff, from Akashi down, felt for the Serb point of view. They were absolutely convinced that we had to talk to the Serbs and lift them out of their isolation. Janvier was convinced that the Serbs would *never* surrender in humiliation; they would rather die.

Since the Paris meeting, a lot of sober reflection seemed to have taken place in the concerned capitals. Already discarded were all notions of forcing the way to Sarajevo or of securing access to the eastern enclaves. It was acknowledged in writing that the rapid deployment forces would form an integral part of UN force and operate under UNPROFOR's rules of engagement. But they would not wear blue helmets and their vehicles would be painted green, not white; this was a 'non-negotiable' point for the French! The Serbs received a 'secret' assurance, probably from the French, that there would be no more air strikes. The Secretary General said Chirac had received Clinton's promise about no more air strikes. The media in UK and US alleged that it was the UN that had given these assurances. Willy Claes even wrote to the Secretary General asking for clarification on this point. But this was simply not the case. The UN had no authority to give any such assurances to anyone. Milosevic told Akashi in Belgrade on June 17 that he had been advised by Chirac that Clinton had told him—Chirac—that air strikes would not occur without Chirac's consent.

In a daring and well-executed operation, the Americans rescued Captain O'Grady, the F-16 pilot. The question was: since the Serbs knew all along where the pilot had been hiding, why did they not arrest him?

All the hostages were released by June 18. We also released the four Serb prisoners.

The Bosnian government launched an offensive in June 'to end the strangulation of Sarajevo'. For a while it seemed as if the operation had petered out but it was still alive in July. They did not receive the kind of active support they were expecting from the Bosnian Croat forces— Hrvatsaka Vojna Organizacija (HVO)—who were busy fighting in support of the Croatian government forces in sector south. BiH forces captured considerable territory from the Serbs and over time they received better support from HVO.

In the first week of July 1995, we had in internal meeting in Geneva to discuss Bosnia. The Secretary General, Stoltenberg, Akashi, Goulding, Annan, Ogata, Janvier, Smith, de la Presle, and I attended. Both the political and military assessments were gloomy. Smith said our people in the enclaves and Bihac were virtual prisoners and he was not sure what to do with the rapid deployment force. Politically, neither side was interested in a peaceful solution. The government side had greatly improved its military position and was playing for time. Janvier thought the Serbs still held the trumps; they controlled the enclaves and parts of Sarajevo. He said UNPROFOR was doing precious little in the enclaves; if politically feasible, he would like to pull out of the enclaves 'today'. Ogata said the UNHCR had crossed an important threshold on July 1 when its vehicles were driven by UNPROFOR military personnel. Akashi was pessimistic about Croatia; intoxicated by their success in May, the Croats were itching for another offensive. UNCRO was unable to fulfil any part of its mandate. In other words, we had all those thousands of soldiers and civilians sitting in Croatia and Bosnia, doing nothing at all! Bildt, Owen's successor as co-chair of ICFY, wanted to go to Pale, but the Bosnians, supported by the Americans, forbade him from talking to the Serbs. Holbrooke was in constant touch with Bildt on this and other issues.

Meanwhile, the situation in Srebrenica was fast deteriorating. Bosnian Serbs were making a determined effort to take over the enclave. The 470 Dutch troops there were facing an impossible task. Thirty of them had been taken hostage. One Dutch soldier had been killed by the Bosnian government forces. Srebrenica was finally overrun by the Serbs on July 11. A half-hearted attempt was made in the morning to use CAS, targeting two Serb tanks, but till July 12 we did not know if they had been hit. The Serbs outflanked the blocking position established by the Dutch one and half kilometer south of Srebrenica and occupied it. The Dutch retreated and the whole battalion headed for Potocari. There was no way the Dutch could stand up to the 1,500-strong Bosnian Serb attack. The Dutch defence minister asked Akashi not to use air power once Mladic threatened to kill the 30 hostages. The Bosnian Serbs had got the full measure of the troop-contributing countries; they had no stomach for casualties. UN had been humiliated.

Surprisingly, or not so surprisingly, there was no demand for UNPROFOR's withdrawal or even for a strong action by it. The US which did not have troops on the ground definitely did not want UNPROFOR to be pulled out. The Security Council adopted a meaningless resolution, asking the Secretary General to use all resources to restore the status of Srebrenica as a safe area.

The human tragedy following the fall of Srebrenica dominated the media. More than 40,000 Muslims were displaced from their homes, put in buses, and dropped off at Kladanj which was 5 km from Tuzla in BiH territory. The Bosnian government at first refused to accept them but relented after a couple of days. There were stories of atrocities alleged to have been committed by the Serbs. Thousands of Muslim men were missing. There was a telling picture of a Muslim woman hanging from a tree, after having been raped by the Serbs. We had reports from UNPROFOR and Zagreb on these aspects of tragedy. On the other hand, one report spoke of Serbs distributing sweets and organising the refugees. I rang up Akashi and reminded him that his people had been

175

very active in reporting human rights violations by Croat government forces in sector west, whereas we did not hear much from them about Srebrenica. He pleaded lack of access, but perhaps the main reason was our people were too scared of the lives of our people being endangered.

The meeting of the major powers in London on July 21 produced a mouse, judging by its communiqué. It failed to resolve the differences among the allies and did not contain a credible threat against the Serbs. The Islamic countries, meeting in Geneva on the same day as the London conference, declared that they would no longer consider themselves bound, de jure, by the arms embargo against Bosnia. The North Atlantic Council took a decision calling for expanded air strikes. It asked the Secretary General to delegate the authority for air strikes to the UN military generals instead of Akashi. The Secretary General was loathe to do so, but agreed in the end after personal pleas from Christopher and Mrs. Albright. Akashi said he was relieved at being relieved of the responsibility!

The war in the Serb Krajinas in Croatia started on August 4 and was over within 60 hours with the Croat government achieving full victory. 'Chronicle of a war foretold' is how I described it, with apologies to Gabriel Garcia Marquez. Sectors south and north became history, like sector west in May. The Security Council took no meaningful action; it could not. Bildt issued a strong statement, condemning the shelling of Knin. He said there was no difference between the Krajina Serbs' shelling of Zagreb in May and Tudjman's shelling of Knin. Milosevic did not intervene in the war.

On August 28, five mortar bombs, one of which struck the marketplace in Sarajevo, left 40 dead and 80 wounded—the same marketplace where a shell killed many people in 1994, leading to NATO decision on exclusion zone. (There never was conclusive evidence about who was responsible for that attack in 1994. The Secretary General and many others believed that it was the Bosnian government side.) We could not identify the guilty party since, we said, the BiH government had not given

176

access to the UN people to make the crater analysis, and so on. Everyone else concluded that the Serbs were responsible. On the 29th, UNPROFOR reported that, beyond a reasonable doubt, the mortars had been fired by the Serbs. General Smith decided to turn the key on air strikes.

However, there were some nagging questions. The attack took place at 11:10 hrs on 28th just after 5 a.m. New York time. I reported to the Council at noon that BiH had denied access to UNPROFOR. But on the 29th I learnt that BiH had provided access at 11:50 hrs, that is, before 6 a.m. New York time! The actual report was signed by one Lt Col Brian Powers. His typed report read: 'beyond doubt', but someone had corrected it by hand to read 'beyond reasonable doubt'. It also used phrases such as 'most likely' at least three times. Lt Col Powers was an American officer. This I learnt from Pedauye, a Spanish diplomat, who was the head of the UN mission in Sarajevo. He told me it was generally believed that there were no Americans serving in UNPROFOR, but Powers was an American holding a sensitive position. On further check-ing I found that Powers' report was submitted to Smith at 10 a.m. on the 29th whereas the two Smiths—General and Admiral—had decided to turn the key on the 28th! Several days later, a Russian officer, Colonel Demorenko, said publicly on Bosnian Serb television that the investi-gation was flawed and that there was not sufficient evidence to blame the Serbs for it. This time the air strikes would not be limited; they started 36 hours later. The delay was to enable the British troops to leave Gorazde. But the air strikes did help the peace process move. In fact, after just a few days, the Americans asked for the strikes to stop since they were coming in the way of Holbrooke's diplomatic efforts.

The contact group met with the foreign ministers of Bosnia, Croatia, and FRY in Geneva. Agreement was reached on basic principles. The FRY delegation also represented the Bosnian Serbs. BiH would consist of two entities, the Federation of Bosnia and Herzegovina and Republika Srpska. The 51: 49 ratio would be the basis for settlement, open for adjustment by mutual agreement. Each entity would preserve its own constitution and would have the right to establish parallel special relationship with its neighbours. If the Bosnian Serbs had accepted these terms a year earlier, so many lives would have been saved. The UN had no part in this meeting. Stoltenberg had been invited but the invitation was cancelled the night before. So was the case with Italy at the last minute. The Americans took all these decisions.

Holbrooke came calling on the Secretary General on September 22. This was a big favour on his part, arranged by Mrs. Albright at Annan's request. He gave a good lecture to the Secretary General on how considerable amounts could be saved in the UNCRO operation which, he said, was being run in a most profligate manner. He said he had first visited UN in 1949 with his father who had been medical adviser to Vijayalaxmi Pandit and the Indian delegation. He revealed this nugget of his biography to illustrate his strong support for UN. Regarding his negotiations on Bosnia, he did not say anything meaningful about his future plans. He did give a graphic account of his two protracted, long negotiating sessions with Milosevic in Belgrade. He described the Bosnian Serb general Mladic, as evil. 'Hollywood could not have created a character to depict evil as striking as Mladic.' The negotiations had been more tough than any of the negotiations he had been involved with in the past, including Vietnam. However, Milosevic was determined to have a peace deal. Holbrooke told the Secretary General that UNPROFOR should test the Serbs if necessary by provoking them. UN, he said, was being too cautious, timid.

The Holbrooke shuttle kept rolling, gathering agreements along the way, finally culminating in the conclave in Dayton, Ohio, on November 1, 1995. The Bosnian peace agreement was concluded on November 21, after three weeks of gruelling negotiations. Mrs. Albright announced, with unconcealed and justifiable glee, in the Council: 'We have a deal in Dayton.' The members of the Council were kept very busy for a couple of days since they had to adopt two or three resolutions to keep up the momentum of Dayton. But in a few weeks they would feel frustrated since most of the action would go out of their hands and their control. One resolution lifted the arms embargo against all the states of former Yugoslavia. The Russians had some problem with it; they wanted to amend it so that the embargo would be reimposed against a party that did not meet its obligations under the peace agreement. But, for the US, the embargo had to be lifted once and for all. The Russians said they would not co-sponsor the draft nor support it, but when Clinton called Yeltsin about it, they did both. The second resolution lifted sanctions against FRY, a reward for Milosevic. The third resolution dealt with the reintegration of eastern Slavonia into Croatia.

There were moments in Dayton when the presidents had their airplanes starting to refuel, in the calculation that the talks had collapsed. The Americans set deadlines several times. Many predicted, some announced failure. But the US had invested too much to allow the talks to fail. It showed conclusively that it took American clout, political and military, to solve difficult issues in the post-Cold War era. The UN, whether the Security Council or the Secretariat, had no part to play in this whole exercise, but this was not the first time that the UN had had no contribution in resolving a problem.

6

MIDDLE EAST

IT IS GENERALLY recognised that the Palestine question is at the core of the conflict in the Middle East and that without a just and lasting solution of the Palestinian problem, the region of Middle East will not enjoy durable peace. In 1947, a conscious decision was taken to take up the Palestinian question in the General Assembly in preference over the Security Council to avoid the complication of the veto provision. The General Assembly somehow muddled through the consideration of the item at two special sessions, finally adopting Resolution 184, recommending partition of Palestine into an Arab state and a Jewish state. When hostilities broke out between the new state of Israel and its Arab neighbours, the matter became the legitimate concern of the Security Council. That is where it has remained for the past almost sixty years; peace and stability in the Middle East are as remote today as they were when the Council was first seized of the problem.

Because of the special relationship between the United States and Israel, the Middle East problem has always been the most difficult and frustrating item on the agenda of the Security Council. If on almost all subjects the American delegation in New York has very little discretionary authority to negotiate, it has none when it comes to anything connected with the Middle East. Negotiating the text of a resolution on the Middle East with the Americans can almost always be an exasperating experience. It can even happen that a deal struck with the American delegation in New York, with the approval of Washington, is unravelled under pressure from Israel. One complicating factor is the status of the Palestinian representative. In the United Nations, the Palestine Liberation Organisation (PLO) has a mission which has been accorded the status of an observer. This does not pose any problem in the General Assembly where it enjoys most of the privileges of full members except the right to vote. In the Security Council, however, the PLO has to request the privilege of participating in the discussion every time the Palestinian issue is raised. This means that the Council has to vote every time the Palestinian observer asks to speak. Often, the Americans—and for the past many years only the Americans—vote against the Palestinian request, but since this is regarded as a procedural question, a negative vote by a permanent member does not amount to veto.

When Yasser Arafat decided to support Saddam Hussein in 1990 in his aggression against Kuwait, overnight he lost the political and financial support upon which he had depended to wage and sustain his struggle. It made him weak enough to agree to participate in the Madrid Conference on the Middle East on terms to which he would otherwise have never agreed, namely to form part of the Jordanian delegation, not to include anyone from East Jerusalem, and so on. The launching of the new Middle East initiative by George Bush and Baker in 1991 inevitably had an impact, however marginal, on the consideration of the problem in the Security Council as the following narrative will bring out.

The Security Council met in an informal session on January 10, 1991, to consider the question of deportation of the four Palestinians by

Israel from the occupied territories. The non-aligned caucus met a day earlier to discuss a draft resolution prepared by the Palestinian mission which sought to condemn Israel for the deportation. While Cuba, Yemen, and others agreed to sponsor it, India suggested that it was time for the non-aligned to think of new formulations; one more condemnation would not make any difference to Israel. Instead of condemning Israel, India proposed using the following language: 'Declares that Israel's action of deporting four Palestinians is illegal, contrary to international law and is unacceptable'. To India's surprise, the others accepted this formulation. But when the non-aligned draft was introduced at the informals on the 10th, American ambassador Tom Pickering opposed the very idea of a resolution. He said the timing was not right. He probably knew that the war on Iraq was only days away. He suggested a presidential statement or for the President to call the Israeli ambassador and convey to him the concern of the Council. Pickering later met with the caucus and told them that he had instructions that he could not work on the basis of a resolution; he handed over the text of a statement. The non-aligned would not agree.

The President informed the caucus the following day that the Americans would let him know when they would be ready to negotiate on the text of a resolution. This was not at all satisfactory since the initiative would lie entirely with the Americans. This was only a stalling tactic by the US. On the 14th, the President brought a draft to the Council and said that the US would negotiate only on the basis of his draft. But when he conveyed that the US would at best abstain even on that draft, the non-aligned caucus decided to go back to their original draft. At the informal consultations when Yemen proposed that the Council should immediately proceed to the official chamber for a vote on the non-aligned draft, Pickering exploded. He asked: How could you, the non-aligned, get so idiotic as to produce such idiotic drafts? He went on in this vein for some time. Everybody was stunned at Pickering's outburst, since he was well liked and widely admired for his professionalism. This being my first exposure to the informal consultations—India having assumed membership of the Council only on January 1, 1991—I thought such occurrences were not unusual. Ashtal, the Yemen ambassador, regretted the use of such language the like of which he said he had never heard before. After the meeting, I told Pickering I was glad to learn that during informal consultations, we could speak really freely and frankly. He apologised and said he should not have used those words. I told him he ought to apologise publicly. To his great credit, he did just that the following day.

The Council was in informal consultations on January 16 afternoon on this very subject. The President, ambassador of Zaire, had an ego problem, not unlike everybody else. He was determined to have a consensus text under his watch, however much time and effort that might demand. The members were engaged in bilateral and multilateral negotiations on the subject when news came in just before 7 p.m., that the Gulf War had begun. The Palestinian issue had to take a back seat.

The question of the deported Palestinians was not revived until March 26 and that happened because another group of four Palestinians was expelled by Israel. This time the Council quickly reached an agreement on a presidential statement. What had changed since January? The Gulf War had started. Several Arab states had joined the 'coalition' against Iraq. The US had to be a little more sensitive to Arab sentiments so as not to make the lives of the Arab regimes more difficult internally vis-à-vis their own public opinion.

In May, the Council was faced with another case of deportation. This time it proved even less difficult to reach an agreement on the text of a draft resolution. The Americans were isolated but they never worried about the isolation, they revelled in it. It was the overall situation in the Gulf which made them more amenable to accommodation. In any case, the draft was the one they could live with without much difficulty. The President advised the others that there was no possibility of making the Americans budge from their maximum position. Thus, if the non-aligned nations and Palestinians wanted a resolution, they did not have much choice!

Secretary of State Baker started his travels in the Middle East in March trying out his ideas about an international conference with the Saudis and others. As he has admitted in his memoirs, he felt that in return for Arab support in the war against Iraq, he had to take some initiative on finding a framework for dealing with the Israeli-Palestinian problem. Syria, having realised the impotence of the Soviet Union, was willing to let the Americans talk to Israel on tackling Syria's relations with the Israelis. Syria of course wanted to get back the Golan Heights. Even the Palestinians in the West Bank were reconsidering their earlier rejection of Baker's offer of meeting them. As mentioned above, Arafat had become more 'reasonable' following his weakened position. The timing was propitious for an initiative.

Baker met the foreign ministers of the 'eight'—GCC (6), Egypt, and Syria—in Riyadh. On March 8, he talked with the Israelis and met a Palestinian delegation on the 9th. He felt encouraged enough to state that the nations of the region now seemed ready to write a new chapter of peace instead of a chapter of war. The Palestinians gave him their usual list of demands: PLO as the sole representative, a Palestinian state, international conference, and freeze on settlements. Baker met Syrian President Hafez Al Assad in Moscow for seven hours on March 14. But if Baker felt he owed one to the Arabs, the latter too felt obligated to the US which had rescued them from Saddam Hussein and hence were willing to show flexibility. The Saudis and Kuwaitis detested Arafat for his pro-Saddam stance and Syria never liked him anyway. Egypt was the one country which regarded Arafat as the best bet available; having invested in him over the years, Egypt was not ready to ditch him. Bush, however, came out strongly against Arafat who, according to him, had thoroughly discredited himself in the whole affair.

Egypt and Iran agreed, in March, to open an 'interest section' in each other's capital. The Iranians felt left out from the post-war security arrangements. They were unhappy with the Damascus Declaration of March 6 and with their erstwhile ally Syria. Iran was also concerned at the certainty of continued American military presence—air, naval, and ground—in the region after the war. As for Jordan, its King Hussein was anxious to make up with America after his pro-Saddam stand; he wrote a letter to Bush who was in no hurry to reply to him. As for Israel, its Prime Minister Shamir affirmed on March 18 that he would never talk to PLO and there was no question of his meeting the Palestinians whom Baker had met a week ago. Arafat, who was hardly in a position to bargain with anybody, said he was prepared to meet with the Israelis but only in the presence of the P-5.

By the end of March 1991, Bahrain announced it had agreed to host the headquarters of the US Central Command, till then based in Florida. General Colin Powell, Chairman of the Joint Chiefs of Staff, said the long-held dream of the US to acquire a permanent ground presence in the Middle East would now be realised. (Hardly any one had heard of Osama bin Laden at that time.) A gift from Saddam Hussein to his American friends! At about the same time, GCC announced that it was cutting off all aid to PLO. Its Secretary General, Bishara, said PLO's crime was too big to forget or forgive.

Baker paid another visit to the region in April. He claimed having made some progress. Israel had now agreed to a regional conference to be convened by USA and USSR. Israel's idea was that the conference would hold only one meeting after which individual bilateral talks would be held between Israel and the Arabs. The Palestinians could take part but excluding the PLO and the Palestinians from East Jerusalem. As far as Israel was concerned, there would be no question of including the status of the occupied territories in the agenda. Syria got worried and its foreign minister dashed off to Cairo and persuaded Egypt to confine itself to saying that it supported the idea of a conference in principle and had to study it further. Syria wanted the conference to be held under UN auspices but no one was surprised when Syria showed more flexibility and decided to compromise. Baker generously agreed to meet the foreign minister of Jordan in Geneva; he needed Jordan's co-operation to agree to a joint Jordanian-Palestinian delegation in any future conference!

By August, Baker had made five visits to the region. He made creditable progress in putting together enough consensus on his pro-posal for a regional conference. He managed to get the consent of Israel, Jordan, and Syria to attend the conference. Egypt was already on board. Syria pleaded for at least some role for the UN but all that Baker would offer was an invitation to the UN to send a representative to the con-ference in the capacity of an observer. George Bush and Mikhail Gorbachev, meeting in Moscow in late July, announced that a meeting would be held in October and that invitations would be sent out at least 10 days before the conference. They stopped short of actually issuing the invitations because Israel was not fully on board and, of course, the Americans would not want to embarrass their ally. So, from Moscow, Baker went to Israel. Shamir agreed to attend, but on the same condi-tions: no invitation to PLO, no Palestinian from East Jerusalem, and no Palestinian known to be a PLO member. Thus the entire pressure came on the Palestinians who found it difficult to bear the opprobrium of blocking the conference. Arafat argued, with logic on his side: how could Israel dictate who should form the Palestinian delegation? But logic is not always relevant in international affairs.

On October 19, the US and Soviet Union issued invitations to Egypt, Syria, Lebanon, Jordan, Israel, and the Palestinians to attend a Middle East conference to be held in Madrid on October 30. The invi-tation to the Palestinians was handed over by the American and Soviet consuls to Feissal El Husseini in Jerusalem. This was announced by Baker and the Soviet foreign minister Pankin on October 19. This was Baker's eighth trip to the region since the Gulf War.

As for the Security Council, it hardly devoted any time to the ques-tion of the occupied territories for the remainder of 1991, except briefly on September 13 when the President informed the members of the contents of a letter he had received from the observer of Palestine, requesting the Council's help in enabling Palestinians from the occupied territories to attend a meeting of the Palestinian National Council in Algiers. The President, on his own, spoke to the Israeli ambassador, and the latter absolutely refused to even read any letter from 'a terrorist organisation'.

To everyone's surprise, the Council adopted, unanimously, a resolution on January 6, 1992, on Israel's deportation of Palestinians. The US agreed to 'strongly condemn' Israel for the deportation. This was a big gain for the Palestinians who readily agreed to accommodate the Americans on a couple of minor points. This was the first time the Council strongly condemned Israel on the question of deportations. The US objective, no doubt, was to clear the decks for the meeting of the peace process in Washington which would be in continuation of the Madrid conference. The Arabs had reacted very strongly against the deportations and had threatened to boycott the Washington meeting. A quick condemnation by the State Department and support for a tough resolution would guarantee Arab participation. The Palestine observer said as much in his statement to the Council. The Council would have preferred if no statements had been made by anyone in the official meeting, but Israel insisted on speaking. The Israeli ambassador told British Ambassador Hannay that even a condemned man had the right to be heard before his execution.

Four Palestinians were killed in Rafah in Gaza Strip on April 1 by the Israeli security forces. The Security Council met and consulted all through April 3. The PLO had prepared a draft presidential statement which the non-aligned members agreed to support. The President put forward the draft as his own at the consultations meeting in the afternoon, which, predictably, invited strong objection from the Americans. Negotiations dragged on until 1:30 in the morning. The US had to continuously check with Washington. At one stage unpleasant words were exchanged between PLO and Morocco who was negotiating on behalf of the non-aligned. The US position was so strong that at one point the non-aligned members proposed suspending the negotiations until after the weekend when they would propose a draft resolution. The US realising its isolation, relented; even UK was ready to go along with the original draft statement. Agreement was reached at 1.30 a.m. and the statement was read out in the official meeting immediately thereafter.

A major crisis broke out in the occupied territories in December 1992. On the 16th, Israel expelled over 400 Palestinians in retaliation against the escalating acts of terrorism which caused the deaths of nearly a dozen Israeli soldiers and policemen in the preceding weeks. The trigger for this drastic action was the abduction and subsequent stabbing to death of a police sergeant, Missin Toledano. The murder of Toledano caused an uproar in Israel. The Israeli cabinet decided on the deportations; only the justice minister did not support the decision. The idea was to push the Palestinians across the border in Lebanon into the so-called Israeli security zone of the 'no-man's land'. The plan was to carry out the expulsions in the middle of the night so as to avoid publicity and possible pre-emptive action in Israeli courts. However, the news invariably leaked out. Friends of the deportees and human rights organisations woke up a senior judge in the middle of the night who wrote out a stay order in longhand. The intended deportees were taken in 22 buses and were held at the border while the Supreme Court considered the matter. After long hours, the court ruled in favour of the government and the deportations were carried out.

This was the largest deportation since the 1967 war. The deportees, mostly from Gaza and some from the West Bank, occupied leading positions in Hamas and the Islamic Jihad which had claimed responsibility for the terrorist acts. The deportations raised a storm of protests and condemnation all over the world. In the Security Council, the non-aligned members prepared a draft resolution which became the subject of intense negotiations with the Americans. As mentioned earlier, the American delegation in New York did not have much flexibility on any issue, but on the Palestinian issue, it had none. On this occasion, an added complicating factor was Lebanon's firm refusal to admit the deportees into its territory, that is, the territory under its control. The Lebanese wanted a couple of paragraphs included in the resolution which necessitated further negotiations firstly among Lebanon, PLO, and the caucus and subsequently between the caucus and the Americans. The PLO was not enthusiastic about including references to Lebanon. Finally, an operative paragraph was accepted by the US reaffirming Lebanon's sovereignty and territorial integrity. This was the first time that Lebanon was mentioned in a resolution on this subject. Resolution 799 was adopted unanimously at 11.30 p.m. on December 18, asking Israel to rescind the deportations and requesting the Secretary General to take up the matter with the government of Israel.

As 1992 drew to a close, the deportees were still on the wintry hillside in Israeli-occupied security zone. Their condition was on the verge of being critical since neither Israel nor Lebanon would permit the International Committee of the Red Cross or any other agency to deliver aid to them. A battle of wills was on between Israel and Lebanon. The Secretary General sent Under Secretary General James Jonah to the region to negotiate with Israel as mandated by the Security Council but Israel gave him a negative response. Separately, Israel said that 10 of the deportees had been included in the list by mistake and would be allowed to come back; they would of course face prosecution and stiff prison sentences. As for the rest, Israel said that a third country could offer to take them in and Israel would permit them transit through Israel. The PLO and the non-aligned members attempted to issue a presidential statement but gave in, in the face of American unwillingness to agree to any but the mildest text. As it happened, the Americans, together with the French and the British, were extremely keen to have a presidential statement on Iraq on that very day—December 30. A linkage was quickly established between the two statements. The Americans were told that the Arabs and Muslims would not accept a situation wherein the Council would condemn Iraq and let Israel completely off the hook.

Significantly, throughout the day-long consultations and discussions, the Russians did not say one single word about the Palestinian problem, though they felt obliged to speak in support of the draft statement on Iraq.

I joined the Secretary General's office as Under Secretary General and senior political adviser on January 1, 1993, and left on my first assignment on January 5 for Cairo en route to Israel to talk to the Israelis about the 400 plus deportees. In Cairo I met the Secretary General who invited me and Lisa Buttenheim, a senior and seasoned political officer, and an expert on Middle East, for a briefing to his house overlooking the city. Lisa was of great help to me on this assignment. The Secretary General advised me about my mission in some detail. 'This is not a humanitarian issue; if it was, the Red Cross would deal with it. The solution lies in implementing Resolution 799; do not visit Lebanon since it is not Lebanon's problem. The return of deportees could be step by step. If Israel does not co-operate with you, I will present a very stiff report to the Security Council; there must not be double standards in the Council. Stay at the Hilton hotel in Jerusalem; meet the Palestinians in East Jerusalem.'

In Israel, I met Foreign Minister Shimon Peres and his deputy Yossi Beillin as well the director general of the foreign ministry Uri Savir. But my main, substantive talks were with Prime Minister Yitzhak Rabin. He was the one who would take decisions. I found Rabin honest and straightforward in my negotiations with him. He took tough positions but I felt that if he agreed to some deal, he would keep his word. The Secretary General called me to Paris to brief him and to obtain his guidance on how to proceed further, since I had not made any headway in my negotiations. The Secretary General called Rabin on telephone and asked him to receive me again. As suggested by the Secretary General, I proposed to Rabin that Israel should agree to take back 100 deportees in the first instance and agree to let the others come back in stages. After a couple of sessions with him, I told Rabin that he probably found the deal I had offered him was reasonable, but he would rather give the solution to the Americans than to the United Nations. I added that the threat of the Security Council imposing sanctions would not impress him since Israel could count on their friend US vetoing any proposal for sanctions. He smiled and agreed. I suggested to the Secretary General that I should return to New York since I did not expect Israel to agree to anything at all.

Back in New York, the Secretary General had to submit a report to the Council on the result of Jonah's and my mission to Israel in terms of Resolution 799. We had animated discussions among ourselves about the recommendations part of the report. Some of us, including me, did not want to use threatening or provocative language on the ground that it would not goad the Council into taking any effective action and would needlessly antagonise the new American administration. But the Secretary General was clear in his mind. He persuaded the rest of us to go along with the language eventually used in the report: 'I would be failing in my duty if I did not recommend to the Security Council that it should take whatever measures are required to ensure that its unanimous decision, as set out in Resolution 799, is respected'. The Secretary General was clearly challenging the Council to live up to its responsibilities, to deal with Israel's persistent defiance of its resolutions, and to impose sanctions under Chapter VII. It was a courageous report, certain to provoke the Americans and test the political will of the Arabs. The Arabs were particularly embarrassed; the representative in the Security Council of the Arab group, Morocco, had the unique opportunity to emerge as the leader of the Arab group by proposing a resolution along the lines of the Secretary General's recommendation and prove its bonafides on the Palestinian issue. But Morocco valued its friendship with the US more. Weeks and months went by without   the Council taking any action on the Secretary General's report. The matter faded out of the agenda when the Israelis worked out a deal with the Americans almost exactly on the lines I had offered to Rabin in January!

On February 25, 1994, a fanatic Jew gunned down dozens of Palestinians while they were at prayers in the sacred Ibrahami mosque in Hebron. The Security Council met on February 28 on the Hebron massacre. For the first time, PLO's participation was approved without the US challenging it. The Council was to resume the debate on March 1. There was a long list of speakers. The Americans said they did not want the debate until and unless agreement was reached on the text of a resolution. They told the President, France, that they would break off all negotiations on the draft resolution if the debate was allowed to resume. This totally unreasonable attitude upset the Secretary General who said to the President that denial of opportunity to speak would create difficulties domestically for Arab countries. The Secretary General, being an activist, decided to speak to Mrs. Albright about it. The Secretary General's real concern was with the impact of the Hebron massacre on fundamentalism in Arab countries.

But the Americans changed their mind and the debate was held but there was a peculiar compromise. Only four speakers from out of a list of more than 20 would be given the floor. This was an unprecedented decision even for the Security Council. When the President proposed it at the consultations, no one objected! Such was the clout of the Americans!

The Russians staged a mini drama in March in the Council. On Friday, March 11, they said that they would not be ready for a vote on the draft on the Hebron massacre before Monday, March 14. On Saturday, Vorontsov suddenly asked for urgent consultations and a vote on Saturday itself. Everyone knew that the Russians were playing this game because Kozyrev was in Tunis and there would not be any vote on Saturday since the Americans were not ready for it. The whole act was played out, with members and non-members coming to the UN on a Saturday evening, regarded by UN diplomats as more sacrosanct than by the Jews, cursing the Russians and going home after a five minute consultation showpiece.

There was ample evidence of the Russian frustration at being taken for granted, at not being consulted by the Americans, and of Russian activism asserting and reminding the world of its importance in international affairs. Kozyrev went to Jerusalem in March, uninvited and unwelcome (almost at the same time that Warren Christopher was in China, being rebuffed by the Chinese on the question of human rights), merely to remind everyone that Russia was a co-sponsor of the Middle East peace process on an equal basis with the US.

The Security Council adopted Resolution 804 on the Hebron massacre on March 18, three weeks after the event. A most unusual, though apparently not unprecedented, procedure was followed. Each paragraph, preambular and operative, was voted upon separately. The US abstained on two preambular paragraphs and voted in favour of all the others. Thus, each paragraph was adopted separately. Thereafter, the President declared the resolution as having being adopted, without putting the entire resolution to vote as is the practice. This was done so that the Americans would not have to vote in favour of the resolution. The two preambular paragraphs on which the US abstained described the territories as 'occupied' and reiterated that the Fourth Geneva Protocol applied to East Jerusalem also. Mrs. Albright made it clear in her statement that she would have vetoed the paragraphs if they had been included in the operative section. The Americans reversed their long-held position on East Jerusalem and the territories as being 'occupied'.

There was a lot of activity in the Council in May 1993 regarding the situation in Yemen. The two Yemens had merged in 1990. They had been fighting a bitter civil war for over three weeks to the extent that south Yemen announced secession on May 20. (Ironically, 'President' Egal of 'Somaliland' which has not received recognition from a single country in the world was the first and only one to recognise South Yemen.) Many people suspected Saudi Arabia's hand behind the trouble in Yemen on the theory that the Saudis never reconciled themselves to or accepted the merger of the two Yemens. North Yemen gained upper hand which galvanised the Saudis into action since they wanted to save the south. So Prince Bandar, the long serving and influential Saudi ambassador in Washington, swung into action. With active American encouragement, he began canvassing support for a draft resolution in the Security Council calling for ceasefire, arms embargo, and resumption of negotiations, and asking the Secretary General to send a fact-finding mission. Not surprisingly, the draft did not contain any reference to the territorial integrity of Yemen. Oman, a member of the Council, had the unenviable task of piloting the draft in the Council. Bandar came to New York on May 25 and met the permanent members.

Ashtal, the ambassador of Yemen, a most experienced and shrewd diplomat, met with the Secretary General on the 25th. (Ashtal had represented Yemen for over 25 years.) The Secretary General's instinct was to get involved in everything, certainly in Yemen! Ashtal was not opposed to the idea of a resolution or a presidential statement but insisted on a reference to the unity of the country. The Saudis were not too happy about it but found it difficult to convince the Council not to include a reference to it. It was widely expected that the resolution would be adopted within a matter of days.

But Middle East being Middle East, unexpected developments must always be expected; things were seldom what they appeared to be! Ashtal wrote a pro-forma letter to the Council to the effect that consideration of the situation in Yemen would amount to interference in its internal affairs, in violation of Article 2(7) of the Charter. But he did not lobby at all to stop such consideration. Perhaps he assessed, rightly, that it would not be possible to prevent the situation being discussed. But he did not make a serious effort to try to have included in the resolution points of particular interest to Yemen, the most significant one being its territorial integrity. He did not also raise any objection to the proposal for a fact-finding mission.

A member of Yemen's Presidential Council met the Secretary General on May 31. The Secretary General was always in his element when he met Arab leaders. The conversation was almost always in Arabic. (The Secretary General always said: 'Ambassador Gharekhan understands Arabic though he pretends he does not.') The Yemeni went into a long historical rigmarole, ending up with why he was opposed to a draft resolution. The Secretary General was very persuasive and insistent. 'It would reflect badly on you if you simply rejected everything and adopted a confrontationist attitude. The resolution would still pass. You should on the other hand say you have nothing to hide, you should welcome the fact-finding mission, show them that the majority of south Yemenis want to remain in one country, and so on.' Ashtal was nodding his head, in approval, when the Secretary General was trying to convert the visitor to his viewpoint.

Things moved fast in the Council on June 1; they do when Saudi monetary might is combined with American diplomatic clout. The Chinese had no stake in the matter and they had an opportunity to express their gratitude to Bill Clinton for unconditionally renewing the MFN treatment. Permanent members have nothing to fear in the form of creating precedents since they can always protect their interests by using the veto. The non-permanent members often do not understand this. Almost all the discussion on Yemen was among non-permanent members, with the permanent members watching their colleagues arguing as to why certain paragraphs, such as respect for territorial integrity, which ought to be of the utmost significance to them, should not be included in the resolution. The performance of the non-aligned members was pathetic. The French ambassador asked me: Would India have supported such a resolution? He went on to reply that India certainly would not have. (Did he have more faith in India than the Indians?)

The members of the Council quickly reached agreement on the text of the resolution. One reason for the haste was that everyone wanted to bring to an end the embarrassing situation in which Oman found itself. The other and more decisive factor was that the Saudis were running out of patience. New Zealand and Spain made a feeble attempt to include reference to territorial integrity, but everyone knew that the representative of Yemen himself was not too concerned about it. The Council adopted the resolution on June 1. It had become common practice in the Council to adopt nearly all resolutions by unanimity. Immediately after the vote, Prince Bandar went up to Ashtal and warmly shook his hand. That is Middle East! Ashtal said later that he wanted to avoid exacerbating the situation. He was persuading his government to receive the fact-finding mission which Lakhdar Brahimi, a former Algerian foreign minister, would lead. A day later, South Yemen warmly and North Yemen cautiously welcomed the mission.

Towards the end of September 1996, the situation in Middle East exploded following Israel's decision to open the second entrance to the tunnel beneath the Western Wall in the old city of Jerusalem. More than 70 people were killed, 80 per cent of them Palestinians, in the ensuing violence. The interesting thing from the point of view of the functioning of the Security Council was the isolation and eventual setback to the Americans. The initial US position was to oppose a public meeting. The line they took, a pretty standard one, was that there must be a clear idea, in advance, of the outcome of the meeting before they could agree to the meeting. But they were decisively outnumbered with even the British not standing with them. The Council met on Friday, September 27 and listened to 51 speakers, many of them foreign ministers— Primakov, Rifkind, Moussa, and others. The US did not want the Council to meet over the weekend but had to give in to others on this point too. As was the usual practice, the PLO prepared a draft resolution which the non-aligned adopted as their own, knowing it would be a non-starter for the US.

The main negotiations were between the Egyptian ambassador Nabil El Araby and Mrs. Albright and between her and the Israelis in the person of Foreign Minister David Levy. After interminable hours of waiting, during which the bar ran out of refreshments, agreement was finally reached. Or so it seemed. Mrs. Albright announced in the consultations that there was a deal. But when members moved to the main chamber, Mrs. Albright received fresh instructions and they all moved back to the consultations room. More negotiations followed. Mrs. Albright had a long telephone talk with Levy and seemed to have got him on board. Once again she announced that a deal had been struck and that she was ready to vote. I was surprised since the draft was distinctly more favourable to the Palestinians. We trooped to the chamber but trooped right back to the room! Mrs. Albright said she needed more time and suggested postponement until Monday the 30th. There were loud protests. The president of the Council, Indonesia, said Mrs. Albright's suggestion was an insult to the dignity of the Council and insisted on a vote the same night. The only country to support Mrs. Albright was Poland, not Britain. Mrs. Albright for once appeared contrite. She apologised profusely and admitted that she had indeed agreed to the text but added, in her defence, that 'such is life in the Middle east'! The vote was taken and the US abstained, everyone else voting in favour. The US could not risk a veto; feelings in the Arab world were running very high against America and the summit which Clinton had announced for September 30 in Washington might not have happened.

It transpired that Mrs. Albright had become the victim of intra-Israeli politics. The hostile relationship between Prime Minister Netanyahu and Foreign Minister Levy was a matter of common knowledge. Levy had complained openly when Netanyahu had not taken anyone from the foreign ministry when he went to Jordan for talks with King Hussein. When Levy gave his concurrence to the draft, Mrs. Albright justifiably announced her own acceptance. But Levy was overruled by Netanyahu who contacted Washington which in turn sent new last-minute instructions to New York.

Arafat, King Hussein, and Netanyahu went to Washington for a summit meeting. Hosni Mubarak declined the invitation in what was clearly a snub to the Americans. Arafat was keen on Mubarak's participation, but Mubarak realised that his main function would be to put pressure on Arafat and he did not want to do that. By refusing the invitation, Mubarak's stock in the Arab World went very high. The summit failed.

The disappearance of the Soviet Union affected the Palestinians more than any other people. Most 'third world' countries lamented the death of the Soviet Union because, they felt, 'the balancing factor' was lost; there was no one any more to restrain the sole surviving superpower. The Palestinians were particularly severely affected since they lost the patronage of a very influential permanent member who, besides, was happy to take on the United States, at least in the Security Council. The Palestinians expressed their frustration when the Russian Federation did not utter a word nor exerted any effort to influence the language of draft resolutions concerning the Middle East. The Palestinians, however, proved quite flexible and pragmatic. Ambassador Nasser Al Kidwa, their able and experienced observer in the United Nations, soon established good working relations with the Americans and others. With the signing of the Oslo Accords on September 13, 1993, he quickly adapted to the new situation. At the same time, he used all his accumulated experience to continue to fight for many technical issues and won many a diplomatic battle.

Subsequent to the signing of the Oslo Agreement, it became standard practice for the Americans to argue that it would not be wise or proper for the Security Council to engage in any discussion or debate of the Israeli-Palestinian issue since the two parties had embarked upon direct negotiations among themselves. Reopening the debate in the Council, they pointed out, would only vitiate the atmosphere because the parties would feel obliged to play up to their respective constituencies and use harsh language which, in turn, would render the task of their negotiators more difficult. By and large, the Palestinian issue as such has not been debated much in the Council since Oslo, except to welcome the 'roadmap' and on a few other occasions.

7

LIBYA—THE LOCKERBIE DISASTER

PAN AMERICAN FLIGHT 103 exploded over Lockerbie, Scotland, in December 1988, killing 270 people in all, 259 on board and 11 on ground. Flight 772 of Union des Transports Aerienne (UTA) exploded over Niger on September 19, 1989, killing all 170 people on board. The trial regarding the UTA flight started in France. As for the Pan Am flight disaster, the initial finger of suspicion was pointed at Abu Nidal, the dreaded Palestinian terror group based in Syria. Later, the British and American governments, which had the main jurisdiction about the Lockerbie disaster, zeroed in on two Libyan suspects in 1991. The theory was that this was an act of revenge by Libya for the bombing of Tripoli in 1986 by American planes based in UK. The French government also suspected Libyan hand behind the UTA crash. The three governments decided to take the matter to the Security Council. The UTA affair was the sideshow, the main focus was on Lockerbie and the principal players were the US and UK.

During the closing weeks of 1991, there was a story in the *New York Times*, datelined Washington, that the US, UK, and France were preparing to bring to the Security Council their case against Libya for its alleged role in the two civil aviation disasters involving Pan Am and UTA. The governments of the three countries had asked Libya to hand over to them certain Libyan officials whom they had identified as responsible for the terrorist attacks and demanded compensation. Since Libya refused to comply with their demands, these three countries had decided to bring the matter to the Council.

The US mission in New York had denied the story when it was first published. According to Paul Lewis of the *New York Times*, the US mission was strongly opposed to the idea. However, I was inclined to give more credence to the Washington story. After their success in the General Assembly in having the resolution on 'Zionism is racism' rescinded with a very comfortable majority, the Americans felt confident that they could use any UN organ for their national ends. A US diplomat told a colleague of mine in the Indian mission: We can do what we like with the United Nations.

Sure enough, the three countries started lobbying in early January 1992 for Security Council action against Libya. They circulated detailed reports by their respective intelligence agencies containing evidence against particular Libyan officials as well as on official involvement of Libyan intelligence. They approached other members of the Council first in the capitals, and after a few days, in New York.

The Libyans got frightened. They were afraid that these three permanent members, before long, would ask the Council to impose sanctions against Libya under Chapter VII. Their fears were well placed. The US, UK, and French diplomats told other members of the Council that if the Libyans did not comply with their demands they would ask for Chapter VII action.

The Libyan permanent representative came to see the non-aligned caucus on January 8. He said that the Council was not the proper forum to deal with legal issues of this nature; however Libya could agree to the Council asking the Secretary General to investigate the matter and suggest ways and means of solving it. Alternatively, the Council itself could set up a committee to investigate the matter in an impartial manner. Libya would accept any decision of the Secretary General or of the Council committee as long as it did not compromise Libyan sovereignty and was within international law.

The Libyan situation was embarrassing for most members of the Council. The three permanent members had picked a country, which was an international pariah, and an issue—international terrorism—on which no country would wish to be perceived as defending terrorism. The three countries had waited until January because by then Cuba and Yemen had gone out of the Council and the ranks of the non-aligned had depleted from seven to six. The main legal and political difficulty for many members was that they did not like the Council to punish a country only on the basis of allegations made by some member states. The Council should have at its disposal an independent and impartial charge sheet on which it could act. The three sponsoring countries argued on the other hand that it was better for the international community that they brought such matters before the Security Council rather than taking punitive action against Libya on their own. They claimed they had the right to do so under Article 51 of the Charter.

The US, UK, and France circulated a draft resolution on January 13, 1992. The draft did not contain any threat of action under Chapter VII in the second phase but said that the Council would remain seized of the matter. It carefully avoided asking for the extradition of the suspects, since several members had conveyed that they could never agree to such a demand. The non-aligned caucus met the following day to consider the Libyan draft. Ambassador Jesus of Cape Verde, who was a lawyer, explained that the main difficulty was the undesirability of the Council acting on the basis of the findings of national investigating agencies. He suggested that the Secretary General could be given some role. The ambassador of Venezuela reminded everyone that the most notorious terrorist of all, Carlos of Venezuela, was in Libya. Ecuador said that the Security Council was not the proper forum to deal with such a matter. Its ambassador, Ayala Lasso, said public opinion was a very important factor in his country; if his president did not support a resolution on terrorism he would lose his job.

The non-aligned members met with the sponsors and pleaded for some role for the Secretary General. The sponsors totally rejected either a judicial role for the Secretary General or any arbitration or mediation by him. Ambassador Jesus, under persistent badgering by the American ambassador, Tom Pickering, diluted the non-aligned proposal and even gave a commitment of non-aligned support if the sponsors agreed to give an opportunity to the Libyans of communicating their response through the Secretary General. Thus, the Secretary General would be merely a channel of communication between the sponsors and Libya. Ambassador Jesus was merely interpreting the unspoken desire of all the other non-aligned members to have some face-saving formula so that they could vote in favour.

The caucus met the Secretary General on January 20 to seek his views and advice. Boutros Ghali made three points: (i) any action by the Council must be in conformity with the principles of international law; (ii) it would be highly desirable to have a consensus resolution; and (iii) he was at the disposal of the Council even if the resolution did not make any reference to him. The non-aligned prepared an amendment which would replace the direct demand on Libya by a request to the Secretary General to seek Libya's co-operation. Our intention was to create some good offices role for the Secretary General but without saying so in so many words. The sponsors completely rejected the non-aligned amendment and put forward a counter amendment, which the non-aligned could not accept. After a great deal of negotiations the non-aligned came up with an additional paragraph requesting the Secretary General to seek Libya's co-operation. The co-sponsors were glad to accept this proposal since it in fact strengthened the resolution. The non-aligned were satisfied at the specific mention of the Secretary General, in the belief that it would provide an opening for Libya to find a face-saving formula.

Ambassador Jesus said privately that it was very difficult for his government not to vote in favour of the resolution since the Americans had conveyed to them in writing that failure to support the resolution would have serious implications for their bilateral relations with the US. We in India had not been subjected to this kind of pressure, as far as I knew! Interestingly, Boutros Ghali had told me a few days earlier that he would not be surprised if the two Libyans were in fact guilty. He had heard that the two of them were relatives of Qaddafi; and if this was so, the latter would never surrender them.

The resolution was adopted on January 21 as Resolution 731. The vote was unanimous.

The *Washington Post* of February 11 quoted a former CIA official to the effect that the two Libyan suspects had been executed in Libya. According to another report, the two Libyans had been kidnapped by the West. If the two had indeed been done away with one way or another, it would have defused the crisis for the Security Council. To the regret of most members, the reports turned out to be unfounded!

The permanent representative of Libya returned to New York after consultations in Tripoli. On the basis of what he told the Secretary General, the latter issued a report on February 14. In terms of that report, Libya expressed its readiness to comply fully with the French demands. As for Anglo-American demands, the Libyans stated their readiness to co-operate with the Secretary General and asked him to set up a mechanism for the purpose. Libya probably calculated that by satisfying French demands, it would manage to cause a split between the French on the one hand, and the British and the Americans on the other. This was only wishful thinking and naïve on their part. In a meeting with the non-aligned, the Libyan permanent representative,

Ambassador Elhouderi said that in the final analysis, Libya would be ready to surrender the two suspects, but it needed a mechanism to deal with the two countries since it did not have diplomatic relations with them. The non-aligned went to see the Secretary General who, though irritated with the Libyans, said that he would ask France and Libya to start consultations regarding the French requests. He would engage the permanent representatives of Libya, UK, and US in a discussion of what exactly was required of Libya in terms of Resolution 731. But all this was not going to work. The Americans and the others would not agree to any softening in their position and were not going to be deprived of the opportunity to impose sanctions against Libya.

On the occasion of the summit level meeting of the Security Council on January 31, 1992, President George Bush, Prime Minister John Major and President Mitterrand actively canvassed support for sanctions against Libya. Prime Minister Narasimha Rao of India was particularly good on this subject when he met Prime Minister Major. Hannay, the British ambassador, brought up the subject during the meeting with John Major. Narasimha Rao told Major that as a lawyer, he found it difficult to accept the proposition that the Security Council should act on the basis of allegations of one or two member states. He said that while the two suspects might well be guilty, it would be extremely difficult to establish conspiracy between them and the Libyan government. Giving the example of Mahatma Gandhi's assassination, he said that he was quite convinced that Nathuram Godse, the main accused, had not acted on his own, but it was impossible to prove conspiracy between him and those suspected to be involved in the assassination. Major and Hannay tried in vain to answer Narasimha Rao's argument. In the end, Major was obliged to tell Hannay that the Council ought to consider the general question of criteria which could guide the Council in such matters.

It became clear over the next few weeks that the Libyans were trying, with a measure of success, to take the non-aligned members for a ride. What they had told the non-aligned members in February turned out to be false. Different and contradictory statements came out from Tripoli every day. At one stage, Russian Foreign Minister Kozyrev, after meeting the Libyan leader, announced in Cairo that Libya was prepared to hand over the suspects to a third country. This was promptly denied by Libya the very next day. The Secretary General sent Under Secretary General Saffronchuk to Tripoli, but even before the latter returned to New York, the Libyan permanent representative told me that the Libyan position had evolved since Saffronchuk's visit! According to him, Libya had filed a case with the International Court of Justice on March 2 and the ICJ had accepted jurisdiction in the matter; should the ICJ decide that Libya must hand over the suspects to UK or US, Libya would do so gladly.

Egypt and Malta were extremely concerned at the possibility of sanctions against Libya. President Hosni Mubarak personally had been very energetic on this issue. The Moroccan king also spoke about it to Bush in New York on January 31. In addition to economic consider-ations, Egypt was preoccupied with the backlash of public opinion; failure to soften American position, despite Egypt being a close ally, would inflame passions among the Egyptian people against the Ameri-cans and strengthen fundamentalist forces. The Maltese ambassador told the President of the Security Council that there was absolutely no evidence that the suitcase with explosives was loaded on the Pan Am flight at the airport in Malta and that if Malta were to make a public statement to that effect, it would knock the bottom out of the Anglo-American case. Hannay told the President that he was most unim-pressed with the Maltese threat!

As it became increasingly clear that the three western countries would propose a draft resolution seeking mandatory sanctions against Libya, Egypt and other countries became active in lobbying against it. Libya continued to harp on its thesis, viz, it had the political will to comply with Resolution 731 and to hand over the suspects. However, there were domestic legal obstacles which prevented it from doing so. Libya showed readiness to hand over the suspects even to the UNDP office in Tripoli!

The non-aligned members decided to consult the Legal Counsel in the UN Secretariat for his expert view regarding the legal implications of Libya's reference to the ICJ on Security Council's competence. The Legal Counsel's opinion, as conveyed to me in my capacity as the caucus co-ordinator, was clear. ICJ and the Security Council were both principal organs of the UN, each with its own competence. ICJ was the highest juridical body and the Council was the highest political body. Neither was subordinate or subservient to the other. Reference to the ICJ did not bar the Council from taking parallel action. This was the legal position; however, the fact that Libya had approached the ICJ could not be ignored. This was the profound opinion of the learned counsel who subsequently went on to become a judge in the ICJ!

On March 10, the three countries conveyed to the non-aligned members their position on how to proceed with Libya. The gist of their presentation was that the Council should consider the next step in the form of mandatory sanctions in three areas: severance of civil aviation links, military embargo, and reducing or closing down Libyan diplomatic and airlines representation abroad. The three governments were not pushing for immediate action but they would not agree to any procedure which would establish a precedent that the Council could not consider a matter which was before the ICJ. Thus, there was no such thing as doctrine of 'sub judice' in international relations!

On March 17, the US, UK, and France produced a draft resolution proposing sanctions against Libya in the three areas mentioned earlier. It caused immense concern all round. Non-members of the Council approached members shaking their heads in disbelief that the permanent members should so blatantly abuse their privileged position. The non-aligned members told the Libyan ambassador candidly that if it was ever ready to surrender the suspects it should do so immediately;

once the sanctions were imposed, it might be impossible to have them lifted even if Libya were to hand over the two persons later. Boutros Ghali told us, the non-aligned members, that he had had about a dozen meetings with different Libyans over the preceding two months, but there was total confusion about Libya's position. He doubted if the Libyan permanent representative had any real mandate to negotiate with anyone in New York. The Secretary General seemed to be fed up with the whole affair.

On March 22, the Libyan ambassador called me at my residence. He sounded excited. He said Major Jalloud, the number two leader in Libya, had informed the Indian ambassador in Tripoli that very day of Libya's decision to hand over the suspects to the Arab League. A delegation of seven Arab foreign ministers would soon be arriving in New York. Within five minutes, the Moroccan ambassador called me to give the same information. He too referred to a report that the Indian ambassador in Tripoli was the recipient of this good news.

The Arab League held an emergency meeting in Cairo on the 22nd and decided to send a delegation of seven foreign ministers to Tripoli. The Libyan ambassador confirmed to the caucus that the suspects would be handed over to the Arab League. As the caucus co-ordinator, I met with the ambassadors of the three countries. They reiterated that they would insist on compliance with Resolution 731. They had no objection if the Secretary General and/or the Arab League served as the transmission belt. Details had to be worked out and clarifications obtained but the suspects had to be tried in America under American laws or in Scotland under Scottish laws. They reminded us that the hand over of the suspects was only one, though the most important one, of their demands; there were others. They said it was essential to obtain a written communication from Libya about their readiness to surrender the suspects to the Arab League. Meanwhile, the Secretary General's advisers had persuaded him to give up the idea of acting as the intermediary. They feared that the Libyans might even set the UNDP office in Tripoli on fire once the suspects were transferred there. The under-standing was that the Libyans would hand over the persons to the Arab League which in turn would hand them over to the Secretary General of the UN, who would then surrender them to the British or the Ameri-cans. But by now, Boutros Ghali did not even wish to set eyes on the suspects. Most of us remained sceptical of Libyan intentions.

When the Arab League delegation went to Tripoli on the 24th, it was ridiculed by the Libyan press for having gone there on such an unholy mission in the holy month of Ramadan! Nobody was surprised that the delegation returned empty-handed. Qaddafi lectured them on international law and sovereignty. We thought the Libyan permanent representative had been disowned by his government and would lose his job. But he said that the Arab League itself had proposed in Tripoli that the whole thing ought to be postponed! Who could discern truth as far as intra-Arab politics was concerned!

As the three governments were pressing ahead with preparing a resolution on sanctions, a new idea came up. Borrowing from Resolu-tion 678 of November 1990 dealing with Iraq, which had given a 45-day grace period to Saddam Hussain, why not include in the sanctions resolution a provision of a moratorium of 20 or 30 days, a pause of goodwill, before the sanctions would take effect? This would convey the sense of the seriousness of the situation to the Libyans and give them time to hand over the suspects. Of course, certain other demands of the three governments were almost impossible to comply to their satisfac-tion such as the one relating to terrorism. Hence, even if Libya were to surrender the suspects, the sanctions would probably still go into effect, but the idea was perhaps worth a try. On 27th evening, the three co-sponsors made changes in the draft, the most significant of which was the inclusion of a pause of goodwill of about two weeks, until April 15, before the sanctions would become operational.

The vote on the Libyan resolution was scheduled for the 30th but was postponed by a day because it coincided with the holiest day for the

Muslims. This was the first time ever that any organ of the United Nations, that too the most important organ, would observe a Muslim holiday and not work on that day. The resolution was adopted as Resolution 748 on the 31st by ten in favour and five abstentions—India, China, Zimbabwe, Morocco, and Cape Verde. The sponsors exercised considerable pressure in the capitals and succeeded in obtaining a couple of positive votes, which made all the difference. Zimbabwe's initial instruction was to vote against, but when it learnt that India and China would abstain, it too decided to abstain. As for India, I was given the discretion to vote against if China did, but I was quite clear that India should abstain even if China voted against. At one stage, I was asked to check with the sponsors whether they would support us if we were to take a similar initiative in respect of the hijackers of the Indian airlines plane in Pakistan, in which case we would vote in favour. I firmly advised the government against it and to stick to abstention. Snoussi, the ambassador of Morocco, lamented that the Arabs were being subjected to a trauma for the second time in less than two years. The Arabs could not understand why the US and UK seemed determined on a course of action guaranteed to inflame fundamentalism throughout the Arab and Muslim world.

After the adoption of Resolution 748, the caucus met with the ambassadors of the three countries to ask them about their requirements in respect of 'terrorism'. Hannay said that they would not mind if the suspects would be handed over in less than direct manner, that is, through the Arab League. If some way could be found to bring them to the courts in Scotland or the US, it would be a massive step forward. He then mentioned some specific demands: surrender of unused timers obtained clandestinely by Libya from Switzerland one of which was used to blow up Pan Am Flight 103, cessation of all support to the Provisional Irish Republican Army (IRA), full details of the contacts and supplies given to IRA, stoppage of all financial and material support to Abu Nidal and other terrorist groups, and so on. The French demand was for Libya to transmit all the documentation asked for by the French judge.

The Secretary General decided to send Under Secretary General Petrovsky to Libya to give them a copy of Resolution 748 and to explain to the Libyans the seriousness of the situation. But on April 2, crowds in the Libyan capital, Tripoli, attacked diplomatic missions of countries that had voted in favour of 748. The Venezuelan embassy was set on fire. The Council met in emergency informal consultations where everyone condemned the incident. The President briefed members about what the Libyan ambassador had told him, viz, that Libya condemned the attacks, the police had used teargas against the mob (apparently for the first time in 22 years), Qaddafi regarded the attack on Venezuelan embassy as an attack on Libya itself and would fully compensate the Venezuelan government. A presidential statement was drafted. Considerable time was spent on whether to use the word 'terrorism' in the statement. Ecuador preferred to say 'violence', but Venezuela insisted on 'terrorism'. Diego Arria explained that terrorism denoted premeditation whereas violence could be spontaneous or unorganised. In the end, the original language 'acts of terrorism and violence' was retained.

The Arab League wrote to the Secretary General suggesting a postponement of the sanctions coming into force, to give more time to its efforts to find a diplomatic solution to the Libyan crisis. At the informal consultations on April 9, the President asked if any member had any observation on the Arab League request. Only China supported the request. The UK and the US reminded everyone that Libya was far from complying with Resolution 731. Without doubt, the sanctions would come into effect on April 15, as they did, not to be removed for a long time, if ever.

It was eventually left to Secretary General Kofi Annan to evolve a formula to settle the Lockerbie affair. The two accused handed themselves over to the United Nations in April 1999. A special court consisting of three Scottish judges was set up in the Netherlands, not in the

International Court of Justice, but in a place called Camp Zeist. The trial was conducted under the Scottish law. The camp was converted into a prison and a court. The trial began in May 2000 and ended in January 2001. In the verdict, the judges convicted one accused, Al Migrani, and acquitted the other, Fhimah. The arguments in support of Migrani's conviction were not very convincing even to the judges!

In October 2002, Libya announced an offer of compensation amounting to $2.7 billion, working out to $10 million for each victim of the Pan Am crash. The trial in Camp Zeist had cost a whopping 75 million pounds, but it was more than matched by the amount of compensation. In August 2003, Libya formally accepted responsibility for the disaster. By this time, Libya was so anxious to end sanctions and its isolation that it was prepared to agree to anything and everything. When France complained about the amount of compensation for the UTA victims being less than that for the Pan Am victims, Libya took little time in offering the same terms to France. As a Libyan minister said, this was a business deal and a price was paid for peace. The Security Council lifted the sanctions on September 12, 2003.

8

HAITI

THE ELECTED PRESIDENT of Haiti, Jean-Bertrand Aristide, a former priest, was overthrown in a military coup at the end of September 1991. Aristide came to the United Nations for help. It took him three years to get back to his presidency. He spent those years in Washington, goading the administration and Congress into taking forceful measures against the Haitian military. He was lucky that Haiti was a neighbour of the United States and he had a weapon in the form of the threat of Haitian refugees swarming Florida. The Americans had to do something to stop the almost certain flow of refugees, and the return of Aristide to Port-au-Prince was essential for that.

Late on September 30, 1991, the President of the Security Council for September, French Ambassador Merimee, called me at my residence in my capacity as President for October. He said he had received a request from the permanent representative of Haiti for an urgent meeting of the Security Council to consider the situation in Haiti following a military coup in which President Aristide had been deposed. Merimee called a consultations meeting for 10:30 in the evening.

When I went to the UN, the First Avenue was packed with Aristide supporters, about 3,000 of them, chanting, dancing, and shouting pro-Aristide slogans and demanding UN support for him. As I entered the building, the British ambassador whispered to me that Merimee had no business to convene the meeting; he could easily have consulted everyone on the phone. I did not blame him for having had to arrive for a meeting at night. He said he had strongly advised Merimee against convening the meeting and had told him that he was against issuing a presidential statement or a resolution. China and the US held similar views.

By this time, Merimee seemed to feel that he had not been wise in convening the consultations. He spoke individually to members in his room. I was the first to be consulted since I was scheduled to take over the presidency within a matter of hours. He showed me a three-para-graph statement and asked if he could issue it. My advice was in the negative; I suggested instead that the Secretary General could be per-suaded to issue the statement as his own, and that he, Merimee, could merely tell the media that he supported the Secretary General. This is what happened in the end.

An interesting procedural point came up. I should have taken over as President one minute past midnight. I was asked whether I would like to assume presidency straight away or if I wanted 'to stop the clock'. I inquired about the precedents of stopping the clock. I was assured there were some, but was not provided any specific examples. I decided to stop the clock for several reasons. Firstly, Merimee had not associated me with his bilateral consultations. This meant that if I took over as President, I would have had to start the process all over again. Secondly, it was clear that Merimee would conclude his consultations latest by about 12.30 p.m. Thirdly, Merimee, as a representative of France, was anxious to conclude the work he had started, given France's special interest in Haiti. This suited me fine since I was not anxious to get involved in the messy situation.

The permanent representative of Haiti called on me on October 2 and indicated a strong desire for a meeting of the Council for the next day. I also received a note from the Secretariat informing me that Aristide wanted to address the Council at 8 p.m. Vorontsov, the Soviet ambassador, was the only one to have expressed reservations to me; his concern was that giving a hearing to Aristide would inevitably drag the Council into the internal affairs of a member state. By the time we met on the 3rd in informal consultations, he too had fallen in line and in fact supported immediate action by the Council in the form of a resolution.

We had to decide whether non-members of the Council should be allowed to speak in the official meeting. We quickly decided in favour. We had to have another round of informal consultations to consider what action, if any, the Council should take following Aristide's address. Many, especially the South American ambassadors, felt it would be disastrous for the prestige of the Council if it were not to respond to him in some form. Ecuador proposed that since a resolution or even a presidential statement might be difficult to prepare and agree upon in a short time, a statement by the President to the media incorporating a few elements would be the most practical and effective means of responding to Aristide's appeal. Vorontsov strongly supported the idea of a resolution, reminding everyone that the Soviet Union was the best expert in the world on coups d'etat! Ashtal of Yemen urged caution against the Council being dragged into the internal affairs of a country; it might constitute a precedent for similar situations in future. He also made the point that to be effective the Council had to act with unanimity.

There was thus a deadlock. I said there was consensus on what the Council should say, but there was a difference on the form in which those sentiments should be expressed. It would be a pity if Aristide were to go away without getting any reaction from the Council. Hannay suggested that I, as president, could immediately convey the sentiments of the Council to Aristide at the official meeting, after Aristide's intervention. I made it clear that I would not negotiate the text of my remarks. This was readily agreed. The official meeting convened at 9.30 p.m. Aristide made an uninspiring speech of about 15 minutes. My response to him was widely appreciated, naturally!

By 1994, Aristide was still in the wilderness, out of power and out of Haiti. The military was ruling the country and the 'international community' had been able to do precisely nothing to reverse the coup. The Security Council adopted its first resolution only on June 16, 1993— Resolution 841—in which it imposed oil and arms embargo against the military regime. These measures had been recommended by the Organisation of American States (OAS). Co-operation between UN and OAS was a marked feature of the Haitian crisis. Resolution 867 of September 23, 1993, established the United Nations Mission in Haiti (UNMIH), following the Governor's Island Agreement of July 23, 1993. The Clinton administration brought Aristide and the military together on Governor's Island, New York, and got them to conclude an agreement in which Raul Cedras, the military strongman gave vague assurances to relinquish power, but found it most bitter to agree to the return of Aristide. The military reneged on the agreement.

On October 11, 1993, USS *Harlan County* sailed to Port-au-Prince with marines to help in the restoration of law and order in Haiti. The ship retreated post haste when a group of Haitian hoodlums fired on it and chased it away. This incident left a deep wound on American pride. President George W. Bush must be having this humiliation in mind when he talks, frequently, about America never again being forced to quit.

Aristide came to see the Secretary General on March 5, 1994. The two of them met alone for 75 minutes. Later, the Secretary General told us that Aristide was against the initiative of the parliamentarians in Haiti, and was negative about and opposed the Governor's Island agreement. He said he had tried to persuade the US president to the contrary, but had failed. Aristide said he had respected the Governor's Island agreement. Even President Bill Clinton admitted that! Only if Cedras left Haiti could the process move forward. The military were the main obstacle. Aristide was unshakeable in his position. His distrust and hatred for Cedras were abundantly evident.

According to Dante Caputo, a former foreign minister of Argentina and the Secretary General's special representative for Haiti, Aristide was obsessed about taking revenge against Cedras and wanted the toughest possible sanctions to be imposed against Haiti and the military. Aristide was convinced that 'suffering' was good for the people. Aristide told Caputo that children in Haiti were being named 'sanctions'! Separately, Aristide told the Secretary General that he had lost confidence in Caputo who, according to Aristide, was working with the CIA and the Haitian rightists, including the army.

US Defence Secretary William Perry came to see the Secretary General on March 24 to exchange views on several issues. On Haiti, he said there was only one solution and he was opposed to it, namely, a military operation by the US. (Perry made a good impression on the Secretary General and others as a modest, unassuming, soft-spoken person, not an 'I-know-it-all' type.)

On April 21, Aristide criticised the American policy towards Haiti as 'racist'. His criticism produced immediate results. Late in the evening of the same day Madeleine Albright gave me a set of talking points, the burden of which was that the US would soon sponsor a draft resolution calling for the resignation of Cedras and company as well as for comprehensive sanctions. Thus, Haitian people would have to continue to be punished because of US domestic compulsions. If there was a secret vote, most members would not support any UN action relating to Haiti since what was happening there was strictly an internal matter for that country and posed no threat to international peace and security. But decisions are taken in the open and countries are anxious not to jeopardise their relations with powerful countries and end up voting in favour of sanctions.

On May 5, the Americans circulated a draft resolution calling for comprehensive sanctions and other tough measures against the military in Haiti. Clinton was being severely criticised for the 'inept' handling of the crisis in Haiti. So he had to yield. He sacked Pezzulo, his point man for Haiti, and no longer ruled out use of force. According to Caputo, the Americans were preparing contingency plans for a military intervention in Haiti. The administration would do everything to improve opinion polls. A quick military action in Haiti, a la Granada, would boost Clinton's image. The US would endeavour to obtain at least OAS's endorsement for what would be a unilateral American intervention. The American assessment at the time was that it would be difficult to get Security Council approval, but they were being unduly and untypically modest about their clout in the Council. Haiti was far too unimportant for Russia and China for them to waste their veto on. The Council adopted the resolution unanimously on May 7.

The reaction of the Haitian military was to arrange for the illegal parliamentarians to elect an 84-year-old former judge as provisional president, thus formally stripping Aristide of his office. Strong rumours were in circulation about the US having prepared a force of 600 marines to land in Haiti to 'restore democracy'. Clinton, who had been under attack by human rights groups, had revised his policy on the forcible repatriation of Haitian refugees. The floodgates would soon be opened. The one thing that the US wanted to avoid and which drove US's Haiti policy from the beginning, namely to prevent the mass influx of Haitian refugees, would happen before long.

Caputo spent a couple of days in Washington in the third week of May and came back convinced that Americans had decided to launch the military intervention in the near future. Aristide would be restored to the presidency; Cedras and company would be exiled; the Americans would get out after a month or so. In the meanwhile, they would try to persuade a few Latin American countries to join in a multilateral peace-keeping force under UN auspices to replace US troops, leaving the UN to hold the baby, a la Somalia. Caputo believed that the Latinos would not oblige the Americans, except perhaps Argentina. (Caputo felt embarrassed about his country's foreign policy of pledging, in advance, whatever the US wanted.) The Secretary General thought, and I agreed with him, that the Americans would not face too many problems in this regard. All of us in the Secretariat were convinced that it would be a disaster for the UN to be saddled with such a mess.

We had an internal meeting about Haiti on June 2. Caputo repeated his earlier conviction that the Americans were committed to a military expedition and that the UN would have to take care of 'Rosemary's baby'. He said we, the UN, should not oblige the U.S. The question was: was there anything the UN could or should do? Alvaro De Soto, the Secretary General's adviser for Latin America, suggested that we should prepare a list, pointing out all the things that would have to be done post-restoration of democracy, such as rebuilding of the army and police, judiciary, economy, and so on. Further, we should present the list to the US and other 'friends of Haiti' to place our position on record. ('Friends of Haiti' was an informal but recognised group of five countries—US, Canada, France, Argentina and Venezuela.)

The Secretary General did not want a confrontation with the US on this issue. I agreed, adding that if the matter was of such vital importance to the US they would go ahead irrespective of other's reservations. But we all agreed that we must somehow place our views on record. Towards the end of the meeting, Caputo told us that Leon Wirth, senior adviser to Vice-President Al Gore, had categorically told him, over a glass of Scotch, that Cedras would be informed about the military action 8 hours in advance. Caputo believed that Aristide would condemn the invasion but return to Haiti a month or so later. Aristide would never agree to write a letter to Clinton inviting the US help to restore democracy in his country but would be happy to oblige the Americans by going back to Haiti. We decided that the Secretary General would write a letter to Secretary of State Warren Christopher and we would discuss the matter again a few days later.

The author presiding over the Security Council meeting on Haiti. Secretary General Perez de Cuellar is on his right. On his left is Saffronchuk, the Director in Charge of Security Council in the Secretariat.

A week later we reviewed the matter. At our earlier meeting, I had expressed some reservation about the Secretary General writing a letter to Christopher. I was not in favour of the Secretariat taking any initiative; it was for member states to react if the US decided to intervene. The Secretary General observed, 'Are you suggesting that we should do nothing and that we should just sit back and enjoy while being violated?' My response was, 'We did not have to enjoy it!' Anyway, it was decided that a letter should be drafted. My reservation remained, but I was in a minority of one. All others—Goulding, Alvaro and Caputo— were in favour. Fortunately, Aime, the Secretary General's Chief of Staff, himself a Haitian, spoke up strongly against the letter. Eventually, the Secretary General decided not to send the letter. I had anticipated that the Secretary General would not want to go out of his way to annoy the US even though the election of the Secretary General was still two and a half years away. In any case, it would be wrong for any Secretary General to write such a letter. I asked Caputo whether Aristide would like to return to Haiti on an American tank. Caputo was very clear. Aristide, he said, would gladly accept a ride on an American tank and condemn the Americans the very next day.

By about June 10, it appeared to us in the Secretariat that the US had abandoned the idea of military intervention in Haiti for the time being. Instead, they decided to give more time for the sanctions to work. More and more doubts were being expressed in the op-ed pages of the *New York Times* and *Washington Post* about the advisability of a military venture. Another reason must have been the reluctance of the countries in the hemisphere to help out the US by agreeing to participate in the invasion of Haiti, merely to lend respectability to US action; they were ready to send military personnel *after* democracy had been restored through peaceful means.

Late in June, the Americans drafted a resolution on Haiti asking the Secretary General to make recommendations regarding a new mandate for UNMIH which would include assisting the legitimate government of Haiti (after it was restored to power) in maintaining law and order, protecting international presence, protecting senior government leaders, and so on. Earlier, the Secretary General had submitted a report drafted in such a way as to accommodate the US concerns. Vorontsov dug in his heels, in an act of defiance to the Americans. The Russians were fed up with being treated without respect by the Americans, particularly at their insensitivity to issues of concern to the Russians. Vorontsov got his chance when Mrs. Albright came to the Council with her resolution on Haiti. He said unless the Council 'welcomed' Russian and CIS 'help' to Georgia in dealing with the Abkhaz situation, he would not agree to the US draft on Haiti. Hannay offered some clever, technical points, which Mrs. Albright promptly supported, as to why the Russian proposal was not appropriate 'at this time'. But Vorontsov, veteran that he was at these games, openly and repeatedly, spoke of double standards and reminded everyone of the French intervention in Rwanda just the previous week. Mrs. Albright was disconcerted. She badly needed the Haiti resolution, which was not at all a straightforward one. Vorontsov won the substance of his point. The resolution on Georgia/Abkhazia noted with satisfaction the initial deployment of the CIS forces.

On July 11 the Haitian military authorities asked the International Civilian Mission in Haiti (MICIVIH) to close down and ordered its staff to leave within 48 hours. (MICIVIH was a joint UN–OAS operation set up by the General Assembly as opposed to UNMIH which was established by the Security Council. Its mission was to monitor the human rights situation in Haiti.) The Secretary General consulted with the acting Secretary General of OAS. They decided they had no alternative but to close down the mission since the paramount concern was the safety of the personnel. (The OAS official, on return to Washington, said to his constituents that it was Boutros Ghali who insisted on evacuating the staff!) The action of the military regime strengthened the

222

pro-invasion lobby in Washington. Strobe Talbot was said to be the most hawkish on this issue.

The Secretariat was in a dilemma. The American game plan was to launch their own military invasion (for which 2000 marines had carried out a much-publicised mock exercise the previous week), drive out Raul Cedras, Francois Mitchel and company, and hand over the baby to an expanded UNMIH. They had approached a number of countries in the region, and also as far as West Africa, for potential troop contributions. Indeed, their entire plan depended upon the UN taking over from them in a relatively short time of two to three months. They knew only too well that there was no way the UN could raise the required troops in such a short time frame. They, therefore, took it upon themselves to find the troops for the UN.

The whole thing was blatantly unprincipled. The US concern remained with the influx of refugees, and that too with black refugees. William Gray, Clinton's Advisor on Haiti, an African American, admitted in a TV show on July 11 that there was an element of racism involved in this affair. There was very little support for the invasion in the US as far the Secretariat could judge. The Republicans were opposed and the Democrats, at best, were divided. The only way in which the administration could soften the opposition was by getting the UN involved in the operation. The UN must allow itself to be used in the service of the US! True, the political decision would be taken by the Council and there was no doubt that the US would have its way. But the members would act only on the basis of a report that the Secretary General would have to furnish before July 15.

The Secretary General wished to avoid a confrontation with the Americans on an issue of such vital importance to them. At the same time, he was keen to protect the organisation's credibility. He issued strict instructions, during an internal meeting, not to discuss the report with the Americans. (He seemed to be aware of the practice in the 'House' of showing reports in advance to the countries most interested in a particular subject. Thus, the Moroccans and the Algerians, even the Polisario Front, knew well in advance, even before the concerned senior UN officials did, the contents of the report on Western Sahara. The department dealing with the report felt that it would only be prudent to get the principal interested country, particularly if it happened to be a major power, on board before the report was officially circulated.) The task of the Secretariat would become easier if Aristide was to support the whole plan, but he had made it clear to the Secretary General, twice on telephone and once in writing, that he was opposed to the whole scheme. The Secretary General was duty bound to reflect Aristide's views in the report; after all, it was not going to be a Chapter VII operation and a request or at least consent of the legitimate authority of the country—in this case Aristide—was a pre-requisite for a Chapter VI action. The Secretary General's instinct was to include the gist of Aristide's position in the report. He asked three of his aides—Goulding, Kofi Annan, and me—to prepare the report and admonished us not to write it in such a way that 'only I come out as the bad boy'!

The report was distributed in good time. (Paul Lewis of the *New York Times* got a copy even before the members of the Council did. The Secretary General believed that Lewis paid for the reports.) It was written mainly by Goulding but the Secretary General had a substantial contribution in it. It was a courageous report, not likely to or calculated to please the Americans. The Secretary General said categorically in the report that he did not recommend expanding UNMIH up to 15,000 troops because it was impossible to obtain and deploy such a large number within the stipulated time frame. The report said clearly that the traditional principle of no country providing more than about one-third of the total troop strength must not be violated since it would have implications for other operations (such as in Georgia). This point was aimed at the US as the Americans were certain to provide the bulk of any intervention force. Thus, Boutros Ghali did not hesitate to take an independent position on a matter which was of tremendous importance to the US. At one point when I suggested moderating the language of one paragraph, he said, 'Don't worry, I will take the responsibility.' To my surprise and relief, Warren Christopher called the Secretary General at about 5.15 p.m. on July 15. While he did not praise the report, he did convey implicit satisfaction. He requested the Secretary General to defend the report publicly as he had defended French action in Rwanda. In other words, the Americans wanted the Secretary General's help in softening domestic opposition! I complimented the Secretary General on all this. His response was, 'Ambassador Gharekhan, there is no such thing as gratitude in international relations; member states would never acknowledge gratitude.'

For some inexplicable reason, the American reception of the Haiti report was not very unfriendly, as we had expected. On the contrary, they seemed quite pleased. They wanted the Secretary General to recommend a full-fledged UN operation under Chapter VI, whereas the report categorically rejected a UN operation and proposed a multinational force (MNF) under Chapter VII. The Secretary General thought the US accepted the report because they did not wish to create a precedent which the Russians could exploit many times over with the members of Commonwealth of Independent States (CIS). The Vice-President of Dominican Republic came to the Secretary General and told him that Cedras would be prepared to hand over his resignation to the Secretary General but not to Aristide or the Americans.

By the fourth week of July, the US was quite advanced in its preparation for an invasion of Haiti. The flow of refugees had almost died down but there were other grounds such as threat to the lives of 3,000 Americans in Haiti, involvement of Cedras and others in drug trafficking for which they might be wanted in the US courts, and so on. (The analogy with Panama and General Manuel Noriega came immediately to mind.) On the other hand, Mrs. Albright was working hard to draft a resolution and drum up support for it. She produced a draft which selectively quoted from the Secretary General's report. There were several bad features in the draft. For example, the commander (an American) would report directly to the Council on the establishment of a secure environment—an unheard of thing all these years since UN force commanders report only to the Secretary General. Goulding and Annan discussed the draft with Mrs. Albright and pointed out the shortcomings. She clearly conveyed that her government was fed up with the Secretary General and that she would insist on the draft irrespective of what the Secretary General thought.

On the evening of July 26, the Secretary General told me that I would have to make a statement in the consultations meeting on July 27, firmly setting forth our misgivings on the Haiti draft, and emphasising that the provision regarding the force commander reporting directly to the Council was illegal. I winced at this tough and unpleasant instruction. I told him it was up to the Council to take any decisions it liked. He disagreed, and I must confess he was right. Apart from personal unpleasantness, I was concerned at the prospect of open and bitter confrontation not just with US but with the entire Council. Goulding and Aime were equally distressed. The latter said the Secretary General could not afford a running confrontation with the US. Fortunately, the US had not managed, by July 27, to get its friends to fall in line with their draft. We decided to wait for the final draft before speaking to the Secretary General again. Mrs. Albright called me at 3 p.m. on the 27th and requested me not to say anything on the draft during the consultations since the draft was still being negotiated. I complied with her request. At the consultations, many members raised doubts and reservations, two important ones being the request or at least consent of Aristide and the Secretary General's role in recommending transition from phase one to phase two. Later in the afternoon, Albright met with Goulding and Caputo and accepted many amendments to the crucial paragraphs and one to include a reference to Aristide's letter requesting assistance in a preambular paragraph.

But she insisted on an American force commander and the Secretary General continued to reject that.

According to Caputo, the Americans had not even spoken to Aristide about the letter. If Aristide refused to give the letter, the US would have a problem on its hands. Caputo had very poor opinion of the professional and technical competence of the American negotiators in New York, an opinion which the Secretary General shared. At the consultations on 27th afternoon, Mrs. Albright praised the Secretary General's report which she said was the result of many hours of consultations between UN and US representatives! Boutros Ghali was quite upset when I told him about it. Again, according to Caputo, the Americans told the 'friends' that the UN agreed with their draft resolution; they told UN that the 'friends' agreed and they told Aristide that UN and 'friends' agreed!

The Council held consultations on Haiti from 6 p.m. to 11 p.m. on the 28th. The amendments worked out by Goulding and Mrs. Albright were accepted by the Secretary General on condition that Aristide would convey, in writing, his acceptance of the resolution and that the Secretary General would not appoint an American as commander of UNMIH after the departure of the multinational force. The Pentagon was insisting on that. During the consultations, Mrs. Albright repeatedly stated that the two paragraphs had been accepted by the Secretary General and, hence, ought not to be disturbed. (She also mentioned the Secretary General's condition about Aristide's letter.) A number of useful suggestions were made by Spain, New Zealand, Russia, and others. The Americans could have accepted at least some of them, but did not. One of the amendments was to qualify member states participating in the multinational force as those co-operating with the legitimate authority of Haiti (along the lines of Resolution 678—member states co-operating with Kuwait). Another was to give a grace or goodwill period to Cedras as even Saddam Hussein was given a grace period of 45 days.

The Council adopted the resolution—Resolution 940—on Haiti on July 31—12 in favour, 2 abstentions China and Brazil. (Rwanda was not participating in the Council.) The previous two days, the Council held consultations late into the night. It was clear that most members were unhappy at what they were being asked to approve, but the US had its way. The US accepted a few cosmetic changes which Nigeria and New Zealand could use to justify their support (much like what I used to do as India's representative!) Vorontsov asked many questions about the figure of 6,000 for UNMIH, but I refused to answer them on the ground that it was the sponsors of the draft who had proposed the number. Mrs. Albright, thereupon, made some rude remarks about the Secretariat. She told me after the meeting that her rude remarks were not aimed at me but at the Secretary General. And Vorontsov told me that his remarks were aimed not at the Secretariat but at Mrs. Albright! The Secretariat was fair game for everyone.

I told the Secretary General that the resolution was very unpopular in South America. Not a single country from the region supported it except Argentina. Mexico, Venezuela, and even Uruguay had publicly spoken against it. Brazil had abstained despite tremendous American pressure.

In my view, the Secretary General's report, on which the resolution was based, suffered from three drawbacks. (a) The Secretary General categorically rejected the option of a traditional peacekeeping operation under UN command and control. He should have merely mentioned the difficulties and recent experience in obtaining the necessary resources without giving his own recommendation against it; leave it to the Council to reject it. (b) We should have said that further diplomatic efforts should have been made to find a solution. (c) The Secretary General himself should not have put forward the option of a multinational force. There was one more thing. In his letter, Aristide had clearly indicated that he wanted the strength of UNMIH to be the same as mentioned in the Governor's Island agreement, namely, 1,200.

The Secretary General asked me about this letter, after the resolution was adopted. I reminded him that we had agreed, after lengthy discussion, not to mention this letter in the report. I learnt later from Aime that the Secretary General had decided not to send the letter to the Council President at the strong personal request of Mrs. Albright. No wonder the Americans were so happy with the report! For the first time, I saw the Secretary General somewhat on the defensive when Aime and I discussed some of these points with him on August 1. I told him we would have to be very careful when the time came for transition from multinational to UN operation. The situation would be readymade for a clash between the UN and US. Aime thought the Haiti resolution would haunt the UN for a long time. Even the *New York Times* criticised the resolution editorially on August 2.

Having got their resolution, the Americans did not seem to know what use to make of it. They were hoping, and they said so, that the mere fact of the resolution would persuade Cedras to leave Haiti. That did not happen and no one expected it would. Strobe Talbot wanted to fix a deadline for Cedras to leave or else. But Defence Secretary Perry strongly disapproved giving any ultimatums; he had always been opposed to the idea of invading Haiti. The US no doubt felt isolated. Before the resolution was adopted, they had commitment from Argentina to send a contingent to join the multinational force. But President Menem, evidently under internal pressure, reneged on his commitment. (It was a clear commitment. The Argentinean ambassador, Emilio Cárdenas, had openly and voluntarily confirmed it during informal consultations.) He said Argentina would send a contingent to the UN-led UNMIH but not to the US-led multinational force. Even Menem could not afford to toe the US line for fear of being isolated in the region. Canada also refused to join. The Americans tried to persuade even Israel to help them out, but without success!

The 'four sponsors' of 940 came to see the Secretary General on August 11. (This was a new grouping as opposed to 'friends' which had five members. Venezuela had completely disassociated itself from the initiative of the other four—US, Canada, France, and Argentina—which led to 940.) The US was looking for a way out so that it would not have to mount the invasion. They suggested that the Secretary General should send someone to Haiti in a last-ditch effort to persuade Cedras and company to leave Haiti in a peaceful manner. The Secretary General readily agreed and even asked me to inform the Council about it and De Soto to announce it to the media. His condition was that it would be *his* initiative and that it would be a Secretariat mission. In the afternoon, however, Mrs. Albright called De Soto to say that she did not have a green signal from Washington for the idea. This was strange since she had personally come to see the Secretary General along with the other three.

The whole thing was mysterious. Reuters reported in the afternoon that Caputo would lead the mission. Caputo told me that he certainly would not be going. Because of all this confusion, no announcement was made. We had a peculiar situation. We had a special representative with whom the Head of State, namely Aristide would not talk. Caputo would not talk to Cedras; he had not been to Haiti in months. The Americans were very happy with him.

The Secretary General's mind was always racing ahead of others. He was seldom satisfied with keeping to one suggestion or initiative in its original form. He always wanted to modify, improve, amend. The result, often, was that if we had discussed something with him one day, he invariably came up with a revised, at times considerably revised, version the following morning. His was a very creative mind which did not always help him win too many friends.

The 'sponsors' of the Haiti resolution suggested to the Secretary General to send someone to Haiti to talk to the military there. The Secretary General agreed and made it his own initiative. Mrs. Albright made it clear to him that all that the emissary would do would be to ask three questions to Cedras: Where do you want to go? How soon do you want to go? Can we help you get there? The Secretary General agreed, but inevitably the idea took on a life of its own. He thought in terms of a multi-phase mission, which would not necessarily confine itself to asking those questions. Invariably, there would be negotiations and the Americans would become unhappy. The Secretary General thought of not sending Caputo in the first phase. The problem was complicated because Caputo was persona non grata to Cedras. So, a lower level official would be sent in the first instance. In this process, the original purpose of the sponsors would become at best only one of the inputs. The Secretary General insisted he would personally check with Aristide for his reaction before sending anyone. The US would have wished to do the checking out for the Secretary General, but he insisted on doing it himself. He did that, for 45 minutes, on telephone. Aristide's position was that the only objective of the mission should be to tell Cedras to leave within a certain number of days, or else.

One school of thought was that the US would not like this mission to succeed, since they could then justify a military intervention to the Congress and to their public opinion. The other view was that the Americans would welcome a successful outcome, since it would make it unnecessary for them to launch an unpopular invasion. The sponsors of 940 came to see the Secretary General on August 23. The Americans in particular were feeling nervous at the 'pre-mission' which the Secretary General had decided to send to Haiti in advance of the main mission which would be led by Caputo/Goulding. Rolf Knutson, Director in the Executive Office of the Secretary General, would constitute the 'pre-mission'.

The US was anxious that Knutson should not engage in any discussion except the modalities of the military's departure; he should, in fact, only prepare for Caputo's mission. The Secretary General said he agreed 100 per cent. However, he added the media might distort the purpose of the pre-mission and even the Haitian military might do that. The mission as well as the pre-mission would have to play it by the ear. Mrs. Albright said it should be made clear to the military that the presence of the mission did not mean recognition of the regime. The US also was not in favour of giving too large a role to the Dominican Republic. The Secretary General retorted that this was tantamount to micro-management. 'I urge you not to interfere in all those details.' Caputo emphasised the need for a credible threat of use of military force without which he saw no possibility of the military agreeing to anything.

Knutson returned from Haiti on August 29, having 'failed bitterly', in his own words, in his mission. He met the foreign minister of Dominican Republic, an old friend of the Secretary General, who assured him there would be no problem in arranging a meeting for Knutson with Cedras. But the emissaries of the Dominican Republic came back from Port-au-Prince with a message that the Haitian military would not receive Knutson. However, the president of the Senate and the speaker of the lower house were ready to come to Santo Domingo, secretly if preferred, to meet Knutson. They added that they would talk to Knutson about their plan for national reconciliation. Knutson's brief was limited and specific: to talk to the military only about their willingness to receive the high-level visit (Caputo) to discuss the peaceful implementation of 940. In the circumstances, the Secretary General decided that Knutson would return to New York. The authorities in Dominican Republic believed that the military in Haiti simply were not convinced that US was prepared to mount an invasion any time soon. They also believed that the most influential member of the ruling troika in Haiti was Philippe Biamby, not Cedras or Francois. The Secretary General decided to inform the Council that his initiative had failed.

By middle of September, Haiti was moving towards a climax. The Americans were getting ready to launch the invasion within a matter of a few days. Clinton, in his address to the nation on September 15, ruled out any discussion with the dictators who, he said, had to leave immediately. But he announced the very next day that President Jimmy Carter would go to Haiti on September 17 for talks with the 'de factos'. Carter would be accompanied by Colin Powell, former Chairman of the

Joint Chiefs, and Senator Sam Nunn, Chairman of the Senate Armed Services Committee. At the same time, about 2000 US troops would stand ready to deploy. The US had managed to put together an international coalition of 24 countries.

The Americans had been talking to DPKO. They wanted to blur the distinction between phases I and II. Pentagon officials were saying openly that theirs was one integral plan; it was only the UN Secretary General and the Security Council that were talking of phases. Thus, the US wanted to start the police training almost the day the MNF moved in whereas according to Resolution 940 police training was the responsibility of UNMIH in phase II. The US plan was to set up an interim police force of 3,000—half to come from the existing armed forces, after checking their human rights records, and the other half to be recruited from the Haitian refugees in Guantanamo. One Cherubin, former police chief of Aristide, believed to be deeply tainted with human rights violations during Aristide's brief active tenure, went to Guantanamo to recruit the police. A certain potential source of conflict was the decision that the police recruited by Cherubin would be armed and the others would not.

After nearly 22 hours of negotiations on 17/18 September, Carter signed a brief agreement with Emile Jonassaint, the 'President' of Haiti on the 18th. As a consequence, American troops started to move into Haiti in a co-operative mode rather than in a hostile environment. The agreement was the subject of massive controversy. Even after 48 hours, Aristide refused to endorse it. The main point of criticism was that Cedras and others were given one month till October 15 to resign their posts and even after that date they were not required to leave Haiti. US officials said that Cedras and others would find it practically impossible to stay on in Haiti once Aristide returned. But what they wanted to know was: would Aristide return so long as Cedras had not left the country? The US military in Haiti had to depend upon the co-operation of Haitian military! Clinton had had to moderate his rhetoric about 'dictators' and 'de factos'. Clinton had already ordered the 82nd Airborne, on September 18, to move into Haiti and the troops were on the move in 61 aircraft. He claimed that it was this act that finally persuaded Cedras to agree to leave. Carter said he had no idea of this development and that it almost derailed his negotiations. Carter had to feel that this achievement would finally clinch the Nobel peace prize for him.

Clinton told the Secretary General on September 25 that Aristide would return to Haiti on October 15. Aristide confirmed it in his address to the UN on October 4. He had been making the right noises about no vengeance, no bloodshed, and so on. The American operation went well. Michel Francois, the police chief, left Haiti for Santo Domingo. UNMIH reported that Cedras might leave on October 7. Parliament would not announce general amnesty and would not grant amnesty to military leaders, as was agreed in the Carter-brokered deal on September 18. Cedras was liable to be arrested and charged with serious criminal actions.

The Secretary General finally agreed to appoint an American general as commander of UNMIH in phase II. Clinton had made a personal request to the Secretary General on September 25. At that time, Boutros Ghali had merely promised to think about it. It was not fair or reasonable to expect the Secretary General, any Secretary General, to resist a direct request from the president of the US. The Secretary General's relations with US improved, distinctly, during those days. Haiti, no doubt, contributed to the improvement.

Mrs. Albright introduced a draft presidential statement on Haiti on October 13, welcoming the return of Aristide to Haiti and commending the contribution of the MNF. When China objected to the commendation, Mrs. Albright exploded, 'How can anyone object to the countries contributing to the restoration of democracy, an objective which the Council had consistently expounded, being commended for it? In that case, US would not want a statement at all.'

Brazil had a more fundamental objection. Ambassador Sardenberg said that Brazil opposed the very concept of MNF occupying any coun-

234

try in the region. That was why Brazil had abstained on Resolution 940 and that was why Brazil could not support the statement. Many people thought Brazil would come around, but Sardenberg held his ground. He said, referring to Mrs. Albright, that every draft had to be subjected to the usual give and take; nobody could impose any text on a take-it-or-leave-it basis. For once, a non-permanent member won. The US converted the statement into a resolution so that Brazil and China could abstain. When the time for vote came, however, only Brazil abstained. Cedras was allowed to go unpunished to Panama in the early hours of October 13. The US unfroze his bank accounts and rented his houses in Port-au-Prince.

Haiti's travails would never end, it seemed. Aristide made a mess of his tenure. The American troops, which had gone on 'Operation Restore Democracy' in September 1994, finally left only in early 2000. Aristide, whom the Americans had restored to office in 1994, was coerced into leaving in 2004 by the same Americans!

The UN should never have been involved in Haiti. The situation there, while horrible for the long-suffering people, was not one which threatened other countries. The only country which was affected by the events in Haiti was the United States, since the refugees would start arriving in Florida. But it was not like the situation in the former East Pakistan in 1971 when 10 million refugees 'invaded' India. Most people believed that there was an element of racism in American attitude since the Haitian refugees were all black. The Haitian experience also brought out the latent tensions between Latin America and the US, the latter not always having its way. It was revealing the way Russia blatantly bargained a plus point for itself in return for agreeing to the American draft and how China could not be much bothered so long as its 'interests', namely Taiwan, were not affected. Perhaps the real lesson is for the people, or rather, the leaders of Haiti. Unless they genuinely reform their ways and give up short-sighted, selfish policies, their country will never come out of the extreme poverty which has been its lot for the past half century.

9

RWANDA GENOCIDE

THE MERE MENTION of Rwanda evokes horrible images of hate-filled and machete-wielding Rwandans, mowing down fellow Rwandans whose only crime was that they belonged to another tribe, the minority Tutsis. The word 'Rwanda' has become synonymous with 'genocide' just as 'Khmer Rouge' in Cambodia immediately brings to mind pictures of piles of human skulls, neatly arranged one on top of the other. It is also associated with the failure of the United Nations to prevent the massacres and protect the lives of helpless men, women, and children. Somalia too is associated with the failure of the United Nations. The difference is that there was no genocide, no targeting of only one particular tribe or religion in Somalia, and the UN as such was not blamed for the massacres which were the consequence of the personal rapaciousness and ambitions of Somali warlords.

Rwanda, like its neighbour Burundi, got its independence from Belgium in 1962. They are both two-tribe nations. Hutus have a majority of nearly 85 per cent in each, with the Tutsis accounting for the balance of the population. The Tutsis, though in a minority, occupied most of the senior positions in the government and the army; they were supposed to be the favourites of the colonial power. Even during the Belgian era, tribal rivalries erupted from time to time and large-scale killings took place. The presence of security forces of the colonial power, which obviously had all the enforcement and coercive authority and resources they needed, did not prevent bloody tribal conflicts. Belgium was not known to be a particularly enlightened colonial power; no colonial power is. But the Belgian rule was particularly known for not doing enough to prepare the populations for independence. In the Congo, for example, there were only 13 graduates in the whole country, with a population of 13 million, at the time of its independence in 1960. All the three countries—Congo, Rwanda, and Burundi—are far from being settled after more than 40 years of independence. It would not be fair to hold Belgium alone responsible for this state of affairs, but it must share some of the blame.

On August 4, 1993, the Hutu-dominated Government of Rwanda and the opposition Rwanda Patriotic Forces (RPF)—the Tutsi army based, trained, and equipped in neighbouring Uganda—signed the Arusha Peace Agreement under the sponsorship of President Julius Nyerere of Tanzania. It provided for a major UN role in the transition period leading up to democratic elections. The Security Council established the United Nations Assistance Mission in Rwanda (UNAMIR) in October 1993, with a strength of 2,548 personnel to be deployed in stages. By December, 1,260 personnel had been deployed in the country.

General Dallaire, the Canadian Force Commander of UNAMIR, sent a most immediate and top secret coded signal to the DPKO on January 11, 1994. It was a highly significant communication and became the subject of much scrutiny and debate in later years. In it, Dallaire reported that he had been put in contact with an informant by a 'very very important government politician'. The informant was a 'top level trainer with the cadre of Interahamwe—the armed militia' of the ruling party. According to the informant, he was in charge of the demonstrations the previous Saturday which aimed to target prominent Tutsi parliamentarians as well as Belgian soldiers. The idea was to provoke a civil war. He said that the president of the country was not in full control over all the elements of his party. He offered to take UNAMIR to the arms caches hidden all over the city. He admitted he was anti-Tutsi but was opposed to killings. He said hostilities might resume in case the political deadlock was resolved. In return, he asked for protection for himself and his family consisting of his wife and four children.

Dallaire proposed taking action within the next 36 hours and recommended giving protection to the informant. He was, however, not naive. He said he had reservations about 'the sudden change of heart' in the informant and proposed to check personally with the 'very very important political person' the following morning. He added: 'The possibility of a trap could not be excluded, as this may be a set-up against the very very important political person.' When he sent his cable, Dallaire had not yet consulted his civilian chief, the special representative of the Secretary General. Given Dallaire's reservations and DPKO's judgement that UNAMIR had neither the mandate nor the resources to undertake the kind of operation he was suggesting, he was asked to consult the special representative and brief the ambassadors in Kigali of USA, France, and Belgium.

The UN is a leaky organisation. The fact of the cable became known in due course. Questions were asked by the media and delegations about what action was taken by the Secretariat on the warning given by the force commander and why the Security Council had not been briefed about it. Countries that had served on the Council at the time were particularly excited about the cable as it gave them an alibi for not having lived up to their obligation to maintain peace and security.

On page 32, paragraph 86, of the United Nations Blue Book on Rwanda, published in 1996, the Secretary General says that 'On the same day, (namely January 11) in New York, my Special Adviser briefed the Security Council on the reports which had been received from UNAMIR and on the actions the UN had taken in response'. This infuriated some members of the Security Council whose alibi for inaction on Rwanda was destroyed by the single sentence in the book. The media in some of those countries went to town against their governments. Ambassadors sought appointment with the Secretary General to seek clarification, denying the Council had ever been taken into confidence by the Secretariat about the contents of the cable. This is where the practice of not keeping official records of informal consultations showed its worth. There was nothing to prevent the Secretary General from claiming that the Council *had* been briefed, since it said so in the Blue Book.

The ambassadors came to see me since I was the Special Adviser referred to in the Blue Book, and the only one, besides the Secretary General and the head of the DPKO, who could have briefed the Council. I was the personal representative of the Secretary General—his eyes, ears, and voice in the Council—and as such spoke for the Secretariat and regularly kept the members of the Council informed of all the developments in all the peacekeeping operations. The delegations claimed that their own records showed absolutely no indication that I had briefed the Council on the date mentioned in the book. At one such meeting with the ambassador of the Czech Republic, the Secretary General asked me to confirm the veracity of the sentence in the book. I, in all honesty, could neither confirm nor deny the claim in the book; after all, the allusion was to something that was supposed to have happened two years ago. I checked my own notes which I used to write fairly regularly and which provide the main source for this book, but I had no notes at all for the period under question. I maintained that if the Blue Book said something, it must have been so. It was entirely possible, I added, that the Council might have been briefed a day or two after the date mentioned in the book. This made neither the ambassador nor the Secretary General happy; the latter told me, after the ambassador had left, that I ought to have corroborated the statement in the Blue Book unreservedly. The controversy was never resolved. It might have cost the Secretary General loss of some credibility.

The fact remains, however, that the major countries that were on the Security Council in 1994 had a pretty good idea, better than the Secretary General, of what was going on in Rwanda. All of them had embassies in Kigali. Dallaire had been specifically asked to brief the ambassadors of Belgium, France, and US. These countries, especially the most powerful among them, were determined not to get involved in the mess in Rwanda either on their own or through the UN. The US even shunned using the term 'genocide' for what was going on in Rwanda. It was Boutros Ghali who had the courage to describe the events as 'genocide' and was reprimanded by the US for having said so. The US and its allies used their clout in the Council not only to prevent a reinforcement of the UN peacekeeping contingent, as requested by Dallaire, but to reduce its size to a level which was guaranteed to fail to prevent any bloodbath in the country.

UNAMIR reached the strength of 2,539 by March 22, 1994. On March 30, the Secretary General drew Security Council's attention to the fast-deteriorating situation in Kigali. The spark that would ignite the genocide was lit on April 6. The presidents of Rwanda and Burundi were killed in an air crash over Kigali airport that day. They were returning from Dar es Salaam after attending a summit meeting of the regional countries which the president of Tanzania had summoned to persuade them to make the necessary political concessions in the interest of peace and harmony. It had been a successful meeting, and the very success of the meeting perhaps was the signal the planners of the massacres were waiting for. The aircraft was brought down by a rocket fired from the vicinity of the airport. No definitive conclusions have been reached regarding the culpability for this terrorist act. There is, however, wide consensus that Hutu extremists, the Interahamwe militia, were responsible. They were not happy with the president who was a moderate Hutu and who was inclined to reach political accommodation with the Tutsis.

As on April 7, Burundi was calm. But Rwanda was in the throes of widespread violence. The 600–700 strong presidential guard was on rampage. They killed the prime minister and many other personalities. Thirteen Belgian soldiers belonging to UNAMIR were kidnapped of whom three were killed on the spot. Only two days earlier the Security Council had extended the mandate of UNAMIR by four months. The Arusha Peace Agreement, which UNAMIR was to implement, was dead.

During the following days, the massacres continued. The French and Belgian paratroops went to Kigali to evacuate foreign nationals. The French strongly emphasised in the Council on April 9 that they did not want any support or endorsement for their action from the Council. Since the Arusha peace process had been abandoned by everybody, the Council had to decide what to do about UNAMIR.

The Secretary General was in Europe in the second week of April. I was with him. Kinkel, the foreign minister of Germany, told him that Germany had got all its nationals out of Rwanda except 11 journalists who had refused to leave; they would have to be looked after by UNAMIR which might have to fly them out by helicopter. The Secretary General took credit for keeping the situation in Burundi calm. He added Rwanda had no government, like in Somalia, and UNAMIR might have to stay in the country for a year or two. He observed that when Bill Clinton came to power he was pro-UN. 'But when he was told by some conservative Americans that I was deciding US foreign policy, he distanced himself from the UN.'

The foreign minister of Belgium came to see the Secretary General in Bonn. He was in a 'state'. He said the RPF was taking over Kigali. Belgium was going through traumatic times. The 10 Belgian paratroopers captured earlier by the presidential guards were killed in a gruesome manner. He asked for the Secretary General's help. He said, 'Even if you can say that you would investigate the situation it would greatly help at home. There is strong anti-Belgian sentiment in Rwanda. Belgium is accused of being pro-RPF. UNAMIR still controls the airport. All the embassies have closed. The Belgian ambassador stayed till 3 in the morning and then left under UNAMIR protection. UNAMIR itself is in danger. The Ghanaian contingent of UNAMIR has fled to Uganda. If RPF gains control of Kigali, the French would leave immediately. UNAMIR should at least suspend its activity if not leave. UNAMIR should withdraw by road to Tanzania and Nairobi; if it leaves by air, it would have to leave behind all the equipment and arms. Even with UNAMIR presence in the country, 20,000 people have already been killed.' The Secretary General asked if he could inform the Council that Belgium wanted to withdraw its 400-strong contingent from UNAMIR. The foreign minister confirmed this and said his country would prefer to withdraw its contingent as part of a collective decision. 'They will all be massacred. RPF has six to nine thousand very well-organised and equipped troops.' He added, 'The RGF (Rwanda Government Forces, mostly Hutu) has its most important camp about 2 km from the airport. It was probably they who had brought down President Habyarimana's aircraft since they were opposed to the Arusha Agreement.'

I forwarded the Secretary General's recommendations to the Security Council on April 14 from Europe. Based on the recommendations, the Council was expected to take a decision on UNAMIR on the 15th. As was often the case, the Council did not want to take the responsibility but preferred the Secretary General to take the onus of making a recommendation. The Council could then agree to the Secretary General's recommendation. We suggested two alternatives. The Secretary General had to be prudent. What he would really have liked to propose was an increase in UNAMIR's strength by about 3,000 troops and keep UNAMIR in Rwanda for at least another year. Since the Council would not agree to such a large increase (or even a smaller one), the Secretary General would prefer to pull UNAMIR out altogether. Both these options would be unpopular, so some provisional solutions were sent to New York.

The Belgian minister called the Secretary General again on April 15 when the latter was in Madrid. He did not like the provisional solutions. He wanted the Council to decide to withdraw the mission completely and urgently. He said the situation was extremely dangerous. The Tutsis (RPF) would soon gain control of Kigali and there would be a terrible bloodbath. The UN troops would likely suffer heavy casualties. The Secretary General later told the Spanish Prime Minister Felipe Gonzales that Belgium was concerned it would be blamed for the outcome by its decision to pull out its contingent unilaterally. The assessment and information given by the Belgian minister were not shared by our force commander and special representative in Kigali. They maintained that the Arusha Agreement was still alive. They denied the Belgian assertion that the Ghanaian troops had fled; they had not. UNAMIR was continuing to help the parties negotiate a ceasefire. The Secretary General personally was inclined to agree with the Belgian assessment since he believed that Belgium, as the former colonial power, understood Rwanda much better than the special representative or the force commander. But he had to go by the views of his people on the ground.

The massacres multiplied fast and furious in the days to come. We still had to decide what to do about UNAMIR. We, in the secretariat, finalised the report for the Council late in the evening of April 19. The Secretary General put forward three alternatives: increase UNAMIR strength by several thousand, reduce it to about 270, or withdraw it altogether. The Secretary General rejected the withdrawal option though several in the Council favoured it, especially the US and UK. The Secretary General's own strong preference was for the first option and he wanted to recommend it to the Council. But we, his advisers, told him that there was not the slightest chance of the Council embracing it. The Secretary General knew that as well as anyone else, in fact better. But he felt that as an African he had to recommend it. I told him that he would be accused of trying to win kudos with the Africans; he should certainly propose the alternative but not recommend it. He agreed, most reluctantly. I soon developed doubts whether we, the Secretary General's advisers, had been right in persuading the Secretary General to change his mind. Even if we knew that the large number of troops would simply not be approved or be available—in fact troops wanted to get out of Rwanda—the UN as an organisation ought perhaps to have taken a moral, principled stand. That would have upset major powers but would have kept UN's or at least the Secretary General's credibility intact. And Boutros Ghali in any case did not easily get intimidated by anybody.

On the night of April 21, the Council adopted a resolution, endorsing the Secretary General's recommendation reducing UNAMIR strength to 270. The decision was widely criticised by the OAU and the NGO community as the UN abandoning Rwanda and, hence, Africa. The resolution was drafted, agreed upon, and adopted—all in a matter of five hours!

The Council reached the depths of sterile, absurd, and totally meaningless discussion on the Rwandan crisis on April 29. The members had been suffering from a guilt complex. They wanted 'to do something' to demonstrate to others, and to themselves, that they were concerned. So they decided to issue a presidential statement, naturally. Ambassador Kovanda of the Czech Republic produced a draft. It was not one of his best efforts and a lot of work had to be put in to improve it. In the process, it inevitably grew in size to three times the original draft. To complicate their life, the members received a bombshell in the form of a letter from the Secretary General, urging the Council to re-examine its decision to reduce UNAMIR's strength to 270 and to take forceful action to deal 'with the appalling situation'. (The Secretary General had discussed the matter with his advisers. He too felt the need 'to do something'. He regretted he had not thrown his weight behind the first alternative in his report of a week earlier and did not fail to remind us that *we* had persuaded him not to do so.)

The Council sat from 11 a.m. until 1.15 a.m.—14 hours with a lunch break. When the letter from the Secretary General came, they were shocked and did not know how to react. They were disturbed in their cozy little exercise of producing a presidential statement which would have a lot of platitudes but no focus. They would have liked to ignore the Secretary General's letter but the media was already talking about it. Finally they produced a most anodyne draft. Seldom had the Council been seen performing at such a low level. It was the pits. As for the Secretary General's letter, they declared it was their intention to consider it urgently! Never was such rubbish written.

The Secretariat presented a non-paper to the Council on May 13 concerning Rwanda suggesting a force of 5,500 with a humanitarian mandate. Salim Ahmed Salim, the OAU Secretary General told the Secretary General in South Africa, where they both had gone for the ceremonies on May 10 marking Mandela's election as president, that Ghana, Tanzania, and Nigeria had offered to send troops to Rwanda. Interestingly, none of the African countries, including these three, had responded to the Secretary General's request for troops. The Council met continuously for nine hours on May 16–17. Agreement was almost reached on accepting the Secretary General's proposal for 5,500 troops. But the US reopened the whole issue at the last minute. Madeleine Albright perhaps felt embarrassed, because she asked her deputy Rick Inderfurth to sit in the front seat to field and face the storm while she herself sat in the third row. (It is most unusual for an ambassador, if present, not to occupy the seat at the table in the Security Council.)

The Clinton administration had unveiled, with much fanfare, PDD 25 (Presidential Directive Decisions) outlining its policy on participation in UN peacekeeping operations. According to this policy, which was designed to implement Clinton's much publicised and mischievous statement at the General Assembly in 1993—"if the US is to say 'yes' to peacekeeping operations, the UN must learn to say 'no'"—the US must ask tough questions before it would agree to any new PKO or extend existing ones. If satisfactory answers were not forthcoming, the US would say 'no'. On this occasion, the Americans found themselves totally isolated and could not say 'no'. Even the British could not or would not help them out. The French enjoyed watching the American isolation. The US ended up getting the worse of both worlds. It accepted many amendments diluting its proposals and earned the image of being opposed or unwilling to support vigorous action to deal with the tragedy in Rwanda. During the meeting, Inderfurth, like a good professional, attempted to co-opt me on his side and asked me for my views on US proposals but I avoided falling into the trap, pointing out that it was for the Council to decide on them. Later, Mrs. Albright expressed her unhappiness to me at my reluctance to support US amendments.

DPKO Assistant Secretary General Riza and Baril (military adviser to the Secretary General) left for Rwanda on May 19. Not a single offer of troops or of logistics support was received in the Secretariat. So much for the concern of the international community! By the very nature of its work, the DPKO has to have very close cooperation with the US. For most things, the department depends on the Americans—logistics, airlift, equipment, and so on. Of course, the UN pays for everything, and pays well since the Americans, in the shape of the company Kellog, Brown and Root, have a monopoly in this area and insist on being paid upfront, but the dependence of the DPKO on the US is not healthy, certainly not for the UN. There was a perception in the 'House' that the DPKO was too beholden to the US, to the extent of losing its objectivity. Countries such as India, Russia, France, and China also have logistics capability, but they lack the political will to take advantage of such opportunities. There was one occasion when India could have provided airlift for its own troops from India to Angola; the Indian government could even have made some money in the deal, but they refused, leaving the DPKO no alternative but to have the Indian contingent airlifted by American aircraft.

Riza and Baril went to Mulindi, RPF headquarters in northern Rwanda, by road from Kabale in Uganda. General Kagame, chief of RPF forces, refused to receive them since, he said, the UN continued to deal with the illegitimate government of Rwanda. He also refused to let Riza go by road from Mulindi to Kigali, forcing them to go by air from Entebbe. In the meanwhile, the RPF succeeded in gaining complete control over Kigali airport on May 22.

On May 25, the Secretary General held a press conference in New York which was notable for two of his statements. The first was the announcement of his availability for a second term. The other was his comments on Rwanda. He spoke with passion, honesty, and frustration about the horrors in Rwanda, saying everyone, including himself, was responsible. Thus, he accepted moral responsibility long before it became *de rigour* to do so. Significantly, he described the gruesome happenings in Rwanda as 'genocide'; he was the first to do so. He had already used the term 'genocide' in an interview on *Nightline* on May 4. The Americans repeatedly refused to use the 'g' word in respect of the mass killings of Tutsis. The farthest they were willing to go, and that too only in response to a battery of questions and only after the Secretary General had had the courage to call it genocide, was to admit that 'acts of genocide' were taking place in Rwanda. The Senate Foreign Relations Committee wrote a unanimous letter to Clinton urging him to use the term 'genocide'.

There was tremendous public pressure in France for the government to 'do something' about Rwanda. As a result, Foreign Minister Juppe announced on June 15 that France was willing and ready to intervene unilaterally to stop the killings. He wrote an article in *Liberation* on June 16 explaining the French government's decision. Merimee elaborated the French initiative in the Council on the 17th. France would be prepared to act in a UNITAF-type operation (the Security

Council-authorised military intervention by the US in Somalia in December 1992) under Chapter VII or as part of UNAMIR, their preference being the former. The RPF objected to the French initiative since France was perceived, and not just by RPF, as being pro-Hutu. The Secretary General said his efforts had succeeded beyond his expectations; he had spoken to Juppe on the phone the previous week. Juppe also proposed to move a few thousand troops from Mogadishu to Kigali.

The Council adopted a resolution on June 22 authorising France to deploy its troops in Rwanda unilaterally, not as part of UNAMIR. France, the great civilisatrice, could not remain inactive in the face of the genocide. Merimee said later (I was away attending a conference) that it had not been easy at all to obtain Security Council approval for their action. There was stiff resistance particularly from New Zealand and Nigeria. Given France's unsavoury reputation in Rwanda, there was widespread cynicism about French motives, especially since France had supported the so-called interim government which was responsible for the genocide. Boutros Ghali not only supported France, he went to the Council almost to lobby for them. The result was that Merimee managed to obtain 10 votes in favour. Five members abstained—Nigeria, Pakistan, New Zealand, Brazil, and China. The 10 positive votes included Rwanda which should not, or should not have been allowed to vote. Thus France got the barest minimum majority.

The French established a 'humanitarian protection zone' in south-west Rwanda. This was the only way, they explained, in which they could protect the Rwandans and extend humanitarian help to them. The Secretary General fully supported French action. France wrote to the Secretary General asking for his endorsement in the name of the UN. The Secretary General transmitted the letter to the Council without comments but did ask his spokesperson to say that the Secretary General thought the French action was in conformity with the Council resolution. There was not much enthusiasm in the Council for the French action but the French were more than happy that there was no criticism. The humanitarian zone would act like a magnet and would attract hundreds of thousands to flock to it, including many responsible for genocidal acts. The French said they would collect information about these people and hand it over to a UN commission.

Bizimana, the Permanent Representative of Rwanda, stopped attending meetings of the Council from July 19. Thus, only 14 members attended the meetings, formal and informal, from July 19. This was not an unprecedented situation. In addition to the Soviet Union absenting itself from the meetings in 1950 during the Korean crisis, the Council continued to function in 1980 even though the General Assembly could not elect one of the non-permanent members until the end of the calendar year in which the term of the retiring member had expired. Bizimana wrote a letter to the President indicating readiness to exchange its turn for presidency from September to a later date. This was all academic since a new government had been installed in Kigali on that very day, July 19. The ceremony of the swearing in of the broad-based government of national unity in Kigali lasted eight hours. Shahryar Khan, Special Representative of the Secretary General, told me that each speech of the new leaders, who spoke in the local language, had to be consecutively translated into English and French—as used to be the practice in the Security Council until the 1960s.

The Secretary General went to the Council on August 19 to talk about Rwanda and Burundi. We were concerned about Burundi. It was a crisis waiting to explode and yet there was nothing that seemed could be done, in a preventive mode, to stop the explosion. The Secretary General would have greatly liked to deploy a PKO under Chapter VII, but the Council would not hear of it. For an operation under Chapter VI, the request or at least consent of the Burundi government was essential. The acting president of Burundi was keen for UN presence, but the military, largely Tutsi, was dead set against any foreign military presence. The Burundi army was no doubt greatly encouraged by the success of the largely Tutsi RPF in Rwanda.

Just before going to the Council, the Secretary General told us about an idea: why not ask those countries which had troops in Zaire to assist in the humanitarian effort in Rwanda, to keep their troops in Zaire for a while longer? Those troops could be called upon to assist in Burundi in case of an emergency there. The troops in question were not UN troops. By the time he entered the consultations room, the Secretary General had further developed his idea. He presented a concept which frightened many members. He suggested 'as a purely personal thought' stationing UN troops or troops belonging to a regional organisation in Zaire. Inevitably, many doubts were raised: how many troops? For how long would they be deployed waiting for an explosion? How can troops be stationed in country A to deal with a crisis in country B? I passed a slip to the Secretary General suggesting he clarify that all he was proposing for the time being was that the troops in Zaire not be withdrawn in a hurry. He used it, but was not happy to give that explanation. After the meeting, he commented on what he considered to be the very low level of discussion in the Council. I reminded him that after all what he had proposed was revolutionary. His response was, 'What revolutionary? What were they proposing to do in Haiti?'

The French troops pulled out of the humanitarian protection zone on August 21. When they had gone in two months earlier, there was widespread suspicion regarding French motives. While doubts about the French motive remained, the international community, by and large, begged the French to stay on a little longer. The Secretary General spoke to Prime Minister Balladur and Foreign Minister Juppe a number of times. Even the Americans tried. Shahryar Khan was very keen. The French, however, did not agree. Merimee said that his government could extend the duration only by 10–14 days, and that too if the Rwandan government requested it in writing and provided the Council asked for it in a unanimous resolution. There was no question of the RPF government making such a request; they were extremely suspicious of the French whom they accused of aiding the former regime for a number of years. The RPF also alleged that the French helped elements of the defeated Hutu army by providing them with safety in the humanitarian protection zone to regroup. The French, of course, claimed that they had disarmed the former army, but they could not convince too many people of their claim.

The situation on the border with Zaire was horrendous. In the north-west, in Goma, it was bad enough, but in the south-west, facing Bukavu, it could be a nightmare because the terrain was extremely difficult and ill-suited to set up large camps. A large-scale exodus from the humanitarian protection zone towards Bukavu was feared once the French left. UNAMIR, despite tremendous efforts, was still ill equipped and not strong enough. More importantly, UNAMIR functioned under Chapter VI whereas the French had a Chapter VII mandate. Hence there was not much confidence among the people that UNAMIR could protect them.

Many observers were embracing the view that 'a transfer of populations' was the only solution to the periodic ethnic massacres in Rwanda and Burundi. Why not create two new, ethnically pure or homogenous states? The idea was morally repugnant but at least some in the international community were attracted to it.

By August 1995, the new government in Kigali had settled down sufficiently enough for the Americans to propose lifting the arms embargo against Rwanda. There was good reason to lift the embargo which had been imposed against the former genocidal regime. The leaders of that regime and most of its army and militia were now camped in Zaire, busily rearming themselves. Why should the Council deprive the new government of the means to defend itself against a possible and probable invasion by the previous regime? Only the French and, to some extent, the British had doubts about the wisdom of lifting the arms embargo. Zaire was totally opposed to the idea. Its prime minister sent a message to the Secretary General on August 15, 1995, that if the embargo was lifted, Zaire would expel all the refugees to

Rwanda and Burundi by force and would embark on a massive programme of rearmament. The very next day Zaire got fresh instructions from the foreign minister who overruled the instructions of the prime minister! The resolution was amended so that the embargo would be suspended for one year and terminated in September 1996 following a review at that time.

Zaire began expelling the refugees on August 19, 1995. In four days, 15,000 were expelled and 170,000 fled to the hills and forests to escape expulsion. This created an outcry and gave an opportunity to France to say, 'We had warned you about this.' The Secretary General had been opposed to the lifting of the embargo. He did not trust the new regime, just as he did not trust the old one. He believed that the Hutus and Tutsis would always go through periodic cycles of massacres. Having made its point, Zaire slowed down the expulsions.

Within a little more than a year, Zaire was on the verge of losing its territorial integrity. The Secretary General briefed the Security Council on October 25, 1996, about the situation in the Great Lakes region. Members agreed with his description of the situation as threatening international peace in the region but did nothing more than express their concern. The Kivu province of Zaire had witnessed unparalleled human misery, the end result of which could be the setting up of an independent Tutsiland or Banyamulenge land. The whole world knew that Rwanda was heavily involved in this fighting. Assistant Secretary General Ibrahima Fall told us in an internal meeting that the Tutsis were determined to revive an old kingdom known as the Hima Empire; the Banyamulenge were being trained and equipped by Rwanda's army. Rwanda was exploiting Zaire's weakness; President Mobutu was in Switzerland for medical treatment and the Zairian army had not been paid for six months. Zaire's own Tutsis had come to occupy key positions in the government and many others had gone to Rwanda. Rwanda was speaking openly of the right of Zaire's Tutsis to defend themselves and, if necessary, to carve out their own homeland.

When Fall briefed the Council he was not as blunt as he was in our internal meeting. However, he conveyed the essence. The reaction of the members was pathetic. They singularly lacked in imagination and honesty. Not having any ideas of their own, they incessantly ask the Secretary General for recommendations. The Secretary General always maintained that unless we in the Secretariat gave them ideas, the members would simply not know what to do. He was right. The major powers certainly knew what was going on where but never shared information with the Secretary General and were quick to blame him for everything.

Boutros Ghali was not the one to shy away from making recommendations. On November 8, he argued forcefully for a military intervention force to be deployed by a 'coalition of the willing' to prevent what he called 'genocide by starvation'. He left an impact on the audience. The French were delighted with his initiative. Even Inderfurth, Albright's deputy, had the courtesy to express nice sentiments for the Secretary General's constant vigil on this difficult issue. (By this time, the issue of his re-election had created extreme tension between Boutros Ghali and the US.) But the Council was not about to endorse the Secretary General's proposal. The Americans rightly insisted on clarifying all issues before committing to the concept. It was all very well for the non-aligned members to call for military intervention, but they were not the ones to send troops, certainly not on their own. Even the French offer to send troops was conditional on American participation. The essence of French proposal was the authorisation of the dispatch of MNF, for a limited period of two months under Chapter VII. It was a no-go for US and the Chinese were not ready to tolerate any reference to Chapter VII; they insisted on 'consent of the parties'. The British were trying to please everybody at the same time. The Africans supported the French but that did not have much meaning; they might send a few soldiers for whom others would have to pay! American reluctance was understandable.

After a long deliberation, the Council adopted a resolution which seemed to accept the concept of MNF but did not authorise it. The Secretary General was asked for a number of studies and to report by November 20. France tried hard for some mention of Chapter VII but received no support from any meaningful member. The US hoped that during the 12-day period before November 20, the situation would somehow improve. Some members felt that failure to take decisive action was the result of 'double standards'. If it was Bosnia or some European country, we would have had a different position, said Wisnumurthi, the ambassador of Indonesia. Even the fact that the Council had held only two or three late night meetings, as opposed to many more the previous year, was interpreted as a manifestation of double standards!

Canada prepared a draft resolution but there were important differences between them and the Secretariat and the NGO community. Canada, US, and others insisted that the mandate of the MNF would be strictly humanitarian. They would not separate the conflicting parties, nor use force to gain access to any place, nor force anyone to go anywhere. We in the Secretariat felt strongly that it was vital to tackle the basic political problem, namely, the repatriation of refugees. Once the MNF was pulled out in six months, the 'blue helmets' would be saddled with an impossible situation. It would be a recipe for disaster.

On November 15, the Council adopted Resolution 1080 authorising member states to establish an MNF. Within days, massive numbers of refugees went back to Rwanda. This was a welcome development. But the obverse side was that it upset the plans for the deployment of MNF. The US announced that it would send only 600 persons to help run the airports at Entebbe, Kigali, and Mombassa. UK also had second thoughts about troop contribution. France remained keen but the regional countries were not enthusiastic about France. The fact of the matter was that the moment US announced its participation in the MNF, the refugee movement started. Rwanda, which worked closely with the Americans, did not want the MNF to go to the region. Also, the refugee problem was 50 per cent resolved. The Secretary General believed that US was pro-Tutsi and the French pro-Hutu. This alignment also roughly corresponded to linguistic features—the Americans on the side of the English-speaking Tutsis of Rwanda, but also of Burundi and Zaire, and the French on the side of the Francophone Hutus.

The MNF was never deployed, strictly speaking. Canada, which had taken the lead in this entire episode, and worked hard and sincerely, to get the major powers behind the proposal for MNF, and had worked closely with the Secretary General, expressed the view that the MNF did not have any functions to perform and should come to an end on December 31. In the last week of December 1996, the Council decided to send a letter to the Secretary General agreeing with the Canadian view. The South Korean ambassador asked whether technically it was in order for the Council to terminate a peacekeeping mission through a letter when it had authorised the establishment of the mission through a resolution. He was obviously a stickler for proper form, like I had been when a member of the Security Council, but no one wanted to go through the exercise of drafting a resolution at that time of the year. It was for the non-permanent members to be vigilant about such things since the P-5 could not care less about the legality of decisions. Regrettably, the non-permanent members do not realise the significance of these technical points most of the time.

On March 25, 1998, President Clinton, on a visit to Rwanda, apologised to the victims of genocide. Kofi Annan, Boutros Ghali's successor, apologised to the parliament of Rwanda in 1999. Annan was elected to his position to speak for the international community. The president of the United States was, of course, *the* international community.

Could the Rwanda genocide have been averted by sending timely reinforcements to UNAMIR, with the required equipment, and with a robust mandate under Chapter VII? First of all, the section of international community which was relevant for the purpose was in no mood to come forth with offers of military, logistical, and financial resources. The Somalia experience was too fresh in their minds to make them receptive to another involvement in an African country, in another 'failed state'. This was particularly true of the United States which had 18 of their Rangers killed in a most barbaric way in Somalia only a few months previously. It is a different matter that the loss of the Rangers was entirely the result of their own bad planning and execution of the plan to capture or kill Aideed, 'the most wanted man' of Somalia; the UN was in no way responsible for it, much as the Americans tried to pass the blame on to the UN. The American reluctance to get involved in another disastrous situation was understandable. And if America was not on board, there was simply no way the Security Council would approve a peacekeeping operation calling for the deployment of thousands of soldiers and policemen. That was a fact of international life.

In case the Council had mustered the political will and approved a large peacekeeping force, it would have taken months, if at all, before the needed troops, with equipment, would have been found and still more months before they could have been deployed. There are, in fact, not many countries which could spare troops for service thousands of miles away from home. As mentioned above, not a single African country had responded to the Secretary General's appeal for troops.

Assuming that the necessary mandate and troops with equipment had been found and deployed, would the disaster have been avoided? I doubt it. As is known, violent and brutal ethnic strife was not unknown in Rwanda before independence. Belgium, with all its might and enforcement authority, could not prevent those incidents. And would any *United Nations* soldiers open indiscriminate fire, with intent to kill, on anyone, including women and children, and that too on a massive scale? It is not as if they would be fighting an organised military force. Would it not make them parties to the dispute and conflict? Worse, each side would regard the UN as being partial to the other. The countries which would have supplied the troops out of their commitment to the

UN would feel compelled to withdraw them the moment their men and women started getting killed in the line of their international duty. And how long could these troops have stayed in Rwanda?

The US could have taken a somewhat different diplomatic tack and thereby invited less flak for its position. On balance, it was not fair to lay the blame on the UN, or for that matter, on the US alone. Some decisions, such as downsizing UNAMIR to 270, were downright hypocritical and ought not to have been taken. The advisers of the Secretary General ought to have advised him not to put forward that option in the first place, but they had not dissuaded him for practical political reasons. We in the Secretariat should have let the Secretary General follow his instinct and recommend the more robust option. The Secretariat officials are not immune from political considerations.

Is there anything the UN could have done to avert the tragedy? The UN should have taken the decision to significantly strengthen UNAMIR. Assuming the necessary troop contributions had been made available by member states, one or two things could have happened. Either the situation would have been brought under control, albeit with difficulty or with loss of precious lives, including UN soldiers, or the events would have developed exactly as they did. In the latter case, at least nobody could have pointed the finger of criminal negligence at the UN. It is painful but essential to recognise the limitations of the UN or of the international community in dealing with such situations. It is simply not possible for the UN to handle every conceivable contingency. The only long-term, lasting answer to situations such as the one in Rwanda and Burundi is genuine democracy, with respect for the human rights of all sections of the population, without distinction of tribe or religion.

10

ELECTION OF THE SECRETARY GENERAL (1991)

THE OFFICE OF the Secretary General of the United Nations is easily the most prestigious diplomatic job in the world. When people think of the United Nations, they invariably have in mind the Security Council and/or the Secretary General. He—so far only men have occupied the post—is considered by citizens of the world as the conscience keeper of the international community. During the Cold War period, there was sympathy for his predicament, for the pulls and pressures to which he was subjected by the competing ideological alliances. In the post-Cold War era, he is often placed on the high and uncomfortable pedestal of being the moral voice, the defender of the oppressed and downtrodden of the world. He is supposed to uphold the sanctity of the Charter and speak up when its letter and spirit are violated.

Surprisingly, for such an extremely high profile and demanding job, the Charter lays down no qualifications nor any procedure for the appointment of the Secretary General. Article 97 simply says that the Secretary General shall be appointed by the General Assembly on the recommendation of the Security Council and that he shall be the chief executive officer of the Organisation. Curiously, the Charter is silent about the term of his office.

In the year 1991 the United Nations was to elect or select its next Secretary General. Perez de Cuellar was due to complete his second five-year term on December 31, 1991. Though the Charter does not bar a third term, so far the tradition has been not to elect anyone for more than two terms. There is also a resolution of the General Assembly adopted in 1946, which implicitly restricts the tenure to two terms of five years each. Kurt Waldheim wanted and tried for a third term in 1981 and would have got it but for the Chinese veto.

To avoid a repetition of what had happened in 1981, think-tanks had been working overtime throughout 1990 and 1991, devising procedures and guidelines for the election of the Secretary General. One group under former Under Secretary General in the United Nations Brian Urquart of Ford Foundation did very useful work. Two main recommendations had emerged. First, there should be a Charter ban on more than two terms. This would mean an amendment of the Charter. Another idea was to limit the duration of the appointment to one term of six years. Second, the search for the Secretary General should be conducted in a systematic manner, preferably through a search committee or a committee of 'wise men', instead of in an ad hoc manner with the P-5 calling the shots. After all, it was argued, even a corporation or a university goes about the business of selecting its head in a more serious and transparent manner than does the UN in appointing someone to what is undoubtedly the most demanding and delicate diplomatic job in the world. The Urquart group also suggested that a post of Deputy Secretary General should be created to assist the Secretary General shed some of his routine responsibilities, but it was recognised that this would be up to the next incumbent to decide.

The members of the Security Council in 1991 were conscious and excited at the prospect of being in a position to influence the choice of the next Secretary General. Some, like my able and affable Austrian colleague, Ambassodor Peter Hohenfellner, had given deep thought to the matter and goaded others to start the process as early as possible. As he assumed the presidency of the Council in March, he started bilateral consultations with members on the subject. To each member he asked three questions: Do you believe that this time the process of electing the Secretary General should be concluded early, say by October? Do you think we should encourage member states to announce their candidates early? Do you support the suggestion that the Council should set up a screening committee or a committee of 'wise men' to screen the candidates?

The issue was brought up in the informal consultations in March. Hohenfellner informed the meeting that his consultations had shown broad agreement that elections this time should be held sooner rather than later during the next—46th—session of the General Assembly. October was regarded as the most appropriate month by which to complete the process. There was also a general feeling that candidates should be encouraged to put forward their names as soon as possible. However, regarding a search committee, there was not a huge amount of support or interest.

In April, the President, the permanent representative of Belgium, Paul Noterdame was prevailed upon, presumably by Austria, US, and UK, to consult members about a draft letter he would send to all members of the United Nations asking them to present their candidates as early as possible so that the Council could recommend a name to the General Assembly by September or October. My reaction was a satirical one, why not advertise the post in the *Economist*? The American information, as indicated to me privately by them, was that no one was opposed to the idea. I was sceptical about this assessment since I knew that Zimbabwe for one, which had a candidate of its own, was not at all happy. When the President in the consultations brought up the issue, even France opposed it. Only Austria, US, and UK spoke in favour. Since the Secretary General, Perez de Cuellar, was present when the members started discussing the matter, though he left soon after, I suggested that in view of the delicacy of the subject, it should be discussed at a strictly confidential informal get together, where only the 15 permanent representatives would be present—no Secretariat, no interpreters—over a cup of coffee, tea, or a glass of whisky! The President found my suggestion 'full of wisdom'! The discussion ended on that note.

Since the previous five incumbents of the office had come from Europe (3), Asia (1), and Latin America (1), the Africans had staked their claim to the post in 1991. They had even managed to endorse a slate of six candidates after they realised that it would be impossible for them to agree on only one. The Africans found the idea of the letter as a manoeuvre to sabotage the chances of an African Secretary General next time. The West did not acknowledge the 'turn' or right of Africa or the principle of rotation. While their public and hypocritical position was that the best available candidate should be appointed, irrespective of his or her nationality, they were widely believed to be working for the election of another European or someone else—the name of Tommy Koh of Singapore was mentioned. There was general sympathy for Africa's aspiration.

I met the Secretary General on April 30 to discuss the situation in northern Iraq, but he chose to give vent to his frustration with the impending 'new world order' and the place of the Secretary General in it. He was particularly concerned with the dominance of the Five. 'Why should I have 10 eyes all the time looking over my shoulder to see what I am doing?' He went on, 'For nine years, I have been acting absolutely independently. I am a very independent person. Even the President of Peru dare not call me or suggest to me what to do or not to do. Even in the case of the Malvinas, I followed my own line, which was not in harmony with the Peruvian President's. Frankly, I sympathise with my successor; his job is not going to be easy'. Prophetic words!

This led to the question of succession on the 38th floor. De Cuellar told me he was 71 and would be 72 the following January. He was quite clear in his mind that there had to be a new Secretary General. He said the French and some others had suggested to him that he ought to continue, at least for a couple of years more because 'of my long experience and knowledge of the problems the Organisation would be dealing with over the next few years'. 'But I do not get influenced by flattery; flattery does not work with me. It would be very unfair to the Africans to deny them the possibility of providing the next Secretary General. I believe Chidzero of Zimbabwe would be excellent, he would be independent, like me.' (Boutros Ghali had not emerged as a candidate at the time.)

On August 9, the non-aligned caucus met the Secretary General to discuss the French draft dealing with the humanitarian situation in northern Iraq—the draft of what was later adopted as Resolution 706 on oil-for-food. De Cuellar was very candid. He said he had serious reservations about the UN doing all that it was being asked in the draft resolution. He said the UN had no experience in handling such huge and complex assignments. (This was commendable prescience in the light of what happened in the oil-for-food programme a few years later.) The Secretary General's post, he added, had become unattractive and would become more so in future. He told us, "It is amazing that in spite all that is going on, so many people are still interested in becoming Secretary General! They must be very brave people!"

The non-aligned caucus met on September 12 to consider the question of the election of the Secretary General. Zimbabwe was most anxious that the caucus should endorse the list of official African candidates. Cuba was sympathetic as were Yemen and most others. Yemen said the Africans should be given priority. Not surprisingly, and not for the first time, it was an African country, Cote d'Ivoire, which prevented the caucus from endorsing the African list. The representative of Zaire said he had a surprise for the caucus. His president had decided to present the candidature of his ambassador, Bagbeni, at the Organisation of African Unity (OAU) summit in Abuja in May. However, upon arriving in Abuja, Zaire found that the African list was sufficiently representative and contained very good names. Consequently, he decided not to present Bagbeni's candidature. Everyone was most grateful and relieved!

The non-aligned caucus met again on September 16. The Nigerian deputy permanaent representative told the caucus that Africa would be happy if all the six African candidates endorsed by the OAU were to receive the nomination of the Council. (The six African candidates were: General Obasanjo of Nigeria, Bernard Chidzero of Zimbabwe, Dookingue of Cameroon, James Jonah of Sierra Leone, Kenneth Dadzie of Ghana, and Boutros Ghali of Egypt.) The non-aligned members were quite happy to give precedence to the Africans but were not sure how this would be played out in practice. A lot would depend on the President who was going to start bilateral consultations on the subject the following day. The caucus decided, on India's suggestion, that if the President confined himself to procedures, the non-aligned members would not raise the question of the African list, but should he go into specific names, the non-aligned would ask for priority for the Africans.

The President started his consultations with India since India would assume the presidency in October. The most important thing was the preparation of the list of candidates. Should only those sponsored by the governments of the candidates be included in the list? Can governments sponsor candidates from other countries? Should the names sponsored only by governments be included? Can individuals sponsor themselves? For how long should the list be kept open? Should there be a cut-off date or should the list be kept open till the last minute?

I met the President on September 19 and told him that India did not favour laying down any deadline for the submission of names. The Council should retain maximum flexibility during the entire process and should have the freedom to consider any name at any time.

Regarding the African request that its official list be taken up first and separately, the President said that some members had difficulty with it on the ground that it would confirm African contention that it was its turn to provide the next Secretary General. In any case, the ultimate result would not be affected one way or the other.

A suggestion came up to the effect that there could be three categories of candidates. The first could comprise official candidates sponsored by African governments. The second list would consist of candidates sponsored by other governments. The third list would include other names. Voting on all candidates could take place at the same time.

I met American ambassador Tom Pickering personally about this matter since I was to assume the presidency in October. He said he could not see clearly at that stage how the process might unfold. I told him my endeavour would be to remain strictly objective and impartial and to be perceived by others as such. He felt the first thing the Council could do was to delete those names that would be clearly unacceptable to members. I told him that if a government insisted on retaining a name I would be obliged to keep it. I also told him it would be my intention to impart a certain amount of transparency to the process without sacrificing confidentiality. He thought one way to show transparency would be for the President to issue brief press statements, after obtaining broad support of members about their wording, after each informal meeting.

September 20 was the first occasion when the members collectively considered this question at an informal meeting. The President reported on his individual consultations. He said there was general consensus that the practice of 1981 should be followed. This meant that in case of more than one candidate obtaining nine votes without a veto, the Council would engage in a further round of consultations until such time as only one name finally emerged. Regarding the list of names, the basic concern of members was that the Council must retain maximum flexibility. The possibility of having informal consultations before moving to a formal vote should not be excluded. There was, however, a difference of opinion on one point. Some members felt that only names sponsored by governments should be considered whereas others thought that the list should be as open as possible and should include even self-sponsored candidates as was done in 1981.

There was another point of difference. Regarding the African request that its official list be considered separately and on a priority basis, some members were willing to support it. But other members refused to accord any priority or special treatment to the OAU list since it would amount to an implicit recognition of the principle of rotation which they absolutely rejected. The President would continue consultations. He suggested he would inform the media after the meeting that the Council had already started consultations on the procedure for the election of the Secretary General, and the Council would start the process of electing the Secretary General from the October 1 with the intention of concluding it as soon as possible. Regarding the list, Pickering said that the US would prefer openness; following previous precedents, it should be kept open until the last moment. The President said most members shared this view.

October 1 was the first day of India's presidency. September 30 was the last day of the French presidency. However, the French permanent representative called a meeting at about 11 p.m. on the 30th to discuss an emergency situation in Haiti caused by the overthrow of President Jean-Betrand Aristide in a coup. The British and, to an extent, the Americans were upset at the French imposition at short notice. The French realised the mistake. The permanent representative consulted me, in my capacity as the incoming President, as well as other members, and refrained from formally convening the informal meeting. But he was anxious to take some action. He showed me the draft of a presidential statement of three paragraphs that he wished to issue on behalf of the Council. I advised him against it but suggested that the Secretary General could issue it and he, as President, could tell the media that he, and not the Council, supported the Secretary General. This is what happened in the end.

But the evening was interesting for a procedural point. India should have taken over the presidency one minute past midnight. At close to midnight, I was asked whether I would like to take over as president straightaway or whether I would like to stop the clock. I enquired about the precedents for stopping the clock and was told there had been some, though no specific example was given. I decided to stop the clock for several reasons. Firstly, Merimee, the outgoing President, had not associated me with his bilateral consultations. This meant that I would have had to start the process all over again. Secondly, it was clear that Merimee would conclude his consultations latest by 12.30 p.m. Thirdly, Merimee was keen to complete the work he had started, particularly on Haiti, given the French connection with that country.

On October 3 and 4, I held bilateral consultations with members regarding the election of the Secretary General. Everybody agreed that there should be no Secretariat presence while the members exchanged views on this sensitive issue. Accordingly, when the Council met in the informal setting on 4th afternoon, I requested the Secretariat staff, including the interpreters, to leave. I briefed members on my bilateral consultations as follows:

(a) There was near unanimity that the process should be concluded in October. (Only UK and US had said that the Council should make every possible effort to conclude the process in October; others had said the Council must do so.)

(b) The Council should move as harmoniously as possible, without too much divisiveness and confrontation. This would send the right signal to the international community and would also be welcomed by the incoming Secretary General. (Translated into simple English, this meant that USA and UK would like to avoid casting a veto.)

(c) The above point placed a particularly heavy responsibility on the President to engage in an intensive process of bilateral and informal consultations.

(d) The purpose of consultations would be to shortlist candidates.

(e) At every stage, members would be free to add or subtract names. Even a name previously eliminated could be reinstated by a member of the Council.

(f) All members agreed that there was no need to rush into any official voting. There could be more than one straw poll before arriving at the stage of an official vote.

Even at that early stage, it was clear that the Americans and the British would like the process to spill over into November. Hannay in particular referred to the Commonwealth Summit in Harare in late October, saying his prime minister would like to exchange views with his colleagues on this important matter in Harare. This was a reasonable point and even the permanent representative of Zimbabwe saw merit in it.

During another round of bilaterals on the 8th, I, as President, conveyed to members my intention to conduct the first straw poll on the 11th. At that meeting, there would not be a different colour ballot for permanent members, as was the case in the Otunnu formula in 1981, but a single colour paper for all members on which they could indicate their position on the basis of the existing candidates. Members would convey to the President names of additional candidates by the 10th. Zimbabwe did not object but wished that the source of new names should be revealed. US said it would not be ready to express its position on any of the official candidates by the 11th. The principal concern of the US with regard to this proposal was that it would amount to recognition of the African claim of rotation since all the official candidates so far were only from Africa. But the Americans had no hesitation in stating that it would not support any of the non-official candidates.

It did not believe that it would be ready to propose names of its own by that date. I made it clear that by the following week, I would have to move to the next stage of taking a vote on the official candidates.

The first straw poll was held on the 10th. At the start of the meeting, I proposed that, since no member supported any of the six self-sponsored candidates, their names would not appear in any future lists. While agreeing, Pickering suggested a straw poll. I agreed since it would give members an experience of straw vote and it would be a more transparent way of conducting business. Zaire hesitated before agreeing with this and it soon became evident why. The Secretariat staff was asked to leave. I made it clear that any member could reintroduce any name at any stage. A ballot paper with six names was distributed to members. A member wishing to retain any name would indicate it on the ballot. In other words, if a member did not want any name to be retained, he did not have to take any action on the ballot. The result of the vote was that five names got knocked out. One member asked for Terence Nsanze's name to be retained. (Nsanze was the permanent representative of Burundi and had been a candidate for the Secretary General's job even in 1981.) It was obvious that Zaire was the one who had asked for Nsanze's name to be retained.

I announced that at the next meeting a straw poll would be held on the basis of whatever names the Council would have. New names could be added to the list in one of the three ways: (a) any member could openly sponsor its own national; (b) names could be communicated to the President who would respect confidentiality; and (c) names could be added to the ballot paper at the time of the straw poll. I made it clear that in the case of (c), those names would be voted upon only at a subsequent ballot since members should have at least 24 hours to seek instructions on new names.

At a lunch at his residence, the French permanent representative let me know that he expected Americans to propose the name of Sadruddin Agha Khan; everyone knew that the prince was close to

President George Bush. Scowcroft was reported to have his own list which included the name of Olara Otunnu, a former ambassador of Uganda. The Soviets, while in favour of Ghali, might propose two names, viz, Jan Eliasson and Gro Harlem Brundtland. Merimee said that both Chidzero's and Otunnu's French was acceptable!

According to Paul Lewis of *New York Times*, he could guarantee that a black African would not be acceptable to the US. I could not quite agree with him since I believed that the Americans would accept Otunnu; but Otunnu had serious problems with his government in Kampala whose UN ambassador was openly and vocally lobbying against him.

By the middle of the month I had realised that it was best to start consultations with Pickering; his was the most important voice and he was also the brightest of the lot and often came up with useful ideas. The Council was scheduled to have a straw vote in the week of October 14 but Pickering requested postponement until Monday the 21st on the ground that Secretary Baker was away in the Middle East and it would be embarrassing to consider a vote since one of the candidates—Ghali— was from a major country in the region. He added that Baker had not been able to give an indication of additional names that the US might wish to propose. I told him if he was the only one to seek postponement of the straw poll, I could not agree to his request. Sure enough, the next person I consulted with, Hannay, also suggested postponement by a few days, as did Vorontsov. In my consultations with other members, I merely informed them of my decision that the vote would take place on the 21st.

The procedure for the straw poll would be as follows. Members would be given the list of names, including such additional names as might have been communicated to me in advance. There would be only one column in which members would put an 'X' against those names they wished to support. There would not be a separate column for a 'no' or an 'abstention'. After the vote, I would communicate the results, in broad terms, to the permanent representatives of the sponsored candidates. In respect of candidates sponsored by other governments, such as Nsanze, it would be up to the sponsoring member state to inform him of the vote.

A minor controversy developed about the procedure regarding the inclusion of additional names. An official delegation of the African countries conveyed its unhappiness at the Council's decision to keep this matter confidential; they wanted open submission of names. The Africans said that the lack of transparency gave rise to a feeling that some conspiracy might be afoot to sabotage Africa's chances. Since, however, a large number of members preferred confidentiality and since the Council had already taken a decision, I told the Africans that the question could not be reopened. They said they reserved the right to take recourse to the provisions of the Charter and even ask for vote in the General Assembly.

On the 16th, Pickering asked for a postponement of the straw vote from the 21st to the 22nd afternoon on the ground that he would have to go to Washington on Monday and that Baker would be able to give his instructions only on Monday. He added that this matter was being handled directly between him and Baker. But the French, who seemed to have got a hint of the American demarche, strongly urged me not to postpone the vote beyond Monday. I contacted Pickering and told him that many members had insisted that the vote be held on the 21st and added, for good measure, that many members felt that the US was deliberately delaying the whole matter. I therefore informed him that the straw vote would be held on the 21st, but late in the afternoon. This worked.

On the 21st, I wanted to make sure that the US would not ask for a further postponement. So I called Watson, Pickering's deputy, and told him that several members, and many non-members of the Council, had conveyed to me their suspicion that the Americans were deliberately delaying the process and that the American behaviour was generating suspicions about US intentions. Watson called me a couple of hours later to say that my message had been heard in Washington and that Pickering would attend the 6 p.m. meeting with the necessary instructions.

The meeting started at 6.15 p.m. in the evening. I informed members that I had not received any additional names until that moment. I also conveyed to them the concerns of the African group that some members might sabotage Africa's chances by proposing new names at every stage. Two ballot papers were distributed, one containing the nine official names and the other a blank sheet on which members could write additional names. A typewriter was placed in the President's office in case some members were reluctant to write names in their hand for fear of their handwriting being tested by handwriting experts! The atmosphere was light and gay. Members were making a mental note and even talking aloud about the time each member took in the President's office. For example, the Romanian ambassador took longer than anybody else. Hannay also took a fairly long time, as did Vorontsov. Pickering had specifically asked for the typewriter to be kept, but nobody used it. I doubted if any new names would be proposed.

In the event, the straw poll was quite a success in indicating the relative strength of the candidates. Boutros Ghali and Chidzero fared the best, each getting 10 votes. Dadzie received 7 votes, Dookingue, Owono, and Obasanjo 6 each, James Jonah 5, Nsanze 3 and Manglapus 2. Five additional names also came on the table: Thorvald Stoltenberg (Norway), Hans Van Der Brook (Netherlands), Sadruddin Aga Khan (Iran), Brian Mulroney (Canada), and Gro Harlem Brundtland (Norway). Two members proposed Van Der Brook, Sadruddin, and Mulroney whereas Stoltenberg and Brundtland were proposed by one member each. Four delegations proposed these five names. One ballot had only Brundtland's name and it was probably Vorontsov. Another ballot had the names of Sadruddin and Mulroney; it looked like Hannay's handwriting. Yet another ballot had three names: Van der Brook, Sadruddin, and Mulroney and the fourth ballot had the names of Van der brook and Stoltenberg. It was not clear whether the Americans themselves had proposed any names. France and China almost certainly did not propose any names.

Immediately after the vote, I called the permanent representatives of the candidate countries one by one and informed them of the performance of their candidates. I also indicated to them the highest and lowest votes. I hinted to some of them that they might consider withdrawing their candidates to avoid further embarrassment to them.

The next straw vote was scheduled for Friday the 25th. The Africans made a big issue relating to the names that would be subjected to the straw vote on the 25th. Their demand was that the five additional names should go through a straw poll by themselves and that it would be unfair to subject the original nine names to undergo another vote. The main calculation of the Africans seemed to be that none of the new five would come anywhere near the ten votes obtained by Ghali and Chidzero. Thus, they would be able to tell the media that the Africans had better support than the non-Africans. As many as eleven members of the Council supported the African position. Pickering was not happy about it, Austria was definitely opposed to it, Vorontsov did not mind it one way or the other, nor did Hannay.

Another issue on which there was a difference of opinion related to the threshold up to which candidates would be retained in the list. The non-aligned cancus took the position that a candidate must obtain a minimum of five votes, that is, one-third of the Council membership, to remain on the ballot. Anyone getting four or less votes would be eliminated. The Soviets were opposed to the idea of a threshold. UK and USA were not supportive of it. Opinion was almost evenly divided. The President would have to decide the issue.

By now, it was clear that the Council was most unlikely to decide on the next Secretary General before the end of October. Of the 15 members 14 seemed ready to move reasonably fast. Hannay said he had got all his instructions and was ready to move at any pace the President desired. For some reason, the Americans were playing for time. Perhaps they did not wish to support Ghali, an Egyptian, or take any position on him when the Middle East conference was about to get underway in Madrid on October 30. But the way they had handled the matter thus far had almost ensured that a non-African was most unlikely to win the race.

On the other hand, the Africans were being counter-productive for their own cause by their hamhandedness. It was possible that, since none of the six African candidates was confident of winning, perhaps expecting to be vetoed by one or more permanent members, they would not let any African win! When I mentioned to Vorontsov my hope that there would be a new Secretary General before the end of December, he shared my hope and added that in case of a stalemate he had a plan! Of course, the only plan could be to give one or two years' extension to Perez de Cuellar. According to the French, the Americans might be feeling uncomfortable since this could be the first time someone not sponsored by them could become Secretary General. The French, of course, were fully behind Boutros Ghali.

The next straw poll was scheduled for the 25th. Until just before the start of the meeting, the point about a separate vote on the five new names had not been settled. The US continued to have serious reservation about it. I told Pickering I had to follow the normal democratic practice since 11 out of 15 wanted a separate vote. Eventually, I held a meeting of my own Crisis Management Committee, consisting of my deputy Prabhakar Menon, Counsellor Dinesh Jain, and First Secretary Sudhir Vyas to think of how to handle the situation. We came up with a solution that I implemented at the consultations meeting.

I first gave my ruling on the question of threshold to the effect that there would be no threshold. We then decided that we would first vote on the five new names, followed immediately with a vote on all the fourteen. Pickering proposed an alternative whereby the votes on both—the five and the fourteen—would be counted together, instead of in the order in which they were voted upon. He, however, did not insist upon it. The vote on the five produced the following result: Sadruddin 8, Van Der Brook 7, Mulroney 5, Brundtland and Stoltenberg 2 each.

Before we could start on a vote on all the fourteen names, Pickering asked for the 'B' ballot paper to indicate additional names. This was done. Only one ballot paper contained one name, that of Skubiszeswski. I myself knew that he was the foreign minister of Poland, but there was a look of bewilderment on the face of all the other members. Of course, it did not require a wizard to figure out who had proposed this name. We then held a vote on the fourteen. This time we had individual ballots for each candidate. Thus we had a total of 210 ballot papers. I showed all the ballot papers as I read out each one of them to Daele of Belgium who had been helping us out with interpretation into and from French. Boutros Ghali and Chidzero got 9 each followed by Obasanjo with 7, Jonah and Owono 6 each; Sadruddin, Dadzie, Dookingue, Mulroney, and Van Der Brook 5 each; Nsanze 4; Manglapus 3; and the two Norwegians 2 each. We then destroyed all the ballot papers.

I went to see the Secretary General to brief him on the course of events. He was kind enough to compliment me on my ingenuity and resourcefulness but was unhappy at the thought that the process would most likely go on for much longer than was desirable. Secretary Baker had told him in Paris, where they both had gone for the conference on Cambodia, that Perezde Cuellar might have to stay on in the job since the whole process of election was in a mess. The Secretary General told me that he completely ruled it out even if all the five approached him with such a request. He said four out of five, except the British, had asked him to continue and added that he was determined not to do so. One of the reasons for his firm position, he explained, was the extremely frustrating situation in which the Secretary General had now to operate. 'Two of the five insist on my showing them all the reports before I finalise them, the situation was simply terrible,' he complained.

On the 28th, Canada withdrew Mulroney's candidature saying he could not be spared. The permanent representative of Finland conveyed to me that his government was prepared to place Marti Ahtissari at the service of the UN should it become clear at some stage that a non-African would be elected. Finland was surprised that not a single permanent member had proposed Ahtissari's name to the President even though it had spoken to all the five at ministerial level.

It was by now clear that the decision on the next Secretary General would not be taken in October. I sounded out the US whether they would agree to a straw poll on the basis of ballot papers of separate colour for permanent and non-permanent members, but they were not agreeable. Nearly all other members were ready to go to an official vote, but not the US. Pickering admitted that the US was hesitant to take a firm position because of the Middle East peace process. The matter was extremely sensitive and the US could not afford to take any risk. I sympathised with his view. To the credit of the non-aligned members, they took the line that even if one member wanted more time, he should not be rushed. Pickering suggested one more straw poll similar to the one held on the 25th, but there was no support for it. Accordingly, I decided to leave it to the next President, Ambassodor Munteanu of Romania, to carry the process to its conclusion.

The atmosphere got quite vitiated in the following days. The new President did not seem to enjoy the confidence of the non-aligned members and the Africans. He did not help matters by being indecisive and appearing too solicitous about US concerns. He convened informal consultations on November 7 without prior individual consultations with members. The Council was sharply divided on the procedure. US wanted one more straw vote along the lines of the one conducted on October 25, but almost no one else was willing. The non-aligned and others insisted on a vote with different colour ballots for permanent and non-permanent members. After day-long consultations and many suspensions to permit individual and caucus conversations, a deal was struck: one straw poll like the previous one on Monday the 11th to be followed by a differentiated vote on the 12th afternoon.

The straw vote on November 11 produced the following result: Boutros Ghali 11 votes in favour, 1 against and 3 abstentions, Chidzero 10, 2, and 3 respectively; Obasanjo 9, 4, and 2; Dadzie and Jonah 6 each in favour, Van Der Brook 5; and Aga Khan 4. Manglapus had the distinction of getting the largest negative vote: 10; Nsanze came in a close second with 9 against.

The differentiated poll was scheduled for 12th afternoon. But quite unexpectedly, the President came up with something new at the last minute. He conveyed his intention before the meeting that as for the ballots of the permanent members, he would only announce their vetoes, not their yes or abstentions which would be kept confidential. Apparently this was along the lines of the Otunnu formula of 1981, but no one knew exactly what the Otunnu formula was. During the consultations, there was a lot of confusion and references to the 'Gharekhan formula of transparency'. Pickering came to the rescue of the President who was confused and sweating at the difficult and politically sensitive task at hand. Pickering suggested, and everyone agreed with relief, that exactly the same procedure as on the previous day be followed.

The vote took place at 6.45 p.m. and the counting took half an hour. All the members closely watched the colour of the ballots. The result was as follows: Chidzero got 11 and Ghali 10. Chidzero received positive votes of two permanent members and abstentions from three. Ghali got four permanent votes in favour and one abstention. Thus, both Chidzero and Ghali received the necessary majority without indication of a veto from a permanent memner. Obasanjo received eight votes in favour including two permanent members, and three negative including one permanent member. Dadzie and Jonah got six each, but Jonah got four negative including one permanent member whereas Dadzie got only two negatives. Van der Brook got five affirmative votes including three permanent members, seven negative including one permanent member and three abstentions. Aga Khan had only four yes votes including two permanent, eight negative, and three abstentions;

he did not attract negative votes from any permanent member. Manglapus set a kind of a record: not a single vote in favour.

As the Council got closer to the final stage of official vote, members got increasingly tense and excited. Rumours started floating. The Russians said that if an official vote were taken immediately, both Ghali and Chidzero would be vetoed. France was strongly committed to Ghali and would certainly veto Chidzero. The French believed that the only way to get an African elected was to persuade either Ghali or Chidzero to withdraw; the withdrawing candidate could be offered compensation in the form of the top position of one of the specialised agencies. The US commitment to Ghali, according to some, was restricted to the straw poll.

On November 20, Munteanu convened one more round of informal consultations that went on for six hours in two instalments. The principal point under discussion was how to proceed after the first official vote, whether to have further straw votes and, if yes, on what basis. Another point the President raised related to his intention to distribute the so-called 'B' paper at the official meeting to enable members to propose new names. This was strongly opposed since there was no provision for it in the rules of procedure. Eventually it was agreed that the first official vote would be taken on Thursday the 21st at 4 p.m; if required, another official vote would be held on Monday the 25th. Informal consultations would be held on the 22nd to take stock of the situation. There was some talk of further straw polls at which point Pickering spoke of the 'torture' of straw polls!

The delegates' lounge on the 21st was rife with speculation about what would happen in the official vote in the afternoon. There were two broad schools of thought (a) Ghali and Chidzero would be vetoed by UK, and France/Soviets respectively and (b) Ghali and Chidzero would both obtain the required majority without veto. The first theory was more widely prevalent. It was almost as if people wanted the permanent members to exercise veto!

At the informals before the official vote, the President took us through the drill at the official meeting. Pickering asked two questions: What would be the effect of non-participation in the official vote by a member? Would the ballot papers for all the candidates be handed out in one lot? The President replied that though he had done his homework, he had not thought of the first question. Ayala Lasso of Ecuador said that he could not even conceive of non-participation by anyone on such a serious matter and that non-participation would invalidate the vote. The President agreed and gave it as his ruling. Regarding Pickering's second question, the President said that ballot for each candidate would be given out separately.

Malaysia officially requested participation in the official meeting but was informed it would not be possible in view of Rule 48 of the rules of procedure.

Just before the vote, in the Security Council Chamber, I asked Pickering what he thought would be the result of the vote. He doubted very much if any definite result would emerge. I told him I would not be surprised if we had a new Secretary General at the end of the day. He looked surprised and slighly worried; he did not know what I knew.

The official meeting convened shortly after 5 p.m. The actual vote started at 5.15 p.m. and the counting concluded two hours later. Boutros Ghali was elected on the very first ballot, having secured 11 affirmative votes, none against, and 4 abstentions.

There was a wide body of opinion in the UN according to which UK and US were taken by surprise at the vote. Going by the straw vote, they were banking on the stalemate to continue for a long time so that they could introduce a new candidate of their choice at the right time. It was almost unbelievable that professional diplomats of such high calibre as Pickering and Hannay were not able to make an accurate assessment of the attitude of the members of the Council; surely they could have found out from the capitals. They obviously did not realise that even the non-aligned could play a trick or two. If the US had come to the correct assessment, they or the British would surely have used their veto against Ghali. Be that as it may, Boutros Ghali made it. The black Africans maintained a brave face, but everyone knew that they wanted a sub-Saharan African to be elected as a true representative of the African continent.

Boutros Ghali was formally appointed Secretary General by the General Assembly on December 3, 1991, by acclamation. While all the hard work leading up to the election of the new incumbent of the office was done by Romania and by me before that, the formal action was delayed until December so that the Soviet Union, a permanent member, would corner the glory in the General Assembly. Such is the influence of permanent members!

11

ELECTION OF THE SECRETARY GENERAL (1996)

DR. BOUTROS GHALI'S five-year term was due to expire on December 31, 1996. He wanted a second term. All his predecessors had served for two terms and he was keen not to be the exception.

For the first three secretaries general, the General Assembly had resorted to vote. Trygve Lie of Norway, the first Secretary General, was appointed by the General Assembly in 1946 by a vote of 46 in favour, 3 against, and 2 abstentions. In 1950, the Security Council was dead-locked, with the Soviet Union vetoing Lie for another term and the US vetoing the Soviet candidate, the foreign minister of Poland. On October 30, 1950, the Council rejected a Soviet proposal to suggest to the Assembly that it should postpone consideration of the appointment of the Secretary General. Following intense debate, which lasted more than two days, the Assembly adopted a resolution, by a vote of 46 in favour, 5 against, and 8 abstentions, to appoint Lie for a period of three years.

Dag Hammarskjöld of Sweden was appointed in 1953 by 57 in favour, 1 against, and 1 abstention. He was re-elected in 1957 unanimously, no vote was taken. In 1961, U Thant of Burma was elected for the unexpired term of Hammarskjöld, who had died in a plane crash in mysterious circumstances during his visit to the Congo, by a vote of 123 in favour and 0 against. U Thant was elected to a full term in 1962 by 109 in favour and 0 against or abstentions.

In 1971, Kurt Waldheim of Austria was appointed 'by acclamation' and reappointed five years later also 'by acclamation'. Perez de Cuellar of Peru was similarly appointed and reappointed without vote, as was Boutros Ghali in 1991. (Ghali's successor, Kofi Annan, was appointed in 1996 and reappointed in 2001 by acclamation without a vote.)

By the time Boutros Ghali declared his candidature for the post of Secretary General in 1991, there were already some distinguished Africans in the arena for the job, such as former president of Nigeria General Obasanjo and finance minister of Zimbabwe, Bernard Chidzero. Ghali had an advantage over others since, as minister of state of foreign affairs of Egypt for 14 years, he had been very active not only in Africa but elsewhere too and was well respected as an intellectual. But he was considerably older than the other candidates. He would be almost 75 by the time he finished his term. To allay fears about his age, he let it be known, publicly, that he would be candidate only for one term. The Americans for one would hold him to his word five years down the road.

Half way through his term, Boutros Ghali announced his availability for a second term as Secretary General on May 25, 1994, during the course of one of his infrequent press conferences at the headquarters of the UN in New York. While he made it conditional on the state of his health, he left no doubt in the minds of his audience, which extended beyond those present at the media conference, that he would be a candidate for re-election in 1996. When reminded that he had stated at the time of his candidature in 1991 that he would be the Secretary General only for one term, he responded: 'Only stupid people do not change their mind'. His response elicited much laughter among the immediate audience, but it started a chain of events, most of it unpleasant for him personally as well for the Organisation, that culminated in an undignified end to his eventful but, distinguished tenure as the occupant of the most difficult diplomatic job in the world. The very next morning, the French ambassador told me that Washington was up in arms at Boutros Ghali's announcement. However, his statement on May 25 did not amount to an official announcement of his candidature. That would happen two years later!

Even when he announced his availability for a second term, a good two and a half years before the expiry of his term, he was conscious that he would be facing a hostile USA in his bid for a second term. He had started his tenure with tremendous goodwill from everyone, including all the permanent members. It is worth recalling that the Americans had not positively supported him in the Security Council when his name was put to vote in November 1991, but they gave no indication that they would make his functioning difficult. The summit meeting of the Council on January 31, 1992 gave a big boost both to his ego and to his office. He was asked to prepare an 'Agenda for Peace'; he prepared an Agenda for Development as well as an Agenda for Democracy. This encouraging atmosphere did not last long. By July 1994, the Secretary General–US equation was so bad that Madeleine Albright told two senior UN officials that her government was 'fed up' with the Secretary General.

The circumstances of Boutros Ghali's official declaration of his candidature well explain the state of his relations with the US administration. On June 19, 1996, his Chief of Staff Jean-Claude Aime came into my room just before 6 p.m. and told me that he had asked Ahmad Fawzy, the spokesperson, to officially announce Boutros Ghali's candidature for a second term. While long expected and overdue, I did not understand the rationale for the timing of the announcement. Fayza Abulnaga, a brilliant Egyptian diplomat and a close confidant of Boutros Ghali, shed light on it a few days later. It seems that Barbara Crosette, *New York Times* correspondent, called the Secretary General's party in

Bonn when he was there on an official visit. She told them her paper would be publishing a story on June 20 based on a briefing by Secretary of State Warren Christopher that the US was opposed to a second term for Boutros Ghali and was prepared to use its veto if necessary. The story would go on to say that Christopher had offered Boutros Ghali one more year as a compromise but since the latter had rejected the offer, it was no longer on the table. When informed about this story, Boutros Ghali, without any hesitation, decided to announce his candidature for a second term. He called Aime from Bonn and asked him to tell Fawzy to make the announcement which he did precisely at 6 p.m. The undeclared battle was officially out in the open. It also proved to be an unequal battle for Boutros Ghali.

By January 1995, all of us in the Secretariat were convinced that Secretary General would run for another term even though he avoided giving a categorical answer; he put the state of his health as the determining factor. He would be 79 at the end of a second five-year term in December 2001. Murad Wahba, a bright young Egyptian in the Secretary General's office, who was almost like a son to Boutros Ghali, said that the Secretary General would definitely ask for another term but might step down after a couple of years. Some thought that he was making all these signals because he wanted to warn everyone not to treat him as a lame duck Secretary General. But by early January 1995, the situation had become complicated because the Republicans had gained control of both houses of the US Congress and the Democrats would still be in the White House at the time of the election of the Secretary General in the autumn of 1996.

In April 1995, I was with the Secretary General in Jakarta for the non-aligned conference. We were staying at the Wisma Negara hotel. I asked him about his plans for a second term since interest in his succession had grown enormously, with only a year and eight months left for his tenure. He said, 'Quite honestly, I have not made up my mind; if I decide on a second term, I have the majority, I will get it, the Americans dare not use their veto against me'. I said in any case he should not accept a one- or two-year term. He was categorical, 'No, never, I will never accept that. I will be very honest. If at any time, I feel that I am physically not up to the strain of travelling five months in a year, I will have no hesitation in stepping down'. He said he would have no problem keeping himself occupied. He would write, give lectures, and receive *honoris causa* degrees. He also did not have any problem of money. 'They (in Egypt) took away 90 per cent of my property during Nasser's time, but I am still very rich.' He was asked in New York, before setting off for the trip to Jakarta, about the candidacy of Australian foreign minister Gareth Evans; his reply was, 'I am still the best candidate in the field if I decide to offer myself'.

Boutros Ghali's differences with the US started in his first year in office, over Somalia. The Security Council had authorized the US to send marines to Somalia to help save the humanitarian situation in that unfortunate country. President Bush was prodded into action by the media, particularly by the CNN which brought out the horrible sufferings of the Somali people due to the absence of any government in the country. The Secretary General insisted, publicly, that the US had to disarm the gangs of warlords to create the safe environment essential for the humanitarian agencies to operate unmolested. But President Bush was not prepared to put the lives of his troops at risk and refused to disarm the militias. Boutros Ghali made himself quite unpopular with the Americans by blaming them for not carrying out their mandate. The situation with President Clinton was hardly better, and Somalia was the cause once again. The fundamental difficulty was that the US wanted to use the UN for its purposes and wanted the Secretary General to work with them. The Secretary General was not inclined to oblige them, at least not in a blatant fashion. When American rangers were killed in Mogadishu in October 1994, it was not the fault of the UN. The rangers did not form part of the UN force and were not under UN command and control. The UN force commander in Somalia was not even informed in advance of the operation which resulted in '*Black Hawk Down*'. Yet, the administration had no hesitation in holding the UN, and the Secretary General in particular, responsible for the tragedy, though they knew better. The media and the Congress in America went to town about the UN and Secretary General. 'Black Hawk' was downed because of lack of thorough planning, failure to anticipate all contingencies, and unfortunate circumstances, not mishandling by the UN as the American version presented it. (At that time, no one, not even the Americans, mentioned Osama bin Laden's or Al Qaeda's name in connection with the event.)

Over the next two years, two more points of friction developed— Haiti and Bosnia. Both these subjects have been treated elsewhere in this book.

In September 1995, the Secretary General decided to send Kofi Annan to Zagreb to replace Akashi who had developed serious problems of communication with all major parties involved in the Yugoslav imbroglio because of his courageous stand on the question of air strikes. The Secretary General's initial idea was for a direct swap between Akashi and Annan, but the Americans would simply not tolerate Akashi as head of DPKO. I was thought of as replacement for Annan in DPKO in which case Ismat Kittani would take my place in the Security Council. But the Secretary General did not want Kittani, a Kurd from Iraq, to deal with Iraq which he would have had to do in the Council, so Kittani went to DPKO. Most people in New York were convinced that Boutros Ghali sent Annan to Zagreb because he wanted him out of the scene in the UN, since Annan was getting too popular with delegations and would pose a serious threat to the Secretary General's ambition for a second term. I personally did not buy this argument. The Secretary General was too intelligent to send Annan to Zagreb for that kind of reason since Zagreb in fact would give him more exposure and more opportunities to get close to ministers of influential countries. Of course, I had no idea of what Boutros Ghali really had in mind.

In the fall of 1995, the UN celebrated its 50th anniversary from October 22 to 24. The Secretary General worked hard for its success which was measured by the number of heads of state and government who would attend the commemorative session. By that criterion, it was a big success. As many as 140 heads of state and government turned up for the occasion. All the leaders praised Boutros Ghali's leadership of the Organisation. Even Clinton, in his reply to the Secretary General's toast at the luncheon on October 22, paid a tribute to the latter's stewardship. In his meeting with the Secretary General, at which some of us were present, Clinton was warm and particularly appreciated the various conferences—from Rio to Cairo to Copenhagen to Beijing— 'organised during your beat'. The Secretary General was pleased with the meeting. As of that session, the scene did not look bad for the Secretary General's re-election. However, at the same meeting, Clinton told Annan in the presence of Boutros Ghali and other senior aides, that he had received reports of the good work performed by the DPKO under his (Annan's) leadership. That was as clear an indication as was possible of how the mind of the president of the United States was working.

Incidentally, Clinton's main concern at the commemorative session was to avoid any contact with and any opportunity of getting photographed with Fidel Castro. The Indian prime minister was even more anxious not to be contaminated by even the shadow of the Pakistani Prime Minister Benazir Bhutto. He was equally determined not to shake hands with Rabin, the Israeli prime minister, although it was he who had taken the politically courageous decision to establish full diplomatic relations with Israel.

In just about two months after the commemorative session, the US–Secretary General equation nosedived. One of the decisions of the Dayton accords on Bosnia required Eastern Slavonia in Croatia to be administered by an external agency for a year or two. The Secretary General had been strongly resisting the American proposal that the territory should be run by the UN even though the Americans knew that

Croatia had no love lost for the Secretary General or for the UN. The Americans, already faced with the formidable task of selling to their Congress the Bosnian operation which involved the dispatch of 20,000 GIs, dared not take up the peacekeeping proposal for Eastern Slavonia with it as well. So they pressurised everyone to agree to a UN peacekeeping operation for Eastern Slavonia. The Secretary General would not accept this quietly and frequently expressed his opinion. When he saw he had no choice in the matter—and we all told him it was for the Security Council to decide these things—he absolutely insisted that he needed at least 10,000 troops to do the job. The Secretary General had strong support for his stand from Belgium which was going to be the main troop supplier along with Russia. Our own force commander and the DPKO had a similar opinion; indeed, the Secretary General's position was based on the advice of his military advisers. But this view was contrary to the interests of the Americans and raised hostility of Croatian President Tudjman who did not want a force larger than 3000. The Secretary General, who was out of the country, authorised a report which reflected his position to be issued. Madeline Albright came to know about the contents of the report and urged the Secretary General to modify it. He agreed and told Goulding to amend the report. But something went wrong and the report was issued unamended. However, it was quickly withdrawn and a corrected version issued, but the damage had been done. Mrs. Albright's publicity officer, James Rubin, lost no time in issuing a statement in her name on December 13 which said: 'While the UN should take care not to assume tasks it is unable to fulfil, I believe it is a grave mistake for the Secretary General to shy away from legitimate operations, supported by key members of the Security Council. In particular, I believe it is misguided and counter-productive to argue that the UN should avoid this operation because of the risk of exacerbating a negative image of the UN in the activities of former Yugoslavia'. Strong words those.

We had already issued a statement on behalf of the Secretary General expressing dismay at the US press release. But he decided to say a few words in the Council. Looking straight in Mrs. Albright's eye, and speaking in French, he said he wanted to express his shock at the 'vulgarite' of the statement issued on behalf of the ambassador of a permanent member. In French, it sounded bad enough; in English, it came out much worse. Everybody was stunned at his bluntness. I could sense acute discomfort among the members. Mrs. Albright said that for the Secretary General to describe the statement of a member state as 'vulgar' was unacceptable. After the meeting, the Secretary General asked me if he had said too much. I said I thought so. He said, 'Don't worry; sometimes these things have to be stated'.

Mrs. Albright told Nabil El Araby, the highly respected Egyptian ambassador, on July 22, 1996, that Boutros Ghali would not remain Secretary General one single day after December 31, 1996, and that anyone who thought otherwise was dead wrong. She delivered the same message to the non-aligned caucus. She said the US wanted to set up a Blue Ribbon Search Committee to look for the next Secretary General. The Americans devoted huge amount of time and money to deny a second term to the Secretary General. They told the Africans that they would jeopardise their desire for a second term for Africa if they persisted in their support for a second term for Boutros Ghali. They sent a high level team to Yaoundé to lobby against OAU endorsing Boutros Ghali for another term but Yaoundé backed him. (The Secretary General told me that Yaoundé was a big victory for him and a humiliation for the US. But he was realistic enough to add: 'What this would mean in practical terms is another matter. I know my African brothers'.)

On July 22, Rubin briefed the media and warned unnamed UN officials against campaigning for Boutros Ghali. He said the US would investigate the use of UN resources to bolster the Secretary General's chances for re-election. An idea of the US attitude to Boutros Ghali became evident in the Council the same day. The Council was considering a presidential statement on Burundi. The British and the Americans tried to keep out a reference to the Secretary General's letter which had been the basis of their discussions. The reference was retained at El Araby's insistence and with the help of Russia and China as well as French ambassador Dejammet who was the president for the month.

In the early days after the American declaration of hostility to the Secretary General, there was considerable talk of resorting to the Trygve Lie precedent of 1950, when the General Assembly voted him in office for three more years following a deadlock in the Council. Such talk was encouraged by Boutros Ghali's supporters, one of whom publicly said that the veto can be vetoed. (If at all Lie's precedent would become relevant, it would do so, only if there was a stalemate in the Security Council—a contingency no one expected.)

The Secretary General told me in Moscow in April 1996 that one of the reasons he wanted a second term was precisely because the US was opposed to him. He looked forward to the fight! On the other hand, he did not want the Russians to go public with their support because, he said, he did not want to provoke the Americans prematurely. He would have very much preferred to have the OAU endorsement in Yaoundé before going to the G-7 summit in Lyons. Eventually his hand was forced by the *New York Times* story and he lost control over the timing. Even then he should have waited for the story to be published and then announced his candidacy. By going public before the story came out, it appeared that he announced first and US reacted in response.

The Secretary General asked me why I thought US was so hostile to him. I said it was partially because he had the audacity to give them his views as he saw them. He agreed, 'They want stooges'. But the fact was that he had done several things that the US wanted from him, be it the appointment of the commander of the UN Mission in Haiti or the appointment of the inspector general in the UN Secretariat in the person of Paschke from Germany.

Boutros Ghali often said he was a politician, not a diplomat. Once Warren Christopher came to see him and gave him a cheque for a certain amount towards the US dues to the UN. He asked one of his staff members how much the US owed the UN. He was told that the American debt to the UN was about $1.3 billion. Instead of first showing appreciation for the payment, the Secretary General's reaction to Christopher was that it was peanuts and would not pay for more than a few days of UN expenditure.

The Secretary General went to Washington on July 31, 1996, to meet President Hosni Mubarak who, I gathered from Egyptian sources, had spoken to Clinton about Boutros Ghali with some insistence. Clinton apparently did not respond at all. The Egyptians interpreted this as a positive indication; if he was negative, he would not have raised the matter at all, as he did. In interviews with *Der Spiegel* and *Hindustan Times*, Boutros Ghali spoke about what he would do if he were denied a second term. Thus, he acknowledged the possibility of not getting another term. He also admitted that it would be impossible to function without America's support.

On August 5, 1996, Tono Eitel, the German ambassador, as President of the Council, informed members that the US would like to raise the question of the Secretary General's election before the end of August. Egypt said it did not agree and would not agree to the subject being discussed before October. Legwaila, the permanent representative of Botswana, said that the mother of all wars had started; he felt this matter ought to be settled outside before being brought to the Council for decision. Wisnumurthy of Indonesia said nothing should be done to impair the effectiveness and dignity of the present Secretary General. Mrs. Albright's response to all this was typical, 'The issue will not go away. It will have to be faced, it is up to you, gentlemen, if you want to sit here right through Christmas, the US will not manage the issue, but you should know that the American decision is irrevocable, there will have to be a new Secretary General on January 1, 1997'.

France conveyed to the President that it would not take part in his bilateral consultations on the subject of the Secretary General. Egypt also took similar position. It was unprecedented that members would officially decide to boycott the President's invitation to bilateral consultations. France and some others wanted the Council to consider the question, even informally, only after the American presidential elections on November 5.

As the General Assembly session opened, there was intense curiosity and speculation whether Clinton would make any reference to the Secretary General in his address, as is customary for all delegates to do, and whether he would make the usual courtesy call on him. In the event he did not refer to the Secretary General in his speech but made a 10 minute call on him during which neither brought up the subject which was uppermost in both their minds. To avoid an embarrassing situation, the traditional lunch hosted by the Secretary General in honour of visiting heads of state was brought forward by a day, thus enabling Clinton to skip the lunch since he would not be in town in time for the lunch. Clinton had attended the lunch the previous year and had said nice things about Boutros Ghali in his toast.

By the end of September, Boutros Ghali had realised that the American position was pretty much irrevocable. He knew other countries were not going to fight the Americans on this issue. He seemed to have mentally resigned himself to not winning, but outwardly maintained a tough posture.

There was some talk of a difference of opinion between National Security Adviser Tony Lake and Mrs. Albright. Lake was believed to be more flexible and believed that Boutros Ghali could be given an additional two years.

An African ambassador told me that his president received a letter from Warren Christopher, asking him not to mention support for Boutros Ghali in his UN statement. Surely, other African leaders would have received similar letters! The problem was that Boutros Ghali had alienated the incumbent Secretary of State Warren Christopher as well as the incoming Secretary of State Madeleine Albright, and President Clinton was not going to go against them.

Mrs. Albright and the Secretary General had a tête-à-tête over dinner on October 7 at the latter's residence at Sutton Place. Apparently, they met somewhere and agreed to meet over a meal. Mrs. Albright told him her own role in the affair had been greatly exaggerated by the media, that she personally liked him and respected him, that it was the State Department which had influenced the decision. The Secretary General told her that it did not change anything. She suggested under the circumstances the best thing would be for him to step down. He told her that was out of question. She also said she wanted to have good relations with the Arabs (in the expectation of becoming the next secretary of state). He told her it was too late for that.

In spite of being under stress, the Secretary General regaled his audience at the annual UN Correspondents Association lunch when he started his speech by saying, tongue in cheek, "It is good to come back from vacation. Frankly I get bored during vacation. It is much better to come back and demoralise the staff, terrorise people by riding in black cat helicopters, and levy international taxes!"

He felt greatly encouraged by Mandela's public endorsement for him for a second term. Mandela was known to be close to Clinton.

Boutros Ghali was keen to avoid American veto. His calculation was that once US vetoed, they would not be able to back down, even to a compromise solution. I suggested that, on the other hand, a veto might be essential to stimulate search for a compromise. The Egyptian strategy was to postpone the vote as much as possible and then get a few heads of state to bring pressure on Clinton.

Warren Christopher visited Africa in the second week of October to lobby against Boutros Ghali. This was his first visit to Africa! He totally failed to win over a single country to his point of view. In South Africa, Mandela, sharing the platform with Christopher, declared his support for Boutros Ghali, adding that he would not be a party to a US move to unseat him. The final rebuff came in Angola where Savimbi, whom the Americans had nurtured for over 15 years, refused to go to Luanda to meet Christopher. Not a successful visit for the foreign minister of the sole superpower. One of Christopher's objectives in Africa was also to cut into France's privileged position in that continent.

At a 'casual' lunch of the Security Council on October 14, Mrs. Albright said that in case of a deadlock, rather than agree to a compromise formula of giving a couple of additional years to Ghali, the US would accept a situation where there would be no Secretary General for some time in January.

As the fateful month of November came, I felt sorry for Boutros Ghali. He had taken on the US in a head-on confrontation. The odds were stacked heavily against him. When he decided to announce his candidature on June 19, he had not consulted anyone, not even Mubarak. Happily for him, Mubarak and many others such as Chirac and Mandela had come out in his support. The OAU also had endorsed him though not in as ringing a tone as he might have wished. He talked to Aime and me on October 31 about his problem. The issue was: Which was better? Should his name be allowed to be presented first, and alone? Or, should his name go forward as one in a list of several names? If his name came first, and was vetoed by US, that would be the end for him. If his name was one among several, there might be a similar result but he felt that the second alternative bought more time. I said that Mandela and others had to do their bit. If they succeeded in working out a deal, the question of one or the other alternative became academic. On the whole, Aime and I preferred his name to come first. The Secretary General said he felt like a man condemned to execution; all he could hope for was to buy time through various stratagems, hoping in the end to receive a presidential pardon.

I talked to Ambassador Albright about Boutros Ghali for a few minutes in the Security Council chamber. She said, 'Boutros and I are good friends. [!] We get along well with each other. I had dinner with him the other night. I hope he has got the message by now. We do not want to embarrass him. I do not know what he plans to do, but if you have any ideas on how to find a graceful exit for him, please let me know'. I told her he did not confide in me, certainly not on such matters. She said, 'It is a pity. He should, in particular, have confided in you and some others when Secretary Christopher was having conversations with him a few months ago'.

Clinton won his second term on November 5. Around that time Wisnumurthy started his consultations with members. His plan was to bring up Boutros Ghali's name as speedily as possible so that other names could be brought into the play. The Secretary General had hoped that after his election, Clinton would be less hostile to him. Mrs. Albright dashed his hopes in no time; a beaming Albright told media there was no change in the administration's position.

According to the *New York Times* of November 7, the Secretary General spoke directly to Senator Feinstein and representative Lee Hamilton urging them to join retiring Senator Paul Simon in affirming support for him. He acted as his own campaign manager which was a mistake. The White House was reported to be furious with him for interfering in the internal affairs of the country. Senator Simon did say publicly that the decision to deny a second term was 'a gross diplomatic blunder'. All of us advisers to the Secretary General were very unhappy with him for personally lobbying with Congressmen.

Mrs. Albright invited Mrs. Ghali to lunch. They ate at a restaurant at the Waldorf Astoria, so she obviously wanted to be noticed by all concerned. Her purpose was perhaps to persuade Mrs. Ghali to talk to her husband and prevail upon him not to be so difficult. But Mrs. Ghali used the opportunity to 'really give it' to her. She told Mrs. Albright that her husband was not looking for an elegant way out, because for him a veto would indeed be a very elegant way out. She asked her, 'Tell me, what has he done to you that you treat him like this?'

Some people felt that the very fact that the Americans were trying so hard to arrange for Boutros Ghali to withdraw suggested that they were not keen to use their veto. Botswana's ambassador Legwaila told me on the golf course that his foreign minister had received a letter from Christopher pleading for their help in getting rid of Boutros Ghali. Legwaila asked Mrs. Albright, "What is your problem? All you have to do is veto him and he is finished".

I was surprised to hear from a Honduran diplomat that the Americans had mentioned the name of the Nigerian ambassador Ibrahim Gambari to them three times. I was not surprised that Gambari should be considered—he was a very able diplomat and a former foreign minister—but that the US should think of any Nigerian, given Nigeria's pariah status in the American eyes at that time was surprising.

The final act in the drama started on November 13, a day before Boutros Ghali's 74th birthday, when Egypt sent an official letter to the President of the Council, formally proposing Ghali for re-election for a five-year term. The decision-making process would start on November 18. On the 15th, the Council members met among themselves and agreed that they would have interpretation facilities on the 18th but no other Secretariat staff. Mrs. Albright exploded, saying the US position was not going to change by delaying tactics; she was prepared to repeat her position from the streets, and so on.

Chirac called Boutros Ghali and told him he was very upset with Clinton's reply, that this was not the way to treat a fellow head of state of a friendly ally. Mandela tried to speak to Clinton a few times but the latter refused to take his call. China publicly reiterated its support for Boutros Ghali.

The first straw poll in informal consultations took place on the 18th. The count was 13–1–1, the US casting the sole negative vote and UK the sole abstention. One hour later, the count was 14–1. British ambassador Weston surprised everyone, and devastated Mrs. Albright, by voting in favour of Boutros Ghali. After the straw vote, the African group declared their continuing support for Boutros Ghali.

Ten members of the Council sponsored a draft resolution recommending to the General Assembly the appointment of Boutros Ghali up to December 31, 2001. These members were: Botswana, Chile, China, Egypt, France, Germany, Guinea Bissau, Honduras, Indonesia, and Russia. According to one report, France would veto Kofi Annan who had quietly emerged as the favoured candidate of the Americans. The first official vote took place on the 19th on the 10-power draft resolution. The count was 14 in favour and one against—the US. It probably was a proud day for Albright for having vetoed Boutros Ghali. I told the Secretary General that he got more positive votes this time than in 1991! At that time he had received 11 in favour but no negative from anyone. It is worth recalling that in 1991 the Americans were caught by surprise since they had expected a deadlock between Boutros Ghali and Chidzero, the Zimbabwe candidate.

It was again decision time for the Secretary General. Should he keep his name in the ring or should he make a dignified withdrawal? I told him that he had reached the peak of his support and from now on he should expect the support to dwindle. But he was not the withdrawing type; he still felt that a compromise could be worked out. For the present his plan was that he would not make any announcement. At the same time, other names could come on the ballot and his own name would not figure on the list for the time being. Boutros Ghali had no intention of releasing the OAU from the Yaoundé decision, which meant that no African name would be forthcoming as long as Boutros Ghali remained in the field. But already murmurs of dissent were being heard from some Africans. Ghana, Kofi Annan's home country, in particular was anxious to put forward Kofi's name. The Secretary General did not want a second official vote since he knew that Korea, UK and Poland would not vote for him again. Kittani advised him that as and when he decided to withdraw, he should do so in a statement to the General Assembly; the Secretary General did not seem to appreciate the advice.

Salim Ahmed Salim, the Secretary General of OAU, was reported to have offered himself for the UN job on November 25 in case Boutros Ghali was no longer under consideration and provided the P-5 agreed on his candidature.

I asked the Secretary General why Heikel, a prominent Egyptian journalist, had been writing articles in the Egyptian press advising him to step down. His reply was, 'You must not underestimate the power and influence of the US. They can influence media in any part of the world. I am convinced that the US will remain the sole superpower, not just for the next 10–15 years but for a long, long time. They are ahead of Europe in technology and finance by 50 years. Europe is divided. Germany, France, and UK, though prosperous, are individually too small to affect American dominance and in any case they are divided and the Americans will make sure that they remain divided'.

I suggested that India, Russia and China, if they were to join forces, could, to some extent, act as a check on the US, but that was for the distant future. He said the US could easily prevent any of 'our countries' from joining up with others. He continued: 'This organisation will come even more under US sway in future; they will insist on seeing every report before it is issued and they will insist on agreeing to their contents. If I have to put in percentages, the Secretary General will have only 10 per cent room for manoeuvring. And if he tries to exercise independence within this 10 per cent, he would run into serious difficulty with the Americans'.

In addition to Annan and Salim, other African names began to appear—foreign minister Amara Essy of Cote d'Ivoire and foreign minister Abgabid of Niger. But OAU as such maintained its stand of Boutros Ghali being its sole candidate. Prime Minister Zelawi of Ethiopia wrote a letter to the chairman of OAU stating that Africa must not lose the second term and that Africa could suggest other worthy names.

When his letter was published in the *Washington Post* on November 26, most people believed that it was written at US initiative. Though a realist, Boutros Ghali kept hoping for a compromise.

According to Aime, Dejammet had instructions from Chirac to veto every candidate so long as Boutros Ghali was in the fray.

The Cameroon mission circulated a letter from President Bia to his African confreres saying he believed time had come for interested African states to present other qualified candidates directly to the President of the Security Council. It appeared to be an internal letter of the OAU, but the mission circulated it as an official document. It was either a mistake, or was done on instructions from the capital or from somewhere else!

There was a bombshell on December 3 in the shape of a media report datelined Tunis, which quoted Mubarak as saying that Egypt could not do anything more for Boutros Ghali. 'The issue is now over and if Boutros Ghali wants to maintain his candidacy, it is up to him.' This caused more than a flutter and the US and the interested Africans seized upon it. The Secretary General called Mubarak in Cairo who told him that he was quoted out of context and that Boutros Ghali continued to have his support.

At the beginning of the consultations on the afternoon of December 4, Ambassodor Fulci of Italy, President for the month, informed members that the Secretary General had told him that he was 'suspending' his candidature. A heated discussion reportedly took place. Weston asked what 'suspension' meant. Legwaila made it clear that Boutros Ghali remained a candidate. Lavrov said Russia supported the Secretary General but wondered if the suspension would be an obstacle if by end of December, no one had been elected. It was left to Mrs. Albright to deliver yet another categorical message, "Boutros is leaving, he *is* leaving, there *will* be a new Secretary General on January 1, Bia's letter is very clear. New names from OAU are only a matter of time..." Ambassador, Cabral of Guinea Bissau reacted equally frankly. He said members had to be courteous to one another; they should not insult each other's intelligence. He told me later that Mrs. Albright kept referring to the Secretary General as 'Boutros' and he thought he had no choice but to react. 'Members ought to refer to the Secretary General at least as 'Dr Boutros Ghali'.'

On December 5, Fulci hosted the traditional monthly lunch for Security Council members at his elegant residence. The pasta was good and the discussion lively. The Secretary General gave a comprehensive, excellent analysis of the situation in Central Africa. But the most interesting feature was the absence of any American at the table. Mrs. Albright was in Washington—her appointment as secretary of state was being announced that day—but her deputy 'Skip' Gneim was expected to replace her at the lunch. Every one interpreted American absence as a deliberate snub to the Secretary General since these lunches were technically in his honour him. Gneim, however, showed up just as coffee was being served. Fulci proposed a toast to the UN and to the health of 'our great Secretary General'. Gneim, deliberately and ostentatiously, did not join in the toast and did not raise his glass; he kept his hands firmly folded.

An interesting sideshow was going on alongside the election drama, between the French and the Americans. It was a reflection of the bad relations between the two. Dejammet never missed an opportunity to get at the US. During the discussion on the situation in the Great Lakes region and the deployment of MNF there, he said, clearly hinting at UK and US, that some countries never had any intention to send troops there even though they had voted for the relevant resolutions.

The battle for influence in Africa between France and US, which France was losing, was being waged with no holds barred. French language also was losing ground to English. The divide between Anglo and Francophone countries was more accentuated than ever before. The President of Congo (Brazzaville) had convened a meeting of the heads of state of Central Africa which the English-speaking countries did not attend. The English-speaking Africans seemed to have decided that their bread was buttered on the American side.

A similar battle was being fought in the Council. The French insistence on the next Secretary General being fluent in French was resented by the English-speaking countries. Would the French really veto a non-Francophone candidate?

The Council received four names on December 6—Algabid (Niger), Kofi Annan (Ghana), Amara Essy (Cote d'Ivoire), and Ould Abdullah (Mauritania). Olara Otunu of Uganda would have been a strong candidate but his problem was that his own government was strongly opposed to him. He tried to find a sponsor country for his candidacy. Norway was said to be ready to do so but it would not do to have a non-African sponsor.

The Council held two straw polls on the 10th. Only the second one was relevant since the permanent members were given a different colour ballot. The suspense was over. France did indicate it would veto Annan who received 10 votes in favour, 4 against including one permanent member, and 1 abstention. Amara obtained 7 in favour, 4 against including two permanent members, and 4 abstentions. The other votes were not relevant. Dejammet was upset that Amara had received 2 negatives from permanent members, UK and US. Between Annan and Amara, Annan was the favorite of most members and his French was better than Amara's English. The American veto against Amara seriously affected its credibility in Africa because it had been saying that it would support any candidate from Africa other than Boutros Ghali. Three more straw polls were conducted the next day. Annan improved from 10 to 12 but France maintained its veto in all of them. Lavrov suggested that in view of the deadlock, it was time to look for a compromise on the incumbent Secretary General. If he intended to provoke Mrs. Albright, he succeeded. She repeated her usual line, adding that her new capacity should remove whatever little hope people might have had on this issue. Dejammet felt that it was a case of Russian-American collusion to give Mrs. Albright an opportunity to finish off Boutros Ghali once and for all.

One more name appeared—Lakhdar Brahimi, a former foreign minister of Algeria. Brahimi was a well-known, highly respected, and popular personality. But there were two problems. The sub-Saharan Africans would not agree to another north African Secretary General and Morocco would not agree to an Algerian. Salim was ruled out by Chirac because he did not speak French.

Two more straw polls were held on the 12th. Annan consolidated his position. He got 13 in the first and 14 in the second poll. France indicated veto in both. A 14 in the second vote indicated clearly that Boutros Ghali's own country had abandoned him. This must have been a terrible blow for him. Nabil Al Araby, who was so close to Boutros Ghali, would have hated to carry out his government's instructions. But Fulci told me, and he swore to it, that Italy was the last non-permanent member to have changed its vote in favour of Annan, thus implying that Egypt had abandoned Boutros Ghali even earlier.

The United Nations had a new Secretary General on Friday, December 13, 1996. The Council reached consensus just before 1 p.m., 15 to 0 in favour of Annan. Fulci started the meeting by stating that he understood there was consensus on Annan's candidature. 'If I hear no objection, it is so decided.' And it was so decided. Weston sneaked out of the consultations, informed the media that the Council had reached consensus on Annan, and went back to the consultations. Kofi Annan should have no problem that he won the coveted job on Friday the 13th! He went on to win the Nobel Peace Prize. Some one told me that Kofi in Ghanaian language means Friday; he was born on a Friday! The Council also adopted a resolution placing on record its appreciation to the Secretary General for his dedication to the principles and purposes of the Charter and commending his efforts at reform. Boutros Ghali issued a gracious statement congratulating Annan and the latter called on the Secretary General on the 16th.

Outwardly at least, Boutros Ghali did not appear shattered. He maintained a reasonably, though not artificially cheerful face. After all, he came from a 5000-year-old civilization and would not let this experience destroy him. And he was no doubt lucky to have become Secretary General in the first place; if the Americans had been vigilant in 1991, it was highly likely that they would have used their veto then. He had won the most prestigious UN position. And he *had* declared that he would want only one term. He put up a very good fight. The Americans had to work very, very hard to defeat him. They invested enormous effort and prestige in the anti-Boutros Ghali campaign. It was in the teeth of their opposition that the OAU endorsed him. And all their pleas did not persuade Africans to put forward alternative names until after the 14-1 vote for Boutros Ghali.

Annan's selection was widely and enthusiastically welcomed by countries around the world as well as by members of the Secretariat staff. Boutros Ghali almost never dealt with the permanent representatives in New York. He did not refuse to meet them but he made it evident to them that he did not need them, that he could do quite well without them. Over the years he had got used to dealing with only Presidents, Prime Ministers and Ministers. This attitude of his did not endear him to the ambassadors. The support he got in the last few weeks of his term was because of the patently unfair and arrogant manner in which the US treated him. Several of us, his senior advisers, told him, many times, that he should pay more attention to the ambassadors, try to cultivate them, and so on. He would agree with us but did not bother to act on the advice. He did not want to make the necessary effort. That was just it; for him it would be an effort whereas for Annan it came naturally.

With the staff, Boutros Ghali could be sweet. But his problem was he had almost never been just a staff member. Except for when he was a lecturer in his early teaching career, he had always been a boss. He did not believe in vacations. He said he had not been to a movie in over a decade, 'not that I am proud of it' he would hasten to add. He was a very kind person, compassionate and helpful. He was strongly supportive of his special representatives. My own task in the Security Council was made less stressful because I knew he would back me up no matter what. He was always accessible to his senior staff, though they were not completely at ease while meeting him. Perhaps he believed that the subordinate must not be allowed to forget that they were just that—subordinates. He was niggardly in approving travel by his senior advisers and often said no. He reacted even more negatively when asked to bring his special representatives in the field to New York to brief the Council. Once an African ambassador, in his capacity as President of the Council, suggested bringing the special representative from Angola to brief the Council. Secretary General said, "Never, over my dead body!" The poor ambassador did not know what had hit him.

Boutros Ghali was an intellectual giant. It was always fascinating to attend meetings, with him in the chair. He provoked us into thinking along new, creative lines. He frequently liked to act as the devil's advocate. His own contributions were original and unorthodox. He had convinced those of us working closely with him, by his actions, that he welcomed criticism. He was fond of saying he was a politician, not a diplomat. But the job he held for five years demanded high standards of diplomacy. Even he admitted he had accommodated the Americans on most issues. How, then, did he manage to alienate them? Why did he not manage to charm Madeleine Albright who would, perhaps, have liked him to try to charm her I am sure? He discounted her importance and influence with Clinton. He said only Christopher and Clinton mattered on the issue of the election of the Secretary General. For a politician, this was difficult to forgive.

Boutros Ghali was an activist. He had no interest except his work. But he also enjoyed company and his 'Scotch'. He told me a few times he had been highly successful with women in his younger days. Every time the subject of attractive women came up, his eyes had that gleam in them. He could be charming on social occasions, and was full of stories. I recorded two.

'An Egyptian diplomat who served 12 years as chief of protocol requested me to post him as ambassador to Berne. So I posted him to Berne. Then he asked me to replace a couple of his officers. So I gave him officers of his choice. Then he said I must pay an official visit to Switzerland. I said 'Are you mad? How can I come in the midst of all these Camp David negotiations?' He said, 'Excellency, you must remember that we are from a country where the regime will always be unstable or uncertain, you don't know when you might have to flee, you should keep in good terms with the Swiss, and you never know when you might need them'. 'Ah, 'I said,' in that case, I will certainly pay a visit to Switzerland'."

And the other story went like this. 'When we had rapprochement with Libya, Gaddafi had hosted a dinner. I did not eat spaghetti. Gaddafi asked Mubarak why. Mubarak said because his wife did not want to him to eat spaghetti. 'Why does he not get rid of his wife?' asked Gaddafi. 'Because, Excellency, I am afraid of her', I said. Thereafter, Gaddafi sent me a gift of 200 kilos of spaghetti.'

Kofi Annan delivered an excellent acceptance speech, just about 10 minutes long. There were a couple of references in it to the need for healing the relations between member states and the UN. From what I heard, his chief of staff-designate, Riza, suggested to Annan to delete those references since they implied criticism of the incumbent Secretary General. Kofi Annan apparently agreed but Ted Sorensen, who was the principal drafter of the speech, insisted on retaining them on the ground that without them the line of thought would be broken.

Boutros Ghali made what I thought was a pedestrian speech. His speech read like a routine one that he had made many a time in the past. I felt bad. His speech did not leave any impact or impression. He perhaps realised that his speech was not up to the mark. He asked me for my opinion. I told him candidly what I thought. He said the earlier draft was conceptual, but it was he who wanted it rewritten the way it was. He said it was important to repeat and simplify for his audience his work over the previous five years. He got a prolonged standing ovation, not so much for his speech as for himself. On the 17th morning, all 15 members of the Security Council handed over to him the text of Resolution 1091 in which the Council expressed its appreciation to him. Fulci did a fine job in getting it printed in the form of a scroll.

Boutros Ghali met all his senior advisers together on the December 19. This was the first time that he met us all collectively. We gave him a Steuben glass eagle as a memento. He thanked us all and indulged in a bit of introspection. 'What are the mistakes I committed in the past five years? Perhaps one mistake I made was not to pay sufficient attention to the United States. I went to Bundestag five times, but only twice to the Congress. I felt that I should pay more attention to countries far away from New York rather than to Washington. I wanted more countries to be interested in the UN. But may be that was a mistake.' He was offering, perhaps more to himself than to others, an explanation for American hostility. (Despite all that Madeliene Albright did to throw out Boutros Ghali, he invited her to his house in Sutton Place for dinner on the 18th!) He said he attached particular importance to the principle of independence of his office. 'It is very important to preserve the credibility of the organisation. Member states want to use the UN for their own purposes, so it is up to the Secretary General to maintain its integrity and prestige. This is not always easy to do, but the Secretary General has to exercise at least a minimum of independence.'

There was an interesting comment by Robert Kaplan in the *London Observer* of December 22. He wrote: 'The UN functions best as a tool of the great powers. When it comes to peacemaking and peacekeeping, let the great powers make the decisions. He (Secretary General) should not worry about being led by the US or other Security Council members. That is the point—only when you *are* their tool (emphasis in original) can you be effective....The Secretary General should not worry about being bossed around by the future US secretary of state.'

Boutros Ghali leaving his office for the last time. On his left is
Ismat Kittani, and to his right, the author.

Looking back over the previous few weeks, Dejammet told me over lunch on December 27 that it was a mistake for France to have ruled out Salim so early in the game. He said Mrs. Albright was nervous at the prospect of Salim's name being introduced in the fray. 'The Americans would have vetoed him. At that stage, we, France, could have played the role of an arbiter between Kofi and Salim. Perhaps that might have opened up the possibility, however slight, of striking a deal for Boutros Ghali for one or two years.' He said he had reached a personal agreement with Albright for one more year for Boutros Ghali, with an understanding that after that Kofi Annan would get a full term of five years. But Paris felt it would not be fair to Boutros Ghali. When Egypt stopped voting for Boutros Ghali on December 12, he was left alone. Dejammet said he had no doubt whatever, that Nabil had definitely been voting for Boutros Ghali and against Kofi; Nabil changed his vote on December 12 on instructions from Osama El Baz and not Mubarak. In the afternoon, Nabil received instructions from Amre Moussa, the foreign minister, to change his vote again but it was too late by then. Dejammet said things might still have turned around differently if the vote had been postponed until Monday, December 16. It seemed Salim had decided to put in his name on Friday. Mandela was going to write to the President of Security Council proposing Salim's name. That would have created a difficult situation for Mrs. Albright. She learnt of this development from the US embassy in Addis Ababa at 10 a.m. and decided that the vote had to take place that very morning.

On December 31, 1996, Boutros Ghali was given a warm send-off on the 38th floor. He posed for pictures with us, thanked us and wished us a happy New Year. Downstairs in the lobby of the Secretariat entrance, several scores of staff had gathered at 1 p.m. to see him off. There was sadness in the air and I thought I saw a couple of wet eyes. He repeated his favourite phrase, 'I will continue to serve the United Nations as an eminent person'. To the media, he said he wished all success to Kofi Annan.

12

SOME THOUGHTS ON REFORM OF
THE SECURITY COUNCIL

THE IMPETUS FOR the current UN reform movement has come from the events of September 11, 2001 which led to the war on the Taliban regime in Afghanistan and eventually to the second Gulf war in the spring of 2003. When the President of the United States questioned the continued relevance of the United Nations in the changed circumstances, the Secretary General, as indeed the international community, had to sit up and reflect on the new situation. The Secretary General appointed a High Level Panel on Threats, Challenges and Change. The Panel submitted its report in December 2004. The Secretary General presented his own report entitled 'In Larger Freedom' in March 2005. In his words, the Secretary General limited himself to those items on which he believed 'action is both viable and achievable in the coming months. These are reforms that are within reach—reforms that are actionable if we can garner the necessary political will'.

Is the United Nations capable or amenable to reform? Can the Security Council be reformed? And what is it that a reformed United

Nations or Security Council is expected to do better than the present United Nations/Security Council?

One set of answers has been provided in the Report of the High Level Panel as also by the Secretary General in his report 'In Larger Freedom'. These documents define the risks and challenges facing the international community in the early decades of the 21st century which, it is stated, can be tackled by the same international community acting together through the United Nations. The Panel has examined the threats under six clusters: economic and social threats, inter-state conflict, internal conflict, nuclear, biological and chemical weapons, terrorism and transnational organized crime. The Panel has recommendations for dealing with each of these threats. It has made some useful suggestions. Its proposed definition of terrorism is particularly well drafted. The Secretary General has utilized his long and distinguished service in the United Nations to endorse some of the recommendations of the High Level Panel and to reject or modify others. For instance, the Panel's proposal to create a second post of Deputy Secretary General has wisely not found favour with the Secretary General. (Perhaps, what is needed, without in any way casting any reflections on the present incumbent of the position, is to evaluate the utility of the already existing post of a Deputy Secretary General.) In the field of human rights, the Panel recommended a much larger Human Rights Commission consisting of all 191 members of the United Nations. The Secretary General has come up with his own, much improved concept of a smaller Human Rights Council which would need further refinement. If, however, the objective behind reforming the human rights machinery is to keep 'undesirable' countries out, it is not likely to succeed.

I shall only deal with the recommendations dealing with the Security Council and its mandate to restore peace and security. On the subject of the enlargement of the Security Council which has attracted the bulk of governmental and public attention, the Secretary General has thrown his weight behind the proposal to expand its membership so as to better reflect the current political, economic and military realities. He has stated that such an expansion is essential to lend more legitimacy to the decisions of the Security Council. He has demonstrated his political skill by suggesting that member states were free to propose any formula, without feeling themselves restricted to the two models presented in the report of the Panel.

The preceding chapters should have shown that 'we the peoples' have hardly anything to do with the manner in which 'their' United Nations functions or in which 'their' Security Council discharges its mandate of preserving peace and security. It is an inter-governmental body and its decisions reflect the balance of political equations prevailing at a given time. To expect anything more might be natural and legitimate but it is not realistic.

This is not to suggest that the men—and occasionally women— sitting around the horseshoe table in the Council chamber or the rectangular table in the consultations room are all, or always, total cynics. Once in a while, some of them are genuinely moved by compassion or anger or a sense of frustration. On the whole, however, it is true to say that the representatives of members of the Security Council, or for that matter of the General Assembly, are guided solely by considerations of the national interests of the countries they represent.

Nowhere does the Charter of the United Nations prescribe that the Security Council should decide between right and wrong. The function of the Security Council is to promote peaceful settlement of disputes between member states and to restore peace in case it is breached. In Chapter VI of the Charter, which deals with pacific settlement of disputes, there is no provision asking the Security Council to promote a settlement on the basis of either the merits of the situation or of justice and equity. The representatives of countries serving on the Council, thus, are expected to discharge their responsibility of maintaining peace in the world without being overly concerned about the rights and wrongs of a conflict. 'Peace before everything else' is their guiding approach. Peace for the United Nations means absence or discontinuance of armed hostilities.

Broadly speaking, the Charter demands that the Security Council act under one of two possible scenarios: either at the request of the parties to a conflict or in an enforcement mode, in case of aggression by one state against another. The first scenario is dealt with in Chapter VI of the Charter and the second in Chapter VII. Chapter VI is in a sense more basic since it would involve the Security Council in actually promoting a settlement of dispute through establishment of good offices, mediation, and so on. Chapter VII, on the other hand, comes into play when one country uses force to impose a settlement on the other. The mandate of the Security Council in Chapter VII is restrictive, though important, in that it is required to bring the armed conflict to an end without necessarily dealing with the root causes underlying the conflict. The Security Council is not a court of law. This has been amply clarified in Article 36 of the Charter which states that legal disputes should be referred by the parties to the International Court of Justice. Article 40 further amplifies this principle and states that any provisional measures that the Council might call upon the parties to comply with to prevent aggravation of the situation shall be without prejudice to the rights, claims or position of the parties.

It is essential to understand the role of the Secretary General and the Secretariat in the field of maintaining peace and security. It is normal and to some extent natural for the international community to blame the Secretary General when the UN fails to resolve a conflict or to restore peace to a troubled country. Dr. Boutros Ghali, the former Secretary General, often said that one of the functions of the UN was to act as the scapegoat for the mistakes of member states. When most people speak of the failure of the United Nations, they are not very precise in their thinking. Do they refer to the Security Council or its individual members? Or do they have the Secretary General in mind? Quite often, they seem to direct their disappointment or anger at the

Secretary General. It needs to be emphasised that the Charter has given only two specific functions to the Secretary General, namely, to act as its chief administrative officer and to bring to the notice of the Security Council any matter which, in his opinion, is likely to threaten international peace and security. The Secretary General does have responsibility in matters of peace and stability since it is he who has to implement the decisions of the Security Council. Most often, the decisions of the Council are based on the assessments and recommendations of the Secretary General. The members of the Council prefer to formulate their judgements on the basis of objective information, and not on the basis of what the parties to a dispute or other members of the Council convey to them about the facts of a given situation. It is entirely reasonable for the members of the Council to depend on the Secretary General to provide such dispassionate information. The difficulty arises because in most cases, the Secretary General lacks the capacity to furnish such information. He has limited, if any, means of getting at the facts on the ground. Those member states who have much more information than the Secretary General can ever hope to gather on his own, either do not share the information with the Secretary General or, what is worse, might provide selective information which might suit their national purposes. On the whole, members of the Council have seldom complained about the quality of the reports presented by the Secretary General, though often about the delays in their submission.

Reform has two aspects: 're-form', and 'reform'. The former would deal with the structure and the latter with ways and means of achieving the purposes and principles enshrined in the Charter. A change in the form, in the structure, is essential, but would not necessarily facilitate the accomplishment of the objectives.

The current debate about the Security Council reform has been dominated by the various proposals to enlarge its composition. The need for increasing the membership is recognized almost universally, except for the five permanent members whose attitude seems to be that the current composition reflects the best possible compromise between efficiency—the need for retaining the capability to arrive at quick decisions—and representativity—the need to ensure adequate representation to the other 186 members of the United Nations. A solution to the problem of numbers has been hampered by two factors. Firstly, none of the P-5 want any addition to their category. The P-5 is the most exclusive club in the world. It was also the exclusive nuclear club until first Israel, and then India and Pakistan broke into it. It is understandable that the permanent members would wish not to admit any new member to their privileged club. This seems to be the position even when the aspirants for permanent membership have come to terms with political realities and given up the demand to be treated on par and without discrimination, with the present permanent members. The second factor is the inability of the under-represented regions—Asia, Africa and Latin America—to forge a unified front to press their claim for better representation for their regions in the Security Council.

The African countries are right in principle to insist on veto power for new permanent members. But they ought to bear two aspects in mind. Firstly, there is absolutely no possibility of the P-5 agreeing to an additional veto-wielding member. Secondly, the insistence on veto, in effect, amounts to a perpetual self-denial ordinance. They will forever deny to themselves as well as to others, the possibility of acquiring permanent seats on the Council. The other route to eliminate discrimination by abolishing or even diluting the existing veto rights will also not work. Moreover, veto is becoming increasingly irrelevant, it has been exercised most infrequently in recent years. Finally, what would the new permanent members use the veto for? There are not likely to be many situations where the candidates for permanent seats would want to exercise veto power to defend their national interests. Since the United Nations, in practice is not an overly principled body, insistence on principles will not yield practical results. The Security Council, in the coming years, will be dealing with a wide range of issues of concern to developing countries and it is important for them to obtain seats at the horseshoe table. The African stand has only facilitated the continuation of the privileged position of the P-5. Permanent members would prefer not to have new permanent members even without veto. They realize, better than most others, that permanent membership even without the power of veto would confer enough weight to the new members to influence decision-making in the Council.

It is argued that an enlarged Security Council would only provide added legitimacy to its decisions which would continue to be dominated by one or two, or at best all the five veto-wielding members. Since countries represented in the Council will only pursue their national interests and since none of them would want to risk harming its bilateral relations with the permanent members, an expansion would only enable the P-5 to claim more legitimacy for their actions. Dr. Boutros Boutros Ghali has made this point in the foreword to this book. The international community, on the other hand, supports the principle of expansion in the conviction that new members, even without veto authority, would have enough weight and influence in international relations to be able to take independent positions. The people and government in most countries would hold elected permanent members to higher standards in the conduct of their UN diplomacy than non-elected P-5. This expectation is not unreasonable. At least some among the candidates for the permanent membership should be able and willing to assert themselves, without jeopardizing their relations with P-5. In fact, this may be an additional reason for the reluctance of P-5 to invite new members to take permanent seats at the horseshoe table. It is then all the more reason not to abandon the 're-form' movement.

Incidentally, the High Level Panel has recommended, and Secretary General Kofi Annan agrees, that members of the Security Council should meet certain criteria such as financial, military, and diplomatic contribution. It is also suggested that developed countries should have achieved or made substantial progress towards achieving the internationally agreed target of 0.7 per cent of GNP for Official Development Assistance. Apart from the Nordic countries, not many developed countries would satisfy this criterion.

If it is difficult to 're-form' the Security Council, it is even more so to 'reform' it. Increasing the size of the Council would need amendment of the Charter. Some permanent members are extremely allergic to the idea of adding to or subtracting from the Charter. Sixty years after the end of the Second World War, they frown upon the perfectly legitimate demand of Germany and Japan to delete the so-called enemy clauses from the Charter. Nevertheless, they did agree to amend the Charter in the 1960s to enlarge the Security Council from the original 11 to 15 members. Thus, it is conceivable that at some stage of their choosing, they might go along with the growing demand to enlarge the membership of the Council and make appropriate amendments to the Charter.

When it comes to reforming the Council, however, the situation is entirely different primarily because it is not easy to define with a degree of clarity, what it would imply. If reform means improving the working methods of the Council, increasing transparency in its decision-making processes, enabling non-members of the Council to keep themselves better informed of its proceedings, giving more access to troop-contributing countries regarding deployment of their contingents in peace-keeping operations, and so on, these are all possible things. Indeed, much has been done during the past years in this respect and perhaps more can be done. The one area where at best a limited improvement can be expected is the actual decision-making process. There is no possibility, and nor should there be any, for non-members of the Council to actually participate in the meetings of the informal consultations; these are confidential and should remain so, otherwise, the Council will not be able to discuss issues frankly.

The real reform should address itself to the question posed earlier in this chapter. What is it that a reformed Council would be expected to do better than the present Council? I believe that the 'peoples of the

United Nations', if they had their way, would have wanted their organisation to have done the following. They would have wanted the UN to prevent, stop or at the least minimize the genocide in Rwanda. They would have wanted the UN to stop the rampaging warlords in Somalia from massacring men, women and children of the country; to deal with the famine and force the warlords to establish a stable and democratic government in the country. They would have wanted the UN to end the bloody civil war in Angola. They would have wanted the UN to eradicate the hated Pol Pot regime in Cambodia well before Vietnam did it in 1979. They would probably not have wanted the UN to get involved in the internal situation in Haiti in the 1990s. They would certainly have wanted the UN to relax the sanctions against Iraq which had taken a heavy toll of the vulnerable sections of Iraq's population. And, they would have, equally certainly, wanted the UN to prevent the military intervention in Iraq in the spring of 2003. Since it did not do any of these things, in the eyes of the peoples of the world, the UN has failed.

It is easy to see that the United Nations, however reformed, can not pass such tests at the bar of public opinion. Only a world government, with powers to raise an army, levy and collect taxes, pronounce and enforce judgements can hope to come close to these kinds of expectations of the people. It is equally obvious that such a government will never come into being. Consequently, some argue, it is legitimate for governments, when they have the capacity and political will, to take it upon themselves to set things right. Public opinion does at times tacitly accept unilateral actions of governments when they lead to eradication of an obviously evil state of affairs. For example, when Tanzania, under President Julius Nyerere, intervened in Uganda in the 1970s to get rid of the Idi Amin regime, nobody protested even though the military action was undertaken without the authorization of the Security Council. Similarly, Vietnam's intervention in Cambodia in 1979 was not objected to much even though its action was not inspired solely by humanitarian considerations and nor was it sanctified by the Security

Council. Indeed, the United States has endeavoured to justify, *post facto*, its intervention in Iraq on the ground that it brought about the removal of the dictatorial and oppressive regime of Saddam Hussein. Unfortunately for the US, the peoples of the world, by and large, have not embraced this explanation.

It can be asserted, without fear of being contradicted, that a military action by one state against another can be regarded as legal only in one of two cases. Either it is an act of self defence or it is sanctioned by the Security Council of the United Nations. The traditional scope of the right of self defence was perhaps somewhat wider than the latitude allowed under the Charter of the United Nations. Article 51 is unambiguous: the right of self defence is available 'if an armed attack occurs against a member of the United Nations'. Pre-Charter, a state could invoke what the Charter refers to as the 'inherent' right of self defence in situations where it anticipated an imminent attack, but not so, since the coming into existence of the United Nations.

The other avenue of legitimacy for military action is the Security Council. In case the Council were to authorize use of force even when public opinion would regard it as unnecessary or illegitimate, it would become legal. Thus, if United States and United Kingdom had managed somehow to get the 'second resolution' adopted by the Council in March 2003, the Second Gulf War would have acquired legality even if it had produced the same consequences as witnessed today.

Is there a third source of acquiring legitimacy, if not legality, for armed intervention? Perhaps there is, in the form of public opinion. It did not take long for the international community to come to terms with and accept the result of India's intervention in East Pakistan in 1971; facts on the ground became India's justification for its action, in addition to it being an act of legitimate self defence. If President Bush had unilaterally sent the marines into Somalia in 1992 on operation 'restore hope', the international community would have not only accepted it but applauded it. The situation was so horrendous that such an action by the American leader would not have attracted the slightest doubt about his bonafides. But he decided to play it safe and obtained Security Council's authorisation for his action. Similarly, the French action in Rwanda in the shape of 'operation tourquoise' would not have invited much adverse reaction, but they too thought it prudent to obtain Security Council resolution for the deployment of their troops. Again, the NATO bombardment over Kosovo in 1999, consciously undertaken without even trying for Security Council authorisation, did not provoke the kind of hostile reaction that the 2003 war in Iraq had. Such *post facto* acquisition of legitimacy, however, will remain an exception to the general observation that there are only two sources of legitimacy for military action.

The other principal organ of the United Nations intimately connected to the task of preserving peace and international security is the Secretary General. During the current debate on reform, hardly any attention has been given to the office of the Secretary General. In the eyes of the international community, an ideal Secretary General would be someone who would function independently, on the basis of recognized principles of morality and fair play and who would not let any country influence his actions. It is sometimes proposed that the Secretary General should have at his or her disposal sufficient armed forces, with all the required equipment, which can be deployed speedily to the required locations to ensure peace. One of the proposals doing the rounds in a similar debate about UN reform in the late 1980s was to restrict the Secretary General's tenure in office to one non-renewable term of six years. It was believed that such a provision would remove the temptation of a second term and enable the Secretary General to function independently.

The reality in the United Nations is such that no Secretary General can afford to completely ignore the interests of member states, especially the richest and most powerful among them. The Secretary General can exercise a measure of independence, but the maxim that he who

SOME THOUGHTS ON REFORM OF THE SECURITY COUNCIL

pays the piper calls the tune, applies to the United Nations too. The very nature of his work compels the Secretary General to depend on the co-operation of member states. In implementing Security Council decisions on peacekeeping operations, for example, the Secretary General is entirely dependent on member states for troop contingents, financial contributions and so on. Very few countries have the logistical capability to airlift troops and equipment from the countries of origin to the areas of conflict. The United States has unmatched capability in this regard. It has been willing to place this capability at the service of the United Nations, albeit for a hefty price. The few other countries which have this capacity have so far been reluctant to make it available to the Secretary General. It simply would not do for the Secretary General to strain his relations with the United States to a point where he is not able to implement the mandates given to him by the Security Council. And it is not quite fair to single out the United States in this context. Every member of the United Nations would like to use the Organisation for its own purposes if it could; the commitment of members to the UN is principled and firm, so long as its national interests are not harmed.

The answer does not lie in establishing a force over which the Secretary General would have total authority in terms of deployment. First of all, it would be practically impossible to create such a force. Would the force consist of units made available by member states which would be brought together and kept ready in one place? If not, how would such a force be recruited? Would there be national quotas in it? Would there be quotas among the officer cadre? Where would such a force be stationed? Would member states be willing to pay for the upkeep of the force even if it would remain unutilised for a long period of time? If governments have no control over their nationals serving in such a force, would it become a purely mercenary army? Would the Secretary General exercise authority over such a force all by himself or in consultation with or as decided by the Security Council? While many governments have agreed to earmark specified units to serve in a UN operation, no one is prepared to agree that the Secretary General can deploy the unit without its consent. It is doubtful if any Secretary General would wish to have absolute authority over such a peace-keeping force. It would not be advisable, since in the real world, the Secretary General will always be subjected to all kinds of pulls and pressures.

The idea of restricting the tenure of the Secretary General to one fixed term of five or six years deserves further consideration. It will certainly not transform the office of the Secretary General into a fully independent one. It would nevertheless remove some of the human constraints and temptations and would perhaps give a more favourable perception of the office to the international community.

Some thought needs to be devoted to the procedure for the election of the Secretary General. As can be seen from Chapters 10 and 11, there is scope for improving the process. It is, of course, unrealistic to expect the permanent members to give up their veto right on this question. Indeed, the veto can at times play a positive role. If China had not exercised its veto in 1981, Mr. Kult Waldheim would have become Secretary General for a third term. Apart from any other consider-ations, it would have set a bad precedent. It should perhaps be possible to introduce one element of reform. The Security Council could send a panel of two or three names, instead of one single name, to the General Assembly. Such a procedure would not need an amendment of the Charter and would give an important role to the General Assembly which is after all more democratic in its composition and functioning than the Security Council.

A needless and potentially divisive issue has been introduced in the debate on UN reform, namely, the doctrine of humanitarian interven-tion or the principle of the responsibility to protect. Nobody can seri-ously disagree with the proposition that the international community has a duty to intervene when a government is either incapable or un-willing to stop the massacre of a section of its population. By elevating the proposition to the level of a doctrine or a principle, however, what was always within the purview of the Security Council has been rendered a subject of controversy. The Council has always known that it is its responsibility to protect innocent civilians who might become or have become victims of their own government's wrath. When Somalia became a failed state in the early 1990s, the Security Council did not hesitate to adopt truly historic decisions. A strong peacekeeping force, with the necessary enforcement authority was dispatched to Somalia to help the people who were caught in the ruthless and bloody game of the warlords. The absence of a formal doctrine of humanitarian intervention or of the responsibility to protect did not act as a handicap in the Council's decision-making capacity or willingness. The same was true of Rwanda where the UN was willing to act to prevent the genocide but was prevented from acting, not by the absence of the necessary doctrine but by some member states.

In recent months, proposals have been put forward to define the parameters for the use of force which the Security Council should embody in an official resolution. The High Level Panel has suggested five criteria: seriousness of the threat, proper purpose of the proposed military action, whether means short of the use of force might succeed in stopping the threat, proportionality, and whether there is reasonable chance of success. These parameters, it is suggested, would guide the Security Council in dealing with future emergency situations in failed states. Embodying these criteria in a resolution might add transparency to the deliberations of the Council. But it is entirely probable that the adoption of such criteria would create excuses for delay and procrastination since any written text can always be interpreted in more than one sense. There is no reason to believe, going by past practice, that the Security Council would act contrary to the five criteria which have been recommended by the High Level Panel for the use of force. It would be better to leave flexibility to the Security Council rather than prescribing parameters for action, however well intentioned and well drafted. This is precisely the conclusion which the world leaders reached at the Summit meeting in New York in September 2005. The declaration stated: 'We are prepared to take collective action, in a timely and decisive manner, through the Security Council, in accordance with the Charter, including Chapter VII, on a case-by-case basis, should peaceful means be inadequate and national authorities manifestly fail to protect their populations from genocide, war crimes, ethinic cleansing,' and so on. In other words, the leaders declared that there was no need to change anything.

An unfortunate fact of the debate on UN reform is that the civil society and the NGO community is not involved in it to the extent that it should be. Apart from a few think tanks, only interested governments and sections of media are reflecting on the issues concerned. The civil society has demonstrated in the past that it can be a potent force for reform when it mobilizes itself behind a cause as was the case on the issue of banning land mines or climate change or women's issues. The international civil society has not evinced the kind of interest that it ought to on the subject of UN reform. Without such interest, it might be difficult to reform or even re-form the Security Council. In recent years, welcome steps have been taken to create a sense of partnership between the United Nations and civil society organizations. Within countries, public opinion manifests and asserts itself. The Spanish Government's decision in 2005 to withdraw its contingent from Iraq was in direct response to the sentiments of the Spanish people. What is required is a mechanism to enable 'world public opinion' to influence the decisions in the world organisation.

INDEX

INDEX